The Queer Games
Avant-Garde

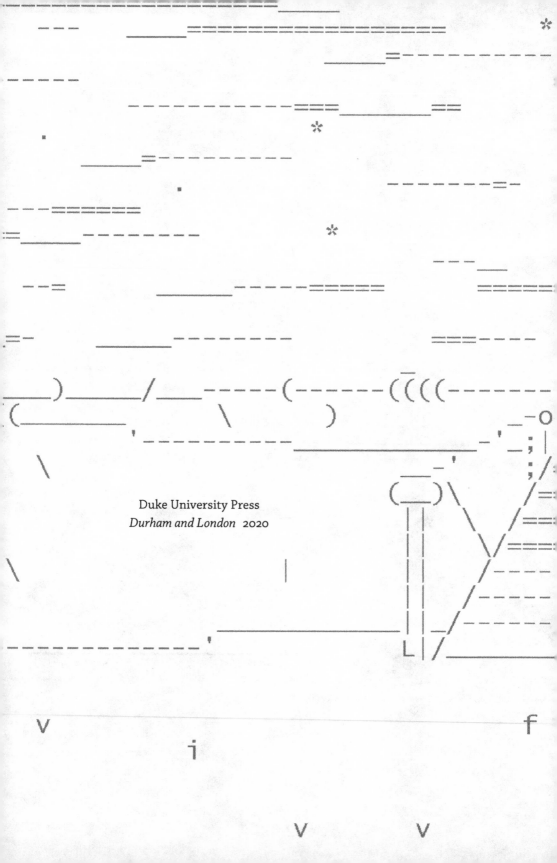

Duke University Press
Durham and London 2020

The Queer Games Avant-Garde

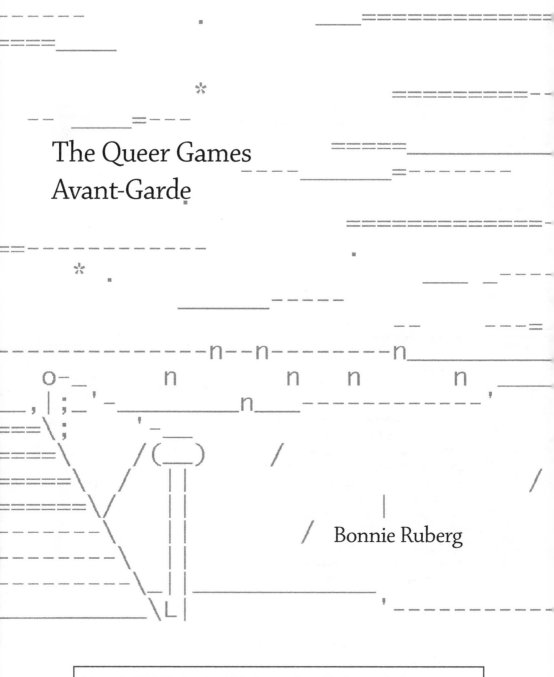

Bonnie Ruberg

How LGBTQ Game Makers Are Reimagining
the Medium of Video Games

Designed by Aimee C. Harrison
Typeset in Chaparral Pro and Lack by Copperline Book Services

Library of Congress Cataloging-in-Publication Data
Names: Ruberg, Bonnie, [date] author.
Title: The queer games avant-garde : how LBGTQ game makers
are reimagining the medium of video games / Bonnie Ruberg.
Description: Durham : Duke University Press, 2020. |
Includes bibliographical references and index.
Identifiers: LCCN 2019041791 (print)
LCCN 2019041792 (ebook)
ISBN 9781478005919 (hardcover)
ISBN 9781478006589 (paperback)
ISBN 9781478007302 (ebook)
Subjects: LCSH: Video games—Social aspects. |
Video game designers—Interviews. | Gay culture. |
Gender identity. | Queer theory.
Classification: LCC GV1469.17. S63 R825 2020 (print) |
LCC GV1469.17.S63 (ebook) | DDC 794.8—dc23
LC record available at https://lccn.loc.gov/2019041791
LC ebook record available at https://lccn.loc.gov/2019041792

Cover art: Ryan Rose Aceae and Heather Flowers,
artwork from GENDERWRECKED

CONTENTS

ACKNOWLEDGMENTS

This is a project that brings together many voices. It reflects a queer community and a network of creators that extends far beyond myself. Fittingly, it has been inspired and made possible by a wide array of people who have generously offered their time, assistance, support, trust, and encouragement along the way. I am immensely grateful to all of these individuals and organizations for helping to bring this book to life and for believing in the importance of this project and the wonderful, artistic, radical, experimental, and complicated queer interactive media making praxis it brings to the fore. Thank you.

The Queer Games Avant-Garde was researched and written primarily in 2017, during my time as a Provost's Postdoctoral Scholar and a member of the Society of Fellows at the University of Southern California. I was able to provide honoraria for interview participants thanks to research funds associated with my position at USC. As a postdoc, I was situated within the Interactive Media & Games Division in the School of Cinematic Arts. This warm, vibrant, creative community contributed immensely to the energy and ethos of this book. Thank you to my colleagues and students at USC, who made me feel welcome and valued—including Kiki Benzon, Peter Brinson, Vicki Callahan, Tracy Fullerton, Kara Keeling, Virginia Kuhn, Richard Lemarchand, Tara McPherson, Margaret Moser, Jane Pinckard, Sam Roberts, and Jeff Watson. Thank you also to Aaron Trammell and Rox Samer, my friends and fellow USC postdocs navigating the world of post-PhD life.

My work on this project was also made by possible by the Department of Informatics and the Donald Bren School of Information and Computer Sciences at the University of California, Irvine. When I was hired for a tenure-track position in 2016, my new department allowed me to postpone my appointment by a year so that I could finish my postdoc—and, by extension, so that I could write this book. Stipends for the graduate students and undergraduate students who helped produce the raw transcriptions of the interviews presented in this book in edited form (an immense task, since the original recordings were each more than two hours long!) were issued through start-up funding associated with my position as an assistant professor at UC Irvine. Thank you to these students, whose assistance with this project was invaluable: Amanda Cullen, Dan Gardner, Heather Faucett, and Gustavo Figueroa.

Thank you also to Courtney Berger, my editor at Duke University Press, who believed in this project and the value of scholarship on queer games and queer gaming communities, and to assistant editor Sandra Korn, who showed infinite patience and wisdom in my moments of anxiety. A very special thanks goes out to Carly Kocurek and Jennifer Malkowski, my peer reviewers, who read the book draft in full (in Jen's case, twice!) and whose feedback on the project was both kind and sharp, and above all immensely helpful. Your enthusiasm for the project has meant a lot to me.

Queer work is often supported by queer community. This project, and my scholarship more generally, has benefited immeasurably from my connections to other queer game studies scholars, queer game makers, and queer community organizers. Thank you, as ever, to the co-organizers of the annual Queerness and Games Conference, now entering its sixth year as of this writing in October 2019. As the organizing team continues to grow and change, I find new and equally amazing collaborators and friends in my life. I am grateful for you all, QGCon co-organizers past and present: Jasmine Aguilar, Meghan Blythe Adams, Mattie Brice, Emma Kinema, Kaelan Doyle-Myerscough, Chelsea Howe, Christopher Goetz, Jess Marcotte, Bahar Moghaddam, Teddy Pozo, Len Predko, Chuck Roslof, Cameron Siebold, Dietrich Squinkifer, and Zoya Street. My thanks go out as well to my writing group, an amazing misfit gang of queer folks and POC. I have come to think of you as my academic family, Alexandrina Agloro, Josef Nguyen, Amanda Phillips, and Adrienne Shaw.

This work also comes into being through support and love from the people closest to me. Thank you, Eli Peterson, for your support in all things, and for listening to me with care and comfort both when my academic work leaves me invigorated and when it leaves me frustrated. Thank you, Jonah Peterson, for being a strange, small, beautiful creature who makes me think in new, queer ways about love, intimacy, bodies, and the future.

Last, thank you to all of the interviewees whose voices and works are included in this book. You are, without a doubt, the biggest inspiration for this project. Some of you are close friends or collaborators; others are creators whose work I have long admired from afar. Thank you for the time you spent with me and for trusting me with your stories, which are often personal, intimate, vulnerable, political, poetic, and fierce all at the same time. You are making the weird, gorgeous fever dream of queer games a reality. Because of you, the medium of video games will never be the same.

INTRODUCTION   Reimagining the Medium of Video Games

Queer people are the avant-garde of video games because we're willing to do things other people aren't. . . . We take the work of disrupting systems farther than other people can. . . . I'm already asking, "What's the next thing that needs to be shaken up?" If you're really interested in queering games, you can never rest.—NAOMI CLARK

Traditional gamers thought indie games would destroy the medium, which didn't happen obviously—but, for this brief period, I was like, "I can destroy something? Great, I have this awesome destructive power!... I'm going to make something so avant-garde it will actually destroy the medium and there will be nothing left." —ANDI MCCLURE

--===---===---===---===---===---===---===---==

The medium of video games is currently undergoing a momentous shift, both artistically and politically—and, in many ways, it is queer, independent game makers who are leading that change. "At this moment, there's a renaissance taking place in games, in the breadth of genres and the range of emotional territory they cover," writes games researcher Katherine Isbister.[1] This renaissance is in large part driven by radical, experimental, vibrant, and deeply queer work from a wide-reaching and constantly evolving network of LGBTQ game makers: today's video game vanguard. These game makers are creating digital (and analog) games inspired by their own queer experiences. This is what I term the "queer games avant-garde," a "movement," loosely defined, that began in approximately 2012 and has continued for more than half a decade. Commonly, the games produced by the queer games avant-garde are scrappy and zine-like, to borrow a term from Anna Anthropy's prescient book *Rise of the Videogame*

Fig I.1 :::: *Dys4ia* (2012) by Anna Anthropy, arguably the best-known video game from the queer games avant-garde

Zinesters, a source of inspiration for many contemporary queer game makers.[2] These are "indie" games, developed largely outside of the traditional funding and publishing structures of the games industry. Though games like Anthropy's *Dys4ia* (2012) (see figure I.1) are among the best-known (and indeed most influential) examples of work from the queer games avant-garde, there are dozens if not hundreds of active queer game makers currently creating queer indie games. The number of games they have developed is growing every day.

The cultural landscape in which the queer games avant-garde is staging its intervention is a turbulent one. Described by some as the most influential media form of the twenty-first century, video games are played by billions around the globe each year and have a profound potential to impact how players view themselves and the world around them.[3] Yet, despite the fact that women, queer people, people of color, and others who are often perceived as "different" have been playing and making video games for decades, games and the cultures that surround them have a long history of underrepresenting, misrepresenting, and at times fostering open hostility toward those who do not fit the image of the white, straight, cisgender, male "gamer."[4] This tension between video games as a progressive and a reactionary medium has culminated, in recent years, in the outbreak of online harassment campaigns against "social justice warriors," such as #GamerGate.[5] Despite this backlash, however, video games are indeed becoming more "diverse." Increasingly, the AAA video game industry, which produces widely popular games with multimillion-dollar budgets, has demonstrated efforts toward greater inclusion in the form of increased LGBTQ representation—for instance, in the popular competitive titles *Overwatch* (Blizzard, 2016) and *League of Legends* (Riot Games, 2009).[6] While many LGBTQ players have celebrated these gestures toward inclusivity, others remain rightly wary of corporate attempts to cater to non-straight, non-cisgender players: such attempts typically operate under the neoliberal logic that "diverse" players constitute an untapped consumer market and that increasing diverse representation will also increase profits.[7] However, queerness is coming to video games in many more ways than one. As the mainstream games industry takes its slow steps forward, the queer games avant-garde—this rising tide of indie games being developed *by*, *about*, and often *for* LGBTQ people—is laying its own claim to the medium for people who have traditionally been made to feel unwelcome, invisible, or even unsafe in games.

Though the games emerging from the queer games avant-garde share a commitment to engaging with queer perspectives, these games are also as varied as the individuals who create them. Some games manifest their queerness through the inclusion of LGBTQ characters, such as Dietrich Squinkifer's *Dominique Pamplemousse in "It's All Over When the Fat Lady Sings!"* (2013) (figure I.2). Others explore queerness in a more conceptual register, playing with embodiment, desire, and intimacy by subverting the standard rules of game design—for instance, Jimmy Andrews and Loren Schmidt's *Realistic Kissing Simulator* (2014). The work of the queer games avant-garde represents far more than video games as we already know them with a rainbow veneer.[8] These are games that disrupt the status quo, enact resistance, and use play to explore new ways of inhabiting difference. Queerness and video games share a common ethos, a longing to explore alternative ways of being.[9] This is nowhere more apparent than in the work of the queer games avant-garde.

Though queer indie games are quickly gaining visibility in North America and beyond, there are still some who would dismiss this work as "niche." Much to the contrary, by demonstrating how games can be a powerful medium for expressing and complicating experiences of identity, the queer games avant-garde is paving the way for artists from a wide range of

Bathroom signs: the bane of my existence. Which one's supposed to be me?

Fig I.2 :::: *Dominique Pamplemousse in "It's All Over When the Fat Lady Sings!"* (2013) by Dietrich Squinkifer, an example of a video game that includes LGBTQ characters

marginalized subject positions to make their voices heard in and through games. The growth of the queer games avant-garde also has notable implications for contemporary queer art-making beyond video games. These games sit at the avant-garde of interactive media as well as at the avant-garde of games. They are regularly shown in galleries and other fine arts spaces; they are also increasingly moving into settings associated with the performing arts. In this way, the queer games avant-garde is pushing the boundaries of how queerness is presented in digital and playful media art more broadly. Whether we see the effects of the queer games avant-garde as a sea change or a landslide, whether we are interested in making video games "better" or simply queerer, this much is true: following the work of the queer games avant-garde, the cultural and artistic landscape of games will never be the same.

This book is structured around a collection of twenty original interviews with twenty-two artists and activists contributing (or working adjacent) to the queer games avant-garde. Rather than approaching queer game-making through the lens of academic analysis, this project foregrounds the voices of queer game makers themselves. Most often, when they have been featured in new reports and other writing, these artists and their work have been referenced in order to tell overly simplified, "up-lifting," and often tokenizing stories about how LGBTQ issues in video games are "getting better." By contrast, the stories presented in these interviews are those that queer game makers tell about *themselves*—their own lives, their inspirations, the challenges they face, and the ways that they understand their places within the wider terrain of video games. These artists speak with insight and candor about their creative practices, as well as their politics and their passions. Their perspectives and opinions vary widely. What emerges across these interviews, however, is a web of related themes, productive tensions, and multiple visions for how queerness can reimagine the future of video games.

LGBTQ ISSUES AND VIDEO GAMES:
IMAGINING OTHERWISE

To understand what makes the rise of the queer games avant-garde so significant, it is crucial to understand the historical and cultural context around LGBTQ issues and video games that surrounds this work. From the release of the first commercial video games in the 1970s to the present, the relationships between gender, sexuality, and notions of legitimacy (that is, who gets to count as a "real" gamer or a "real" game maker and what gets to count as a "real" game) have been fraught, especially for women and other subjects pushed to the fringes of game cultures, as historians such as Carly Kocurek have noted.[10] Over the past four decades, LGBTQ characters in video games have been conspicuously scarce—though scholars like Adrienne Shaw are currently in the process of documenting the presence of these characters across games history, complicating the often-repeated myth that LGBTQ game characters did not exist until recent years.[11] Still, video games' track record of representing queer identities has left much to be desired. Prominent early examples of queer characters in video games, like the transgender dinosaur Birdo first introduced in *Super Mario Bros. 2* (1988), have typically been reductive or outright offensive. In more recent years, as mentioned, AAA game companies have begun introducing more and "better" LGBTQ characters and romance options into their games.[12] Popular titles with LGBTQ content include, for instance, the *Mass Effect* series (BioWare, 2007–2012) and *Dragon Age: Inquisition* (BioWare, 2014). Indeed, the topic of "diversity" in games has been given a growing spotlight, with inclusivity funding initiatives from companies like Intel, numerous media reports on women in gaming, and an "advocacy" track at the annual Game Developers Conference (GDC). The extent to which these corporate efforts, with their questionable motives and arguably conservative identity politics (to draw from Alison Harvey and Stephanie Fisher's writing on the "post-feminism" of initiatives designed to bring more women into the games industry), are enacting systemic change is debatable at best, however.[13] Homophobia and anti-LGBTQ sentiment continue to be rampant and well-documented concerns within the games industry and reactionary sectors of games cultures.[14] Many of the queer game makers profiled here have been among the primary targets of #GamerGate.

The problems of underrepresentation and discrimination in video games are by no means limited to queer and transgender identities. Such issues are fundamentally intersectional. They also deeply affect people of color, for example, as scholars of games and critical race like Kishonna L. Gray, Soraya Murray, Lisa Nakamura, and David J. Leonard have demonstrated.[15] This larger system of marginalization and oppression emerges from what Janine Fron et al. have called the "hegemony of play," an "entrenched status quo" that pervades the games industry and the cultures around it and which dictates what video games should look like and whom they should be made for.[16] In addition, the issues that surround LGBTQ representation and experiences in video games are inextricable from the broader political situation today, both in America and internationally. Video games are far more than a mere entertainment medium; like all forms of cultural production, they reflect and react to the society around them.[17] It is no coincidence that the rise of the queer games avant-garde is taking place alongside the rise of the alt-right or the election and governance of a president who is unapologetic in his racist, sexist, antigay, antitrans agenda. As these interviews demonstrate, the contributors to the queer games avant-garde are acutely aware of the political backdrop to their work. For many of those whose voices are featured here, simply making video games as queer people is a political act. Given the deeply entrenched biases found in video games and the dangers of the current political situation, simply by making games as queer people these creators are engaged in fundamentally radical work.

Luckily, the artists of the queer games avant-garde are not alone in insisting on the value of bringing queerness to video games. The network of game makers profiled here operates alongside other, related queer games networks from areas of academia and community organizing. Queer game studies is a burgeoning scholarly paradigm, led by scholars such as Edmond Chang, Todd Harper, Josef Nguyen, Amanda Phillips, Adrienne Shaw, and many more. Like the queer games avant-garde, queer game studies represents a vanguard, pushing game studies toward a more meaningful engagement with identity and social justice.[18] Many of the game makers contributing to the queer games avant-garde are hybrid artists-academics themselves, and it is common to see collaborations between those who develop queer indie games and queer game studies researchers. These interdisciplinary, inter-industry dialogues are exemplified by the annual Queerness and Games Conference, an event that combines theory and practice and which, along with similar events like the Different Games conference, has become a hub for sharing, discussing, and building community around the production of queer games.[19] Player-oriented expos like GaymerX are also creating supportive spaces for LGBTQ players to express themselves as "gaymers." In the past few years, a handful of indie video games that notably foreground queer representation have even achieved widespread popularity and/or recognition. Some of these include Game Grumps's *Dream Daddy: A Dad Dating Simulator* (2017) (figure I.3), Toby Fox's *Undertale* (2015), and Christine Love's *Ladykiller in a Bind* (2016) (figure I.4). As the queer games avant-garde grows, so does the diverse ecosystem of thinkers, commentators, and players committed to exploring queerness in video games.

At the same time, with increased reach and visibility come new challenges for the queer games avant-garde. As the number of queer indie video games continues to grow, so too do the number of people who play them, creating more room for differences of opinion even among LGBTQ players. For instance, queer game maker Aevee Bee's latest visual novel, *Heaven Will Be Mine* (2018) (figure I.5), recently drew (largely unwarranted) criticism sparked by a much-liked tweet from a queer-identified player who asked, "Can we please have more queer games that aren't visual novels?"[20] In addition, as queer games are increasingly being sold through mainstream distribution platforms, they become susceptible to the often discriminatory whims of corporations. In the summer of 2018, for example, the online game retailer Steam quietly and abruptly erased its "LGBT" tag, making queer games harder for potential players to find and the presence of LGBTQ content on the platform less visible.[21]

To what extent are today's queer indie video games bringing change to the games industry, games culture, and the shifting history of LGBTQ issues in games? How can we understand the forces of influence through which progress comes to the mainstream? Should the purpose of queer

Fig I.3 :::: *Dream Daddy: A Dad Dating Simulator* (2017), a widely popular queer video game developed by the studio Game Grumps

Fig I.4 :::: Christine Love's *Ladykiller in a Bind* (2016), which has earned recognitions like the 2017 Excellence in Narrative Award from the Independent Games Festival

Fig I.5 :::: The 2018 queer visual novel from Aevee Bee and Mia Schwartz, *Heaven Will Be Mine*

indie game-making even *be* to make the broader medium of video games "better," or does that narrative instrumentalize queer art and queer artists, reducing the transgressive potential of their work by making them agents of "diversity" and potentially exploiting their already precarious labor? These are questions that cross many of the interviews found here, and they have no easy answers. Different contributors to the queer games avant-garde understand their roles, the messages behind their work, and the value of speaking from the margins in very different terms. For example, game designer Naomi Clark states in her interview:

> Queer games have already changed the medium of video games quite a bit. [However,] like any process of cultural recuperation, a lot of what is unique about queer games is already being reintegrated into the various parts of the game industry, all the way up to AAA game makers who are not queer themselves. Historically, that's been true of things like queer photography or queer Riot Grrrl punk music. They went on to influence plenty of people who were not queer because they changed how people thought about a medium. That is what is most valuable to me about queer games. Their impact is already rippling back and affecting how games are made today, even in the most traditional parts of the industry.

While the future of video games is still uncertain, the rise of the queer games avant-garde suggests that we are standing at a pivotal point in which, as Clark says, queerness is changing the very ways we think about the medium. Through their work, the contributors to the queer games avant-garde are inviting players to reconsider what the relationship between sexuality, gender, identity, and games can be, to look past long-established standards of gameplay and entrenched norms of discrimination, and instead to imagine video games as spaces for (in the words of queer theorist Jack Halberstam) "living life otherwise."[22]

WHAT IS THE QUEER GAMES AVANT-GARDE?

Curtain, a 2014 game from Llaura McGee, bears little resemblance to the action-packed adventure games and sprawling online worlds that come to mind for many people when they imagine video games. McGee's game is a reflection on an abusive relationship between two young women, Ally and Kaci—punk rockers on the rise in Scotland's music scene. Yet, unlike so-called "serious games" or "games for change," which are often didactic and heavy-handed, *Curtain* and many other works that emerge from the queer games avant-garde are not primarily designed to educate or elicit empathy.[23] Instead, *Curtain* invites players to spend time inside an emotionally complex situation, one which is queer both in its narrative content and its interactive form. While the player explores the women's apartment from the first-person perspective of Ally, a constant stream of commentary from the absent Kaci fills up the screen: the voice of Ally's abuser, which she hears in her head. The game is colorful and shimmering but so highly pixelated that even the most mundane features of the apartment (like a guitar or a napping house cat) become disorienting and strange (figure I.6). In *Curtain*, the passage of time is represented by a magical-realist hallway that appears in the back of the shower. By walking through it, the player enters the future, where Kaci's words continue to haunt Ally long after their relationship has ended. Though *Curtain* draws from McGee's own history, it intentionally refuses to offer the player a direct or immediately comprehensible depiction of her experiences.

McGee's *Curtain* is one of numerous examples of the video games being produced by the queer games avant-garde. Those who are familiar with queer indie games have usually heard of artists like Anna Anthropy, Mattie Brice, merritt k, Christine Love, Porpentine, and Robert Yang. These game makers have been instrumental in exploring how queerness can be

Fig I.6 :::: *Curtain*, a 2014 game from Llaura McGee (DREAMFEEL) that uses pixelated aesthetics to disorient the player

expressed through games and in bringing queer indie games to a wider audience. Yet their work, while foundational and compelling, represents only a selection of the queer games being developed today. Queer game makers are producing their art across a variety of genres, from story-driven games to platformers, from unstructured play experiences to games made entirely of interactive text—such as Porpentine's *With Those We Love Alive* (2014). These games are most often made by individuals or small teams. Typically, they are inexpensive to purchase or free to download (though compensating queer game makers and other marginalized artists whenever possible is crucial). Often, the increased availability of so-called accessible game-making software, such as Twine and Game-Maker, is credited for driving the rise of queer indie game-making, though the interviewees in this volume productively challenge this narrative of technical accessibility.[24] Queer indie game makers build games for virtual reality, for mobile phones, and for multi-interface art installations, to name just a few platforms. This book focuses primarily on digital game makers, but non-digital game design—such as tabletop and role-playing games—is also an important part of the queer games avant-garde.[25]

Though the scale and impact of the queer games avant-garde makes it exceptional in the history of video games, precursors to today's queer indie game-making can be found going back nearly four decades. Graeme Kirkpatrick has documented the game-making practices of "bedroom coders" in the early 1980s in the United Kingdom, for example.[26] Melanie Swalwell has looked at a similar early "home coding" phenomenon in New Zealand. While this coding was largely done by straight, cisgender creators, its "do-it-yourself" quality does resonate with the work of queer game makers, who create video games not with large AAA teams but individually or with a handful of collaborators. Swalwell also describes the development of video games by early home coders as "a highly experimental practice" that "presaged many of the contemporary practices involved in digital culture," such as "appropriation, modification, and remixing."[27] In Czechoslovakia, as Jaroslav Švelch has demonstrated, "homebrew" communities used the Sinclair ZX Spectrum console to create expressive games that were, in their own way, resistant to dominant political power.[28] Anne-Marie Schleiner has argued that 1990s "KiSS" dolls, digitized and user-edited versions of the paper dolls found on the back of manga, can be understood as a "queer, edgy, erotic . . . adult game."[29] Experimentation with the handcrafted, gendered art style seen in work by queer games avant-garde contributors Kara Stone and Llaura McGee has a predecessor in the aesthetics of Theresa Duncan's mid-1990s games for girls, like *Chop Suey* (1995) (figure I.7).

Who are these game makers? More so than in any other area of video game development today, the queer games avant-garde has an overwhelming representation of women, nonbinary people, and transgender people—with a notable presence of trans women. The majority of contributors to the queer games avant-garde are white, but there are also many artists of color working in this field, including eight of the game makers interviewed here. Most of these artists are based in America or Canada, but queer indie game-making is also taking root internationally. In the early days of the queer games avant-garde, roughly between 2012 and 2014, an important "scene" existed in the San Francisco Bay Area, but it later disbanded, and today New York, Montréal, and Toronto are all important hubs for the work of the queer games avant-garde.[30] With a few important exceptions, the artists contributing to the queer games avant-garde are in their twenties and thirties. Though each queer game maker brings a unique background to their work, a number of those interviewed for this project grew up in geographically or socially isolated environments; they found connection to the "outside world" and to queer community through games. The relationship between the queer games avant-garde and aca-

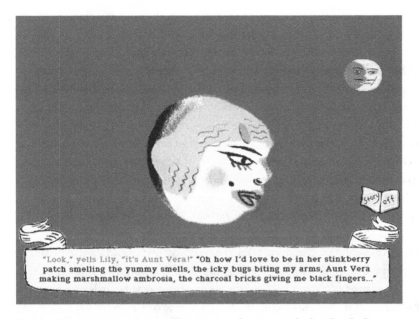

Fig I.7 :::: Theresa Duncan's 1995 *Chop Suey*, predecessor to the handcrafted aesthetics found in the queer games avant-garde

demia is a complicated one, and while some of these artists are employed at universities or currently completing PhD programs, a number of others chose not to finish their undergraduate degrees. Among their commonalities, contributors to the queer games avant-garde often have strong creative skills in a variety of areas, and many bring previous experience in theater, writing, visual art, or music to their work on games.

The socioeconomic realities and undervalued labors of indie game-making are issues that are too rarely addressed. As Stephanie Boluk and Patrick LeMieux have argued, the dominant discourse around "indie" games valorizes the work of game-making only when it "pays off."[31] For the artists interviewed here, creating indie games and the community networks that support them also requires forms of labor that are rarely compensated, are highly gendered, and remain largely invisible, such as emotional labor.[32] Even as queer games inspire change in the mainstream industry, which in turn reaps financial benefits, queer indie game-making itself remains precarious. The artists who contribute to the queer games avant-garde support themselves in a variety of ways, from working full-time jobs at tech companies to relying on crowdfunding and Patreon accounts. In many of these interviews, game makers speak frankly about their experiences with financial hardship and homelessness, as well as their frustrations with the expectation that they should tailor their work so that it changes the hearts and minds of straight consumers. As these interviewees point out, we need to continue to ask: who benefits monetarily from the ways that queer indie games are shifting the medium? In this way, the work of the queer games avant-garde could also be placed in dialogue with other forms of precarious digital labor, much of it similarly performed by women, people of color, and otherwise marginalized subjects whose undercompensated work has driven technological "progress."[33]

It is tempting to call this wave of queer games and their creators a "movement." However, this term raises mixed feelings for the participants in the queer games avant-garde themselves. There is no one, singular group of game makers who are creating queer games today, nor is there one vision of queerness and games that is shared among these creators. It is preferable to imagine the queer games avant-garde as a network or a series of interlocking constellations. Some of the artists interviewed here are actively in dialogue with one another, while others have their primary community ties elsewhere. After the initial #GamerGate attacks, some contributors to the queer games avant-garde chose to stop making video games. At the same time, more and more creators are coming to this work regularly. In truth, the queer games avant-garde is not one entity but multiple, interrelated creative practices. Yet there is still value in thinking of this work as a "movement," at least in one sense. Even in moments when queer game makers feel their own differences keenly, together they represent a force that cannot and should not be ignored. There is strength in numbers, and the sheer number of queer game makers creating work in this area makes the growing prominence of the LGBTQ presence in video games undeniable in its importance.

WHY QUEER INDIE VIDEO GAMES AS AN AVANT-GARDE?

Of all the ways to characterize the contemporary wave of queer indie game-making, why call it an "avant-garde"? Doing so has the potential to make a powerful statement, but it also calls for critical self-reflection. Most commonly applied to forms of artistic production such as literature, music, film, and the visual fine arts, avant-gardism has been widely theorized in classic works like Peter Bürger's *Theory of the Avant-Garde* and Hal Foster's *The Return of the Real*.[34] Indeed, precedents for contemporary queer indie game-making can be found outside of the realm of video games in earlier avant-gardes whose contributors, while working in non-digital media, were similarly interested in playfulness and games. Today's queer game-making shares an investment in the subversive potential of play with movements like Dada and Surrealism, for example.[35] It also brings to mind the Situationist manifesto, which "[calls] upon the revolutionary potential of play, for the 'invention of games of an essentially new type'" in order to "bring about the future reign of freedom and play."[36] The queer games avant-garde could also be seen as part of a lineage of experimental games like those created in the 1960s and 1970s by the Fluxus group, or perhaps as a reengagement with the social critiques found in the 1970s New Games movement, or even as a return to the spirit of game design as counterhegemonic, anticapitalist political statement exemplified by Elizabeth Magie's 1924 board game The Landlord's Game.[37] While there are many echoes between these earlier moments and the queer games avant-garde, the queer indie games discussed in this book also bring something new and crucial to avant-garde game-making. They bring queerness: queer identities, queer politics, queer joy, queer pain, queer resistance, queer worlds of play.

Importantly, the contributors to the queer games avant-garde *see themselves* as building from existing avant-garde traditions. Though not all, many of these game makers used the term "avant-garde" to describe their own work. A number of the game makers interviewed, including Mattie Brice, Kara Stone, Tonia B******, and Emilia Yang, cite feminist performance artists like Yoko Ono and Marina Abramović among their inspirations. Embodiment, vulnerability, and the reclamation of the female body (or, in the case of these game makers, often the queer and/or trans body) emerge as key themes that echo across past avant-gardes. Among the additional avant-garde artists that the interviewees profiled here point toward are musical composers like John Cage (Andi McClure), literary authors like Virginia Woolf and J. D. Salinger (Robert Yang and Aevee Bee), beatnik poets like Allen Ginsberg (Nina Freeman), and directors of nontraditional narrative cinema from the Iranian New Wave (Dietrich Squinkifer).

To call queer indie game-making an avant-garde is also to raise debates around video games and the ontologies of art. If queer games are an avant-garde, then video games must be an art form. For those who approach games as a medium of cultural production, this may seem like an obvious statement, but the question of whether video games should be considered art has a long and rocky history.[38] The work of the queer games avant-garde itself occupies a liminal space between the video game and art worlds, raising questions about how this work is situated and how it is received. Queer indie games, while undoubtedly the products of art-making, fall outside of what was termed in the 1990s "game art," for example. In a 2018 presentation titled "20 Years of Game Art: Reflections, Transformations, and New Directions," Eddo Stern noted that past game artists were not interested in gameplay or the "practice or craft of making games."[39] By contrast, the "younger" (Stern's term) artistic game makers of today make playable games and, I would add, are deeply invested in game-making as a practice. The network of contributors to the queer games avant-garde is also notably more diverse, especially in regard to gender and sexual identity, than the "game art" movement. Perhaps the biggest difference, however, is that today's queer indie games are primarily created not to exist in galleries but to be widely purchased, shared, and played. This is part of the politics of inclusion. Wide distribution is what gives players of a wide range of backgrounds access to queer games.

Admittedly, claiming the term "avant-garde" for queer indie game-making is a way to argue for the legitimacy of this work. This legitimacy, however, has the potential to directly benefit marginalized creators by giving them access to material resources and support from established cultural institutions. If queer indie game-making is an art form, then queer indie game makers deserve to be the recipients of artists' grants, residencies, and other opportunities. At the same time, this strategic bid for legitimacy must proceed with caution. I think most of the game makers interviewed here would agree when I say that the queer games avant-garde, taken as a whole, is not interested in seeking approval from the art world for its own sake. Yet this approval is one potential tool for supporting queer creators and their subversive work.

What does an avant-garde look like for video games and how does the work of queer indie game-making embody that avant-garde? Game studies scholars Mary Flanagan, Brian Schrank, John Sharp, and Alexander Galloway are among those who have theorized the notion of a video games avant-garde—though it is notable that queerness, gender, and sexuality are topics that rarely appear in their texts (with the exception of Flanagan's work). In his 2006 essay "Countergaming," Galloway describes what he sees as a (then) unrealized potential for an "independent gaming movement" that, rather than replicating the existing structures of the medium, will "redefine play itself and thereby [realize] its true potential as a political and cultural avant-garde."[40] Today's queer indie video games, I believe, do realize that potential. In addition to representing LGBTQ identities and experiences, they disrupt the accepted formalist and aesthetic qualities of the medium—scrambling graphics, rejecting win states, and suggesting vulnerable, tangible modes of interaction with machines that are at once "political," "cultural," and deeply queer. Mary Flanagan writes in *Critical Play* (2009) that avant-garde games "rework contemporary, popular game practices to propose an alternative, or 'radical,' game design." Such games, Flanagan continues, are "designed for artistic, political and social critique or intervention, in order to propose ways of understanding larger cultural issues as well as the games themselves." In this way, avant-garde games offer a "careful examination of social, cultural, political, or even personal themes."[41] The work emerging from the queer games avant-garde does just this. It speaks to pressing social issues by drawing from the personal in order to intervene on the level of culture.

Though contemporary queer indie games are conspicuously absent from these later works, more recent writing by Brian Schrank and John Sharp describes avant-garde video games in language that likewise seems tailor-made for the queer games avant-garde. In his 2014 *Avant-garde Video-games: Playing with Technoculture*, Schrank states his vision of avant-garde-ness for video games in this way:

> The avant-garde challenges or leads culture. The avant-garde opens up and redefines art mediums. . . . Avant-garde games are distinguished from mainstream ones because they show how the medium can manifest a greater diversity of gameplay and be creatively engaged in more kinds of ways by more kinds of people. They redefine the medium, breaking apart and expanding how we make, think, and play with games. The avant-garde democratizes games, and makes the medium more plastic and liquid.[42]

The queer indie game makers interviewed in this book challenge and lead culture. They are setting new precedents for inclusive representation and destabilizing accepted paradigms for how and by whom games should be designed and played. In this way, echoing Schrank's description, their work "manifest[s] a greater diversity of gameplay" and models how games can "be creatively engaged in more kinds of ways by more kinds of people." In their interviews, a number of these game makers, such as Avery Alder, Andi McClure, and Liz Ryerson, describe how their creative work is driven by a desire to upend traditional notions of gameplay—making manifest, as Schrank writes, the drive toward "breaking apart and expanding how we make, think, and play with games." While the focus of John Sharp's 2015 *Works of Game: On the Aesthetics of Games and Art* is the relationship between games and art, rather than avant-gardism per se, Sharp's notion of "artgames" offers another productive parallel to the work of the queer games avant-garde. "Artgames [use] the innate properties of games . . . to create revealing and reflective play experiences," writes Sharp.[43] Indeed, like the creators of "artgames," the contributors to the queer games avant-garde use the properties of games as the raw material from which to build play experiences that reflect on culture and identity.

In challenging existing standards of the medium, the queer games avant-garde demonstrates how formalistic experimentation is inextricable from the social meaning of games. Each of the game makers whose voice is included in this volume approaches the work of reimagining the medium in different ways. Nicky Case, for example, erases the "magic circle" by creating playful experiences that directly interface with real-world politics. Says Andi McClure of her work with algorithms and glitches, "Personally, I'm not interested in games themselves. . . . I [make] stuff that reject[s] what a game [is] supposed to be." These discussions about the nature of games and play are far from purely theoretical, however. Arguments about what does or does not count as a video game have been widely used in reactionary sectors of games culture as a thinly veiled excuse to discriminate against games created by and about women, LGBTQ people, people of color, and non-neurotypical people.[44] In short, the stakes of the queer games avant-garde as an avant-garde—that is, as an opportunity to "redefine the medium," in Schrank's terms—are surprisingly high. There are many people who play or even develop mainstream video games who would still dismiss queer games as insignificant: not technically complex enough, not challenging enough (though challenge comes in many forms), too wrapped up in "identity politics."[45] Avant-gardes may start small or initially seem niche, but they have large impacts, and their influence reverberates for artistic generations to come. Laying claim to the title of the "queer games avant-garde" is itself a political act.

CHARACTERISTICS OF THE QUEER GAMES AVANT-GARDE:
MESSY, POLITICAL, INTERSECTIONAL

A number of recurring themes and questions can be traced across the interviews in this volume. While each of the artists profiled here brings their own perspective to queer indie game-making, their stories suggest a set of shared interests. Together, they point toward a picture of contemporary queer indie game-making as enacting cultural critique through artistic expression. The work of the queer games avant-garde is, by nature, a hybrid creative-critical practice, informed at times by queer and feminist theory and at other times by concepts of queerness that emerge directly from the body. Among the most prominent characteristics that emerge from these interviews are the following.

The queer games avant-garde explores queerness beyond representation. The popular discourse that surrounds "diversity" and video games often focuses on increasing the on-screen representation of marginalized people.[46] However, many of the artists in the queer games avant-garde are committed to thinking beyond surface-level inclusion. These game makers move beyond representation into the mechanics, aesthetics, interfaces, and development practices of games, asking, "How can these be queered?" Some of these designers are accomplishing this through what Avery Alder describes as "structural queerness." Others, like Kara Stone, draw inspiration from queer theory. Still others challenge representation itself, like Kat Jones in her game *Glitter Pits* (2016). In some instances, the "beyond" in queerness beyond representation takes on a different meaning, as in the postapocalyptic work of Heather Flowers, which places players in a time beyond time: a queer future that emerges after the heteronormative world has fallen away. There is no one answer as to what queerness beyond representation looks like for queer indie game makers. The power of these alternative visions lies in their multiplicity.

The queer games avant-garde makes identity messy. It might seem that an interest in "identity" would be a common denominator for the contributors to the queer games avant-garde. Indeed, queer, trans, and intersectional identities and the communities that form around them are often explored in these games. However, many of the game makers interviewed here also challenge simplistic notions of identity. Aevee Bee, for example, argues against understanding identity as a series of boxes to check; Andi McClure rejects identity entirely by representing only abstractions in her games. Those game makers who remain invested in identity often complicate the idea that a queer artist should represent their own experiences through their games and that a straight player who picks up their game can or should identify with them. The ways in which these queer indie games represent identity is often less direct. Elizabeth Sampat's *Deadbolt* (2012) seems at first unrelated to Sampat's own queer identity, yet she understands it as queer because she is a queer person. These game makers also bring into question what queerness itself means. Some describe it as a mode of desire, others as a mode of connection, still others as a call to social action. Yet even as many of these artists reject the expectation that they should make autobiographical or confessional work, most describe their games as highly "personal."

The queer games avant-garde is interested in how games feel. These game makers explore affect, embodiment, experience, and intimacy. Traditionally, the discourse around innovation in video games has focused on the formalist aspects of games: their rules, their systems, and their mechanics.[47] While systems also interest many of these artists, the queer indie game makers interviewed here are deeply invested in recentering feeling and the experiences of the body. Many of these artists combine digital games with material elements to create installations that literally reach out and touch the player—or which the players themselves touch, as in the soft tactile interfaces created by Jess Marcotte. Other games reimagine the role that affect can play in the formalistic tropes of gameplay, such as in Mo Cohen's *Queer Quest* (in production), where grief becomes an object that the player collects and carries with them. Intimacy is a key theme across the work of the queer games avant-garde, but that intimacy often takes on unexpected forms—as in Naomi Clark's *Consentacle* (2014), where strangers play out a sexual encounter between a human and an alien, or Seanna Musgrave's *Animal Massage* (2016), a virtual reality installation in the which the player is caressed in front of a public audience, or merritt k's *Hug Punx* (2015) (figure I.8), a game about exuberant hugging. These games build opportunities for queer togetherness and also interrogate what it means to feel alongside others.

The queer games avant-garde questions empathy and looks for its alternatives. As the work of contemporary queer game makers is being more widely discussed among mainstream commentators, "empathy" has become a buzzword for describing queer games.[48] This is a characterization that many queer indie game makers actively resist. A striking number of those interviewed here speak about the problems they see with players thinking that games can—or should—provide them with the opportunity to "step into the shoes" of marginalized people. Some of these artists insist outright that they do not make games for straight people. Others intentionally design their games not as mimetic reflections of queer lives but as explorations of alternative paths that their lives might have taken. Many of these

Fig I.8 :::: merritt k's *Hug Punx* (2015), a game about hugging that models one of many forms queer intimacy can take in video games

games deliberately refuse to package queer experiences as playable consumer products. The few artists who do speak in support of empathy use the term in unexpected ways or as a tool for social justice. Through discussions of empathy, these artists ask, "Who are queer games for?" Not all agree on the intended audience of their work. Some feel that queer games should educate straight consumers, whereas others believe that the goal of developing these games is creating spaces for queer people.

The work of the queer games avant-garde is political. Almost without exception, the queer game makers interviewed here describe their work using this term. What "political" means and how it manifests differs across creators and their games, however. Nicky Case's *To Build a Better Ballot* (2016) explicitly engages with contemporary U.S. politics. Robert Yang, whose games—such as his newest work, *The Tearoom* (2017) (figure I.9)—represent sexual practices between men, describes his work as political because it refuses to desexualize queerness. For other contributors to the queer games avant-garde, the politics of their games are located in the design of consent, or their creation of worlds widely populated by queer subjects, or their rejection of the tenets of what supposedly makes a "good game." Indeed, resistance is a theme that appears in many forms across these interviews. Sometimes that resistance manifests as outright political dissent, but other times it takes alternate forms—like aesthetic abstraction or the exuberance of glitter and dancing in the face of discrimination and hate. Many proponents of mainstream games culture insist that video games are "just for fun" and therefore apolitical. The queer games avant-garde proves that even those games that seem small, silly, sexy, or strange communicate powerful messages. As Shira Chess writes, "The playful is political."[49]

The queer games avant-garde is fundamentally intersectional. For contemporary queer indie game makers, experiences of queerness cannot be separated from experiences of race, socioeconomics, mental health and disability, access, religion, nationality, and numerous other factors of identity, privilege, community, and disenfranchisement. Race and ethnicity play central roles in how many of these game makers experience and express their queerness, such as in the work of Santo Aveiro. Money and issues of poverty are topics that arise in a striking number of these interviews. In some queer indie games, religion is an oppressive force, while in others it is an important form of personal expression. A number of the artists contributing to the queer games avant-garde are non-neurotypical; some of their work reflects on their practices of self-care and healing, while other work serves as an intermediary between the artist and the neurotypical world. As Emilia Yang states, paraphrasing Audre Lorde, "We're not single-issue people because we don't live single-issue lives." One of

Fig I.9 :::: *The Tearoom* (2017) by Robert Yang, a video game about gay cruising in public restrooms

the main goals of this book is to represent and value queer individuals as whole people. Each of the game makers interviewed here brings their own intersectional identity to these discussions and to their games.

LISTENING TO QUEER VOICES:
METHODOLOGY AND BOOK STRUCTURE

The methodologies of the project are a crucial component of its politics. Presenting interviews rather than scholarly interpretations is a way to foreground how queer game makers tell their own stories. This is not to discount the value of academic writing on these games. Excellent work is being done in this area by scholars like Claudia Lo, Whitney Pow, and Teddy Pozo.[50] However, the ways that queer game makers talk about *their own work* is equally if not more important—especially because, as marginalized creators, their perspectives are often overlooked, overwritten, or appropriated. Some of the game makers profiled here speak often at public events, but others have rarely given interviews. The discussions found in this volume offer valuable opportunities to learn about these artists' influences and intentions and the obstacles they have faced. Structurally, this book is inspired by Cara Ellison's *Embed with Games* and merritt k's *Videogames for Humans*, which similarly highlight individual indie game makers and their interlocutors.[51] The book also shares an interest in bringing together diverse voices around sexuality and gender in games with recent collections of analog games like *#Feminism*.[52] In its ethos, this project draws inspiration from disability studies, which conducts research "by, for, and with" people with disabilities and their communities, rather than research "about" or "on" them. The present project is one that has been undertaken "with" and "for" queer subjects; they are equal authors of this book.

In deciding which game makers to interview, I have tried to represent a wide range of perspectives and game-making practices and to highlight those contributors to the queer games avant-garde whose works merit increased attention. When speaking with queer game makers who are already well known, I have endeavored to focus on topics that resist the tokenizing narratives commonly applied to these artists. Some of the figures whose work has been instrumental in the rise of the queer games avant-garde are not featured this volume. Most notably, these include Anna Anthropy, merritt k, Christine Love, and Porpentine, all of whom declined to be interviewed. Their presence is palpable all the same. Many of the artists whose voices do appear here cite these artists among their inspi-rations. As I discuss in the afterword, other artists do not appear here because they are so new on the "scene." There is also the matter of space and scope. The network of the queer games avant-garde is constantly ex-panding. For every queer game maker interviewed for this book, there are many more who could have been included. Any attempt to fully en-compass contemporary queer indie games will prove incomplete. That is a fundamental limitation of this work but also, I believe, an excellent prob-lem to have.

All of the interviews in this book were conducted by me in the spring of 2017, with the exception of the interview with Sarah Schoemann, which I conducted in the summer of 2018. Because these conversations took place within a relatively short period, this book functions as a snapshot: a picture of what queer indie game-making and the questions that sur-rounded it looked like at a precise moment in history. This was not only a moment of change for the medium of video games; it was within the first months of the Trump presidency. During these interviews, fear, concern, and anger weighed heavily in the air, not just for queer game makers in America but also for those living in Canada and Europe. In one way or an-other, LGBTQ game developers have been involved in the process of mak-ing video games for decades. Yet the stakes of developing defiant, ecstatic queer games have never felt more real.

Each interview lasted roughly two hours. Most interviewees received an honorarium as compensation for their time. The interviews were con-ducted either in person or over Skype, recorded, transcribed, and edited down to their present form. In selecting which parts of the interviews to include, I have focused on informative and unexpected moments, mo-ments of excitement and friction, with an eye toward content that will interest scholars, players, and aspiring game makers alike. It is also im-portant to me to acknowledge my own positionality and privilege in these interviews. I am a queer game studies scholar and an active queer games community organizer. From 2013 to 2017, I led the Queerness and Games Conference (QGCon), which is mentioned by many game makers in this volume. Through QGCon, I have had the honor of getting to know most of the artists profiled here. A few are close friends. I am myself queer, I have a background in the arts (creative writing), and I am a faculty member at a large research university. All of these factors, undoubtedly, have had their effects on the interviews. I can also see ways in which these interviews have been shaped by my own internalized biases. Often, I start with questions about the artists' childhood or background and move forward to the present day. In this way, I risk reinforcing "chrononormative" narratives of personal growth.[53] Thankfully, many of these game makers themselves point out the need to tell stories in ways that resist the traditional logics of linearity.

There are two points of terminology to clarify in my framing of the queer games avant-garde. The first is the word "queer." Like many queer theorists, I use "queerness" to signify both the identities of LGBTQ people and more conceptual notions of non-heteronormativity. Nearly every game maker I spoke with said that "queerness" resonated with them on a personal and/or artistic level. However, queerness meant different things to different people, and not all of these artists themselves identify as queer. There is power in describing these games and their creators under the bold, unifying heading of the "queer games avant-garde." It insists on the place of queerness at the forefront of video games. Yet, as Aevee Bee points out in her interview, there is also a potential danger in lumping all folks of non-heteronormative gender and sexualities into one category. When I use the terms "queer games" and "queer game makers," I mean these as a shorthand (albeit one with its own limitations) for indie game makers and their work that emerge from or engage with the experiences of LGBTQ people. This framework is intended to be descriptive, not pre-scriptive. It is only one of many ways to categorize the games discussed in this volume, as well as their creators. The second point of terminology is my use of the words "game maker" and "artist," which I deploy here interchangeably. In writing on video games, it is more common to see those who make video games referred to as "designers" or "developers." I have chosen not to use these as my go-to terms because not all contributors to the queer games avant-garde are designers (some are visual artists, musicians, programmers, etc.) and because "developer" brings to mind the production paradigms of the larger game industry.

It is my hope that these interviews serve as a springboard for game makers, scholars, and players interested in the queer games avant-garde. For those who want to build their own queer games—or any kind of socially aware play experience—think of these interviews like blueprints, not so much for the technical aspects of game development as for the development of what Colleen Macklin and John Sharp have called "design values."[54] A few interviews offer direct advice on *how* to make a video game (see, for example, the interviews with Mo Cohen and with Jimmy Andrews and Loren Schmidt), but all provide invaluable models for *why* to make one, where to turn for inspiration, and what questions to ask before you begin. For scholars in game studies, queer studies, and a number of adjacent fields, these interviews serve as primary material from which to build analyses of contemporary queer indie video games. The artists' discussions of their work have the potential to spark numerous close readings and suggest larger themes that cross the queer games avant-garde, as well as LGBTQ issues in digital media more broadly.

Each of the twenty interviews with contributors to the queer games avant-garde found here forms its own chapter. Every chapter opens with a short essay introducing the artist or activist (or group of collaborators), their work, key elements of their interview, and connections between their work and other queer games. These interviews focus on the artistic, social, and personal influences behind the queer games avant-garde. Together, they present a vision of queer indie game makers as a network of insightful, self-reflective, passionate, and often subversive creators—and as unique people, many of whom feel strongly about their own queerness but none of whom can be defined by any one aspect of their identities.

These chapters have been grouped into seven thematic sections. Part I, "Queer People, Queer Desires, Queer Games," opens the book with interviews from three game makers who directly represent queer subjects in their work: Dietrich Squinkifer (chapter 1), Robert Yang (chapter 2), and Aevee Bee (chapter 3). By contrast, the interviewees who appear in the second part, "Queerness as a Mode of Game-Making," engage with queerness primarily through their art-making practices and aesthetics. These include Llaura McGee (chapter 4), Andi McClure (chapter 5), and Liz Ryerson (chapter 6). Part III, "Designing Queer Intimacy in Games," features Jimmy Andrews and Loren Schmidt (chapter 7), Naomi Clark (chapter 8), and Elizabeth Sampat (chapter 9): game makers whose work creates, celebrates, and complicates queer experiences of intimacy. The game makers featured in part IV, "The Legacy of Feminist Performance Art in Queer Games," emphasize issues of embodiment, materiality, and co-presence in their work. They are Kara Stone (chapter 10), Mattie Brice (chapter 11), and Seanna Musgrave (chapter 12).

Part V, "Intersectional Perspectives in/on Queer Games," highlights artists whose games emphasize the interplays between sexuality, gender, race, and other aspects of identity—including Tonia B****** and Emilia Yang (chapter 13), Nicky Case (chapter 14), and Nina Freeman (chapter 15). In part VI, "Analog Games: Exploring Queerness through Non-Digital Play," the focus turns to queer game makers who develop analog rather than digital games, such as Avery Alder (chapter 16) and Kat Jones (chapter 17). The final part of the book is part VII, "Making Queer Games, Queer Change, and Queer Community." Through discussions with Mo Cohen (chapter 18), Jerome Hagen (chapter 19), and Sarah Schoemann (chapter 20), this section considers how queer games and the organizations that support them are being built from the ground up. It also addresses the influence that queer games are having on the mainstream games industry, while remaining critical of the industry's interests in queer indie games.

Finally, the afterword, "The Future of the Queer Games Avant-Garde," discusses new queer games that have been released as of this writing (in the summer of 2018) and presents short profiles of four up-and-coming queer game makers: Ryan Aceae, Santo Aveiro, Heather Flowers, and Jess Marcotte. This afterword also looks ahead to the work of queer indie game-making that has yet to come. Video games are an interactive medium, and playing them is crucial to understanding them. For this reason, I have also included an appendix of recommended queer indie games, both digital and analog, which can be played at home or in the classroom.

THE (QUEER) FUTURE OF VIDEO GAMES:
CELEBRATING CHANGE, COMPLICATING "PROGRESS"

The future of video games is constantly emerging and changing. Yet what is becoming increasingly clear is that that future is being irrevocably shifted by the work of contemporary queer indie game makers. These game makers represent a true avant-garde: they push the boundaries of the medium and show players and fellow designers that video games can take on different subjects, different forms, and different meanings than many people have ever imagined. In this way, the queer games avant-garde is blazing a trail for ongoing work that will continue to expand and reimagine video games as we know them today. This new work will be done by an increasingly vast and varied array of queer and transgender people, but also by more people of color, non-neurotypical people and people with disabilities, and people of various religious, national, and cultural identities. The history of video games will look back at this moment as a turning point—in ways both hopeful and alarming. Those who are seen as "different" are being openly and at times viciously harassed online by reactionary gamers who believe, as McClure states in the epigraph to this introduction, that queer indie games are "destroying video games." In a sense, they are. They are "disrupting systems," to use Naomi Clark's words, "shaking things up." The video games of the future will not look like the video games of the past, and this is due in no small part to today's queer games avant-garde. This implication is inherent in the very notion of a queer games avant-gardism. That which is avant-garde leads the way forward.

Yet, even as we celebrate this future, it is crucial to remain critical of our visions of progress and change. The politics of futurity are complicated at best. "Video game cultures seem to have a paradoxical relationship to temporality," writes Švelch. "On the one hand, they are obsessed with the future. . . . On the other hand, players and designers alike are nostalgic for the past."[55] This dual focus on the past and the future often leaves little room for the present: for the real, material, embodied conditions of making and playing games *now*. Paolo Ruffino, in writing about the rhetorics of innovation that dominate the discourse of the video game industry, describes how "what video games can do is always . . . projected in an imminent future."[56] Warns Ruffino, these stories about the future of the medium, with its "allegedly liberating and innovative effects," often reinforce rather than disrupt the "economic, political, and social conditions of the present."[57] I too remain wary of losing sight of the here-and-now and its dominant structures of power and privilege. However, the queer future of video games toward which the queer games avant-garde leads is different than the capitalistic future promised by the rhetoric of games industry innovation. It is a future that directly seeks to overturn the economic, political, and social conditions of the present by centering queerness and its capacity to imagine alternative ways of living, desiring, and playing in the world. Queer theory too brings with it critiques of futurity and progress. We can see this in Lee Edelman's refusal of heteronormative reproductivity, in José Esteban Muñoz's queer utopia that remains always on the horizon, in Kathryn Bond Stockton's queer child who grows sideways rather than up, in Jack Halberstam's rejection of heteronormative narratives of success, and in Elizabeth Freeman's critique of chrononormativity, to name only a few examples.[58]

To say that today's queer indie video games are leading the way toward a "better" future for LGBTQ folks and their place within the medium runs the risk of instrumentalizing queer art in the name of mainstream change. Perhaps it is more accurate to say that the power of the queer games avant-garde is not in making the mainstream video games more inclusive but rather in destabilizing the very notion of a mainstream. The future suggested by the contemporary queer indie game makers is one in which the center has not held, in which queer folks cannot simply be said to "speak from the margins" because the margins themselves have been repositioned as new centers for expression. In this future, video games belong to all—or, if not to all (because "democratizing" technologies are rarely as democratizing as they are made out to be), then certainly to more than before. Many of the games that have emerged from the queer games avant-garde themselves explore uncertain futures. These complications are not a weakness but a strength of the queer games avant-garde and its work. Like the game makers interviewed here, the future represented by the queer games avant-garde embraces change but also resists tidy narratives of progress. In this way, it preserves the transgressive spirit of queer game-making as a deeply radical art.

Queer People, Queer Desires, Queer Games

PART I

One of the many ways that the contributors to the queer games avant-garde are bringing queerness to video games is by making games that focus on the experiences of queer people. The LGBTQ characters in these games represent a spectrum of identities, desires, and experiences. This section presents interviews with three game makers whose games foreground characters who are non-heteronormative in their sexuality and/or their gender. In chapter 1, "Dietrich Squinkifer: Nonbinary Characters, Asexuality, and Game Design as Joyful Resistance," one of today's most exuberant game designers discusses how the development of their video games has paralleled the development of their own genderqueer, demisexual identity. Squinkifer argues for using glittery, camp aesthetics to send a message: the homophobic past of video games must die to make way for a fabulous new world of queer games. Chapter 2 is "Robert Yang: The Politics and Pleasures of Representing Sex between Men." Of the games emerging from the queer games avant-garde, Yang's are among the most explicitly and unapologetically sexual. Here, Yang talks about why representing queer sex in video games matters for the politics of LGBTQ presence in games, and how the gay male body becomes an important site of erotic world-building. The third chapter in this section is "Aevee Bee: On Designing for Queer Players and Remaking Autobiographical Truth." Bee's game *We Know the Devil* (2015) uses metaphors of monstrosity and mythical transformation to tell a story about transgender experience. Though the game is inspired by Bee's own history, she explains in this interview how her work resists traditional notions of autobiography and instead offers queer players the chance to remake their own histories. Together, these chapters offer a powerful vision of what queer representation can look like in video games: not the inclusion of tokenized LGBTQ characters often found in mainstream video games but the exploration of what it means to represent oneself and to see oneself represented.

1 DIETRICH SQUINKIFER

--===---===---===---===---===---===---===---==

Nonbinary Characters, Asexuality, and Game Design as Joyful Resistance

Dietrich "Squinky" Squinkifer is a Montréal-based game designer and interactive media artist. Their work explores queer experiences, nonbinary gender identities, and the challenges of building interpersonal relationships as a non-neurotypical person on the asexual (ace) spectrum. Squinky is among the most prolific artists in the queer games avant-garde, and their work spans a number of artistic mediums and development platforms. They are a person of color, genderqueer, and identify as "gay-leaning demisexual." Squinky has been instrumental in bringing increased visibility and support to genderqueer and ace members of queer and otherwise diverse games communities.

Across its varied forms, Squinky's work is marked by playfulness, humor, exuberance, autobiographical self-reflection, and insightful cultural critique. Often it is set to a catchy tune. As Squinky explains in this interview, they strive to capture a sense of "joyful resistance"—to embrace a "silly, proud, ostentatious," and distinctly queer approach to responding to contemporary politics. Among the many themes that emerge in the interviews found throughout this volume is the importance of intersectionality. Hand in hand with LGBTQ issues go questions of race, mental health, and socioeconomics. Also striking is the inextricable connection between Squinky's artistic work and their own queer identity. Often the two have emerged in parallel and profoundly shaped one another. This is true even on the most embodied level. The sales from one of Squinky's newest game, for instance, helped fund their recent top surgery.

Squinky spent their childhood in Edmonton, Canada; their family moved to Vancouver when Squinky was in high school. It was during this difficult transitional period that Squinky began teaching themselves to code and make video games. As an undergraduate, they studied computer science and took part in an educational co-op program that gave them direct experience in the tech industry. After graduating in 2008, they worked for two years at Hothead Games, where, as they describe here, they experienced the discriminatory attitudes of the games industry firsthand. While Squinky points to storytelling as their first love in video games, the shifting landscape of game-making in the early 2010s inspired them to begin creating work that engages explicitly with identity. In 2013, they moved to Santa Cruz for an MFA program in Digital Arts and New Media, and then to Montréal in 2016 to begin their PhD work at Concordia University. With their background in computer science, their extensive portfolio of creative work, and their time spent in higher education, Squinky is uniquely positioned to synthesize technical skills, artistic vision, and an engagement with critical theory. Here, Squinky shifts seamlessly from discussing gameplay controls to Bertolt Brecht to the relationship between social justice and glitter. Their work epitomizes how much of queer game-making today is emerging from dialogues between scholarship and creative practice.

Among Squinky's many games, the best known is their 2013 musical, film-noir-inspired detective drama *Dominique Pamplemousse in "It's All Over Once the Fat Lady Sings!,"* a point-and-click adventure game featuring a nonbinary protagonist. At the time we spoke, Squinky was working on a sequel, which has since been released as *Dominique Pamplemousse and Dominique Pamplemousse in "Combinatorial Explosion!"* (2017) (figure 1.1). In other games, like *Quing's Quest VII: The Death of Videogames!* (2014) (figure 1.2) and *I'm Really Sorry about That Thing I Said When I Was Tired and/or Hungry* (2014), Squinky uses Twine to tell stories that are at once personal, cultural, and political—such as a sci-fi tale of a rogue space captain who must decide whether destroy the toxic planet Videogames, or a series of daydreams from a young child attempting to make sense of cultural difference. Squinky has exhibited their work in a number of venues, including the Babycastles game art gallery in New York. Their game *Coffee: A Misunderstanding* (2014), a work of interactive theater in which participants act out possible versions of an awkward encounter between two convention attendees, has been featured at game events and is the subject of an article that Squinky published in feminist film studies journal *Camera Obscura.*[1] Much of Squinky's recent work, such as *The Truly Terrific Traveling Troubleshooter* (2017), which uses plush controllers to comment on "soft" emotional labor, moves toward hybrid forms of digital and ana-

Fig 1.1 :::: Dietrich
Squinkifer's 2017
sequel *Dominique
Pamplemousse and
Dominique Pample-
mousse* in "Combinato-
rial Explosion!"

Fig 1.2 :::: Built using
the development plat-
form Twine, *Quing's
Quest VII: The Death
of Videogames!* (2014),
which asks players
to decide whether to
destroy the planet
Videogames

log play, pushing the queer games avant-garde to increase its engagement with tangibility and the body.

RUBERG :::: What was your experience like as a queer person of color growing up in a predominantly white part of Canada? Did you think of yourself as different?

SQUINKIFER :::: From a very early age, I realized I wasn't normal. Aside from things like gender and sexuality, which would come much later in my life, my parents are immigrants, both from two different countries, Iran and the Philippines. Even though I wasn't an immigrant, I had an immigrant experience. When you're really young, you don't know how different you are. As soon as I started going to school though, I began to realize. When I went to the houses of my white friends, I thought, "Wow, this is just like what I see on TV."

It has always been interesting to me that that was my reaction—that this is what I've seen on TV and read in books. I understood whiteness through media. I was this very introverted, bookish kid, so most of my ideas about human interaction in general came from books. There are a lot of little social dances that most kids seem to absorb more intuitively than I could. I'm pretty sure that was because my experience was non-neurotypical. What people did in books just made more sense to me than trying to observe and understand them.

RUBERG :::: Do you feel connected to your parents' cultural backgrounds? Have they influenced your creative work?

SQUINKIFER :::: Yes and no. I definitely had the "third culture" experience, where you are between two cultures and you don't really fit into either. For a long time, I found myself not feeling very connected to either Iranian or Filipino culture. For example, my dad's family practiced this Iranian tradition of *taarof*, which is about saving face. It's a hospitality thing where, when someone offers you something, you're supposed to refuse. I didn't get that, so I felt really confused and out of place a lot of the time.

That experience is something I explored in my game *I'm Really Sorry about That Thing I Said When I Was Tired and/or Hungry*. I made it as part of a mini game jam that a friend and I did in Santa Cruz. I knew I wanted to work in Twine. For some reason, what came out was this story inspired by my childhood about these tiresome family gatherings we would go to. I would always daydream, so I wanted to play around with that in the game by allowing the player to skip around in time and explore the future. A lot of my work uses that kind of unresolved ending, because the truth is that there is a lot about being queer and being different that often still feels unresolved.

Actually, the unresolved endings in my games come in part from an Iranian influence. As a kid, I watched a lot of Iranian cinema, which is inspired by avant-garde French cinema. A lot of these movies had no ending. My cousins and I would be like, "What was that?" My dad told us that that was just how movies were in Iran. As I got older and understood storytelling better, I realized that an abrupt, unresolved ending can be so powerful, especially if you want to connote a sense of uncertainty and anxiety about the future. That's something I want my work to communicate.

RUBERG :::: In addition to those influences from Iranian culture, are there ways that Filipino culture has influenced the games you've made?

SQUINKIFER :::: Filipino culture is very celebratory, very jovial. There's a lot of dancing, especially in my mom's family. Music and dancing are themes that appear often in my work—but also there's this bigger spirit of joyfulness.

If you think about my game *Quing's Quest VIII: The Death of Videogames!*, it's about responding to difficult situations with joyful exuberance. At the time I made it, #GamerGate was happening, and that was really rough for me and my community. In response, I made *Quing's Quest*, which came out of a game jam for people who wanted to "ruin video games." In the game, you are a young monarch exiled from the planet Videogames. Ultimately you have to blow it up, destroying video games as we know them. It's a dark topic, but it's also fun and frivolous. There's so much glitter in the game, and I dedicate an entire section to picking out outfits. *Quing's Quest* is about resistance through this destructive sense of joy. It's really queer to respond to tragedy with silly, proud, ostentatious work.

Especially now, in the current political climate, holding onto things that make you happy is more important than ever. For instance, right now, I am in the process of getting consults for top surgery, which is something I've wanted for a long time. Why now? Because things are horrible, and if things are going to be horrible, I want to be more comfortable in my body. People ask me, "Why do you make games? Why do you make games now? Aren't there more useful things you could be doing?" It goes back to this idea of joyful resistance. That's why we make art. Across history, people have been making art in all sorts of harrowing situations.

RUBERG :::: This idea of joyful resistance through game design is a beautiful one. It seems to speak directly to the politics of your art. Do you see your work as political?

SQUINKIFER :::: Absolutely. I see everyone's work as political. Trying to be apolitical is itself a political stance, and not one that I agree with. There is no such thing as being apolitical.

In terms of politics, my games have been compared to the work of Bertolt Brecht. One of the things that Brecht did in his plays was use bad acting to create a sense of alienation or lack of identification, so that you are always aware that what you are watching is a representation. I like that as the antithesis to the idea of "empathy games," games in which you can supposedly walk in another person's shoes. Queer and especially trans game makers have been vocal about how problematic that idea is. Removing players from identification gives them a more critical distance and creates a different way of existing in relation to the work that doesn't rely on immersion.

My earlier works, like the first *Dominique Pamplemousse* game, were also very political, though they were also really personal at the same time. People have mostly talked about the game being about a nonbinary character, but for me it's more about a sense of anxiety about what was going on in the world. Socioeconomics were a big part of it. I started making the game during the Occupy movement, and I wanted it to be a reflection on how to survive under capitalism, how you need to compromise a lot of the time if you want to survive, because being ideologically pure will often put you in danger.

RUBERG :::: You said that *Dominique Pamplemousse* was a deeply personal game for you. How did the game and the process of developing it relate to your own identity?

SQUINKIFER :::: There has been a definite feedback loop. I started working on the game in 2011, and that was the year that I began really questioning my gender. In developing that game, I was actually working out my own identity. I originally was going to have [the protagonist] Dominique use "she" pronouns, but then when I switched to "they" pronouns for myself, I decided that that's what Dominique would use, too. So the character evolved with me. Then, when the game came out, it outed me as gender nonbinary. That was in 2013, when I moved to Santa Cruz to start my master's program, so it was actually a perfect opportunity to start over in a new city and use they/them pronouns. My experience with *Dominique Pamplemousse* was also a big factor in my name change. The game was credited to my old name, and when it started getting recognized for awards, I felt really uncomfortable with the name I had used. That pushed me to finally make the change to Squinky and then Dietrich "Squinky" Squinkifer.

Now I'm working on a sequel: *Dominique Pamplemousse and Dominique Pamplemousse in "Combinatorial Explosion!"* The original game has two different endings, so this game starts from the premise that both of those endings are true, and that there are multiple Dominiques. At first, I didn't want to make a sequel, but apparently there was more I wanted to say.

RUBERG :::: In the same way that the first *Dominique Pamplemousse* game paralleled shifts in your own identity, are you seeing something similar happen with the sequel?

SQUINKIFER :::: Definitely. Dominique's gender gets addressed less in this game, because the experience of being nonbinary has mostly normalized for me. The sequel is more about my experience as an ace [asexual] person. A lot of the scenes are about love and relationships. Romantic relationships are a theme that I didn't feel comfortable covering for a long time. Romance is a big part of a lot of queer games, which is great, but that doesn't reflect my own experience. When I tried to incorporate romance into my games, it felt uncomfortable. Sometimes, when it comes to queerness, being uncomfortable is good—but eventually I realized that the reason I was uncomfortable was because I'm ace. Lately though, as I've come into myself more, I've been wanting to address relationships more in my work. *Coffee: A Misunderstanding*, for example, was about a particular kind of relationship, the whole "I follow you on Twitter so let's be friends" relationship. I actually ended up dating someone I met on Twitter recently, so it's come around full circle.

The feedback loop between my life and the *Dominique Pamplemousse* games is definitely still going strong. For example, my plan is to use the sales from the new *Dominique Pamplemousse* to fund my top surgery.

RUBERG :::: **How did you get started making queer games? In the past, you've spoken about your negative experiences in the games industry. Was that a factor?**

SQUINKIFER :::: I got my start in the games industry as an intern at Telltale, which was a great place to work. When I was there, I was still very bright-eyed and bushy-tailed. After I finished my undergraduate degree in computer science, I worked at Hothead in Vancouver for two years. That's where I started running into problems. I was in my early twenties. I wasn't out as genderqueer yet; by all appearances, I was just a nerdy girl. The only other not-men at the entire company were the receptionist and one of the producers.

Given the state of games and the games industry at that time, I had no real space to explore my gender identity. I knew I wasn't a man, but for some reason I would go to Women in Games International events and not feel like I belonged there either. People were talking about experiences that I didn't share—for example, how they were treated by men. When you're trans, even if you don't know it yet, there's always something about you that people can pick up on. So all the stories about cisgender women getting hit on by men in the games industry, it would very rarely happen to me.

Still, a lot of the challenges I faced were definitely about gender. Young Squinky was very vocal and enthusiastic. However, people didn't like how vocal I was. They thought I was overstepping. It occurred to me that they wouldn't have thought that if I were a white guy. Some people at work were very encouraging toward me, but a lot of people weren't. They were scared of me, especially when I started getting into feminism and sharing feminist articles on the group emails. What I perceived as suggestions on how to make games better were interpreted as signs that I was being confrontational and attacking people.

I was really passionate and dedicated. I worked really hard. Once it became clear that they weren't going to give me what I worked hard for, I started working on side projects. That led to me being let go from the company. After that, I spent a couple years working for a studio that made websites for social change organizations. By then, I had learned not to fall in love with my job. Around that time, Anna Anthropy's *Rise of the Videogame Zinesters* came out and we had the "Twine revolution." Those were catalysts for me coming out as nonbinary. I watched as a bunch of people in games came out as queer and trans and I saw that that was OK. That's when I started working on *Dominique Pamplemousse*.

RUBERG :::: **Given your background, you walk a unique line between the games industry, academia, and the art world. Do you find that players from different contexts respond to your work differently?**

SQUINKIFER :::: I like to say that my work is loved by tenured professors and disliked by "gamers." In my opinion, that's a good thing. The difference in people's reactions has to do with their expectations about what a game is supposed to offer. People who are interested in the weird, experimental possibilities of interactive media like my work. That's in part because it doesn't require as much mechanical skill as a lot of video games do. It's important for game controls to be intuitive for the average person, especially if we want to reach other queer people or trans people or people of color. My material is challenging, but what makes it challenging is form, structure, and storytelling, not mechanical dexterity. This is the same reason why gamers don't like my work. It eschews skill and challenge, and if you expect games to be about mastery, these games won't be for you.

More and more, we're seeing games in galleries and art museums. When I show my games at art spaces, people are often surprised by what games can do. I find arts people are usually more impressed by my work than games people.

RUBERG :::: Do you think of yourself as part of a queer games avant-garde? Are there ways in which your work differs from other contemporary queer games?

SQUINKIFER :::: In terms of the differences between my work and other queer games, I've found that a lot of the queer games that are best known have sexual content. Sex always seems to fascinate people. My work doesn't engage with sex all that much, so it's not as titillating. That relates to larger tensions between aces and other people in LGBTQ communities. People ask, "Can you really call yourself queer if you're ace? Are you appropriating queerness?" However, if we take a queer theory perspective, being ace is absolutely a nonnormative sexuality and is therefore queer. Historically, what made someone "deviant" was not engaging in heteronormative relationships and not getting married or having children. It was the not-doing that raised flags.

As far as a queer games avant-garde, there is definitely a movement going on. The idea of an "avant-garde" is complicated though. Normally that's something that someone calls you after the fact, and I'm not sure we know yet what effects queer games will have in a larger historical context. We're going to have to wait and see.

2 ROBERT YANG

--=====---==---===---===---===---===---===---===--==

The Politics and Pleasures of Representing Sex between Men

Of the video games to emerge from the queer games avant-garde, Robert Yang's work is among the most unabashedly sexual. The subject of his games, which range from the suggestive to the pornographic, is commonly sex between men or related practices. Yang is far from shy about representing the gay male body giving and receiving pleasure. Influential for many other queer game makers, Yang's games have also sparked a variety of responses (from fascination to disgust) from the more mainstream, reactionary sectors of games culture, as he discusses below. Yang often faces censorship; in the past, his work has been banned from online streaming platforms like Twitch on grounds of obscenity. Yet, for Yang, representing gay sex in video games is crucial to the politics of queer game-making. In his writing and public appearances, he has been vocal about refusing to desexualize queerness in order to make it safe or palatable for heterosexual players. He resists "empathy," rejects the instrumentalization of LGBTQ identities by the games industry, and questions the often-heard narrative that video games' relationship to LGBTQ issues is simply "getting better."[1] Yet Yang's games are fundamentally celebratory: funny, at times bizarre, playful, and unapologetically sex-positive depictions of queer sexuality.

Robert Yang grew up in Southern California and attended the University of California, Berkeley, as an undergraduate. He got his start in game-making in high school through "modding," the practice of modifying existing video games. This spirit of remaking games still remains visible in his work, which often draws from and reimagines traditional gameplay experiences. Toward the end of his time at Berkeley, Yang began work on *Radiator 1* (2009), an experimental mod about gay divorce. In 2012, he moved to New York to take part in the Design and Technology MFA program at Parsons School of Design. In 2014, he began work on an ongoing series that he refers to as his "gay sex games." *Hurt Me Plenty* (2014) (figure 2.1), the first game in the series, is about spanking. The second game, *Succulent* (2015) (figure 2.2), invites the player to move a melting popsicle sensually in and out of a man's mouth. In *Stick Shift* (2015), the player's objective is to bring a car to orgasm by stroking its stick shift and progressing through the gears to climax. *Rinse and Repeat* (2016) takes place in the group shower of a men's locker room, where the player rubs down a naked hunk. Next in Yang's series is *Cobra Club* (2016), a game about "dick pics," in which players take and share naked photos of their characters in an imaginary, Grindr-esque app. Yang's most recently released game, which was under way at the time of our interview, is *The Tearoom* (2017), which is about cruising in public restrooms. Yang currently serves as assistant arts professor at NYU Game Center.

Though he is best known for the sexual explicitness of his games, what emerges in discussion with Yang is a nuanced set of artistic and political intentions that guide the representation of queer erotics in his work. An English major in college, Yang was drawn to modernist short fiction. Among his influences he lists Ernest Hemingway, J. D. Salinger, Robert Altman, and Virginia Woolf. When asked how his background in literature has affected his game-making, Yang points to the brief, vignette-like style of his work. "Short work is more interesting to me because it doesn't waste time. I think about Ezra Pound, who cut down his writing mercilessly to find the essence," he says. While the connections between literature and Yang's recent games—which rarely focus on storytelling or textual elements—may not be immediately obvious, Yang draws inspiration from these previous avant-gardes to imbue his work with meaning. "In my games," he says, "I try to mime what literary depth looks like, where you can analyze a text from all these different angles." This depth reveals itself below in Yang's reflections on how sexual desire can be understood through formal design, how erotics can speak back to power, and how the gay male body can become a site of queer world-building. In this way, Yang is challenging how game makers, both queer and mainstream, understand video games by demonstrating that pleasure itself can be a key site of meaning.

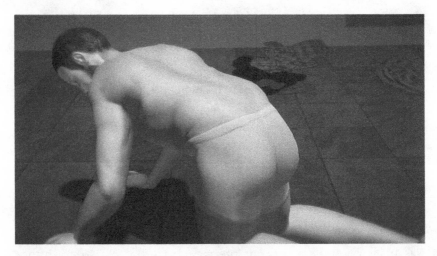

Fig 2.1 :::: The first of Robert Yang's "gay sex games," *Hurt Me Plenty* (2014), about spanking and consent

Fig 2.2 :::: *Succulent* (2015) by Robert Yang, in which players mimic fellatio by sensually moving a Popsicle in and out of a man's mouth

RUBERG :::: How would you describe your identity? Are there elements of your identity that have been particularly influential for your work?

YANG :::: I'm gay. I'm East Asian/Asian American. My family history is that my grandparents had to leave mainland China and go to Taiwan because they were fleeing from the communists. I grew up in Orange County, where my high school was predominantly white, so, at first, I tried to resist politicizing my identity, especially my race, because I felt like no one around me would understand. All my friends were white suburban skater boys. I sublimated that aspect of myself for a long time. In high school, I was much more focused on being gay and being closeted than on my race.

I moved to Berkeley for college because I wanted to get away from my parents and to reinvent myself. I thought that the Bay Area would be a gay paradise. When I got there, I found out it was not. I did meet a lot of other Asian people who felt political about their identities. I also met a lot of gay people. But I started realizing that, when I'd go to gay events, other gay people would treat me differently because of my race. I can't escape my race. I thought I could in Orange County; I thought I could assimilate into white culture. Gay male culture is still very white-dominated though, so I couldn't escape racism, because racism is everywhere. That's when I first recognized that this is all connected.

RUBERG :::: How did you get started making video games about sexual practices between gay men? What was your path to your current work like?

YANG :::: During high school, I did a lot of modding. That's where you build new things on top of existing games, like levels or skins, or ideally a whole new game. Being a good modder was about proving that you could actually work in the games industry. For better or worse, that's the value system that's in place. It's people aspiring to enter the industry and to prove themselves. I was younger than a lot of my peers in the modding community, so for a long time I thought I was some kind of prodigy destined to make important industry games.

Later, when I was wrapping up my undergrad degree, I made my *Radiator 1* mod of *Half-Life 2*, because I was interested in experimenting with personal games. I thought I wanted a job in the industry, so I went to the Game Developers Conference and somehow got an interview with [the games studio] Valve. I brought my laptop, took it out, and showed them *Radiator 1*. They played it and were like, "This is good, this is well made, but this is too weird. This is a gay divorce simulator. If we hire you, are you going to be able to make a game about shooting monsters? Make some 'normal' video game levels and then we can talk."

At the time, I was very upset and angry that the games industry was basically telling me I was too weird. Looking back on it though, I think they were right. I wouldn't have fit in and I wouldn't have been happy. They told me what I needed to hear. I've learned to regard it as this badge of honor—that I was too gay for the industry.

RUBERG :::: **You mentioned that you became more political as you grew up. Have your games become more political over time as well?**

YANG :::: Definitely, my work has become a lot more political. Take *Radiator 1*. It began as a formal experiment. The fact that the game contained gay identities was just incidental. By contrast, my current series of games about gay sex comes from a different direction. They're still formally experimental, but they came directly out of a desire to make games more gay.

The games in my current series are sexually explicit, and that's related to politics as well. A lot of the time, heteronormative forces try to de-sex gayness. We've fallen into this trap of homonormativity and focusing on gay marriage. That turns gay life into this very sincere, earnest, nonsexual domestic arrangement. It's important to put sex acts front and center, because sex is part of what makes gay communities, especially radical gay communities. I think a lot of straight people are OK with gay people in the abstract—like, "Just keep whatever you do behind closed doors"—and I want to fight against that.

I met another gay artist recently who makes even more sexually explicit works, like quilts of two men fist fucking. I felt like he looked down on what I'm doing because I censor myself a bit. Like, in my game *Rinse and Repeat*, which is about men washing one another at the gym, I pixelate the dicks. From this artist's perspective, I'm compromising. From my perspective, I actually feel like he's compromising by working in a medium that readily interfaces with the art world, which is already a safe space for gay people. Meanwhile, I'm trying to work in games culture, which is a much more hostile environment.

RUBERG :::: **As a game designer with an MFA working in New York, have you had other encounters with the art world? Does it matter to you to think of your games as "art"?**

YANG :::: I rarely share my work in arts spaces actually, because the fine art world doesn't understand what I do. Part of my success comes from the fact that my games use the language of video games. That signals that these are gay sex games for gamers. When the fine arts world sees these games, they just see the image, and they think it's boring. Robert Mapplethorpe was taking photos of spanking thirty years ago. Why is a game like *Hurt Me Plenty* more visually interesting? I don't have any response to that. The magic of these games comes from being conversant in games.

Personally, I don't care much about my games being recognized as "art." I used to, but I've learned to survive without that. That's not why I make games, anyways. I make games because some part of me still buys into the utopian premise of technology. I make games because that's my way of talking to a lot of people who I otherwise wouldn't talk to. Through my games I can have a conversation with them.

RUBERG :::: **Do you see yourself as part of a queer games movement? Many artists making queer games today differ in their perspectives on the connections between queer game makers.**

YANG :::: I've always felt like I was in dialogue with other queer game makers, people like merritt k, Andi McClure, Liz Ryerson, and Anna Anthropy. I consider them my friends. But when I think about a movement, I think about community, and for some people the word "community" has a lot of baggage. The Bay Area queer games community [that was active from 2012 to 2014] kind of imploded. Some of the people there feel like community hasn't helped them or they were never part of that community. But if they came back around and said, "No, I was part of a queer games community," I'd be OK with it. It doesn't really depend on me, because I operate from so much privilege. Having a queer games movement wouldn't be about helping me. It would be about helping other people.

RUBERG :::: **Your current "gay sex game" series started with *Hurt Me Plenty*. What's the origin story behind the game?**

YANG :::: *Hurt Me Plenty* started out when I decided to commission a 3D artist to make me a gay, beefcake, hunky character model. One frustration with making diverse games is that it's hard to find diverse art assets. Because I come from a modding background, I'm used to grabbing other people's assets and modifying them. Generic male body types in video games are really limited though. You either have super muscular soldiers or zombies. That's not really what gay men are interested in. That's not relevant to us. So, what is? What would be a character model for a gay male gaze? I think the character I commissioned is more popular and relevant to people who are sexually attracted to men. It's like in Ovid's *Metamorphoses*. Ovid is interested in how bodies suggest worlds of possibility. Each body is a world in itself. In order to represent a gay world, you need a gay body.

Once I had the character, I thought, "What should I do with him?" Then [game interface developer] Leap Motion was doing this game jam. The Leap Motion is a control device where you move your hand above a sensor. I got one and I thought about what game I could base around a hand gesture. I considered making a voguing game, but the Leap Motion is just terrible at fast, complex movement. I simplified it to a giant hand swipe, which became a spanking motion. I'm not into kink myself, so I started doing research, and I found out that BDSM communities have really interesting approaches to formalizing sex. There's always a negotiation or consent phase. Then you play out the scene and there's aftercare at the end. That is basically a game design document. Kinky people generally liked the game, but Leap Motion never even acknowledged that I'd made it, even though I think it was the best game in the jam.

RUBERG :::: In a lot of your games—including your next game, *Succulent*—you use the same character model, and he's almost always wearing sunglasses. What's your artistic intent there?

YANG :::: A month or two after I made *Hurt Me Plenty*, I watched a movie called *Inherent Vice*. There is a scene of the characters sucking on a frozen banana. In the movie, it's played for homophobic laughs, but the camera lingers a while, and it was interesting to watch the mechanics of what was happening. Inspired by that, I made *Succulent*. An important technical element of the game is what I called cheek physics. In video games, there's this dominant trope of breast physics, which is about how bodies deform when they move. In *Succulent*, you're using the Popsicle to deform the characters mouth and face, so I added cheek physics. Video game physics are important in general because that's what makes the body real inside the virtual space: the simulation of interaction and response.

In terms of the character, reusing him is partly about practicality, and partly it's funny to me that this hunky beefcake guy is, like, in my stable of stars in my fictional game studio. Also, by always using the same character, it's like these games exist in one shared universe. As far as the sunglasses go, there's a technical reason. It's hard to do eye rendering in a way that's not creepy. Giving him sunglasses is a shortcut so I don't have to worry about it. It also gives him a sense of character that he wouldn't have otherwise. In *Succulent*, it's very important that he wears sunglasses. It makes the scene much hotter. Eyes make people more vulnerable, more human. In *Succulent*, I didn't want the character to feel human. I wanted him to be a pure embodiment of ideology.

RUBERG :::: Both *Succulent* and *Rinse and Repeat* are about relatively "normal" sexy scenarios, like using a Popsicle to suggest fellatio or washing another man, but they both have very weird, unexpected endings. In *Succulent*, the character's jaw opens so wide it seems like he's going to eat the player, and *Rinse and Repeat* becomes a surreal, psychedelic dream. Why end the games that way?

YANG :::: I do that because I want these games to have more than one note. A lot of short "joke" games hammer on one note and expect to sustain it. A joke is never just one note though. You can't just have a punch line. Then again, I don't really think of these games as jokes. I'm being funny, but I'm also being serious. When people do read them as jokes, especially straight gamer dudes on YouTube, they end up laughing at gay people's expense. What I'm actually going for is more "inside baseball": gay people laughing with themselves. So, I wouldn't call these games jokes because that opens them up to a dominant, hegemonic interpretation of all gay culture as a joke.

These straight gamer dudes performing their gay panic really do annoy me. It's not that they would spit on gay people, but they go on YouTube and demonstrate their disgust because it helps them assert their own heteronormativity. Also, they're all saying the same thing, that gay stuff is gross, and at that point you're basically retelling my jokes and pretending you came up with them—and you're not even telling them right. Or the joke totally goes over your head and you don't know what's going on, but you're going to laugh and pretend to be disgusted anyway.

RUBERG :::: You're currently working on your newest game, *The Tearoom*. What inspired the game? What are you hoping that it will accomplish?

YANG :::: *Tearoom* is about men cruising in public bathrooms circa 1960. I drew a lot from *Tearoom Trade* by Laud Humphreys, the notorious sociological study. It started out with my fascination with video game bathrooms. Video game bathrooms are strange because characters in games rarely need to pee, so a bathroom is usually purely decorative, or it has to take on another function. In video game level design, a bathroom is where you might put a health kit, for example. In that way, there are cultural implications to video game bathrooms, because they don't acknowledge bathroom politics.

I wanted to make a game that tried to actually simulate a bathroom. The first thing I did was model out a urinal in painstaking detail. I also chose the Cadillac of urinals—the biggest, most beautiful urinal ever. When I do things like that, I'm trying to prove that it's worth putting time and resources into a game like this. A lot of queer games follow punk aesthetics. They try to move away from polish. That makes sense, but I also want to start a second aesthetic front. Gay people should be expensive. Gay issues should be expensive. Gay politics should be rendered with high production value. But then, as I thought about what gay sex inside a bathroom looks like, it occurred to me that when men went to bathrooms to have sex, they weren't there to pee. So, in a funny turn, my bathroom still isn't functional, because you're still not there to pee, you're there to have sex.

In the game, the player stands at the urinal waiting for men. Suddenly, you'll hear a car pull up and you'll wonder, "Is that a new guy, or an under-cover cop?" I want players to feel a bit of fear. Men would meet in these bathrooms, but they wouldn't trust each other and they would avoid intimacy. Then there are the social rituals. Part of the game is about glancing at each other: making eye contact or not making eye contact. The act of looking is something totally not explored in games, even though that's what games are about. Eventually all this leads to simulated fellatio. One design challenge I'm facing is that it's really hard to depict something penetrating you orally with a first-person camera perspective. My solution is to have this giant, creepy lecherous tongue appendage attached to the front of your camera.

I also want to be in dialogue with the fact that my games have been banned from Twitch for having sexual content. If I put dicks in the game, it will definitely get banned. So instead the characters are going to have guns sticking out of their pants. I'm trying to make a point about how guns are apparently OK in video games but sex isn't. It's also about how guns are idolized in video games graphics. These are going to be very lovingly rendered guns that you lick.

3 AEVEE BEE

--==---==---==---==---==---==---==---==

On Designing for Queer Players
and Remaking Autobiographical Truth

Aevee Bee is the writer and creative director of the acclaimed 2015 game
We Know the Devil (figure 3.1), made in collaboration with cocreator Mia
Schwartz. *We Know the Devil* sits at the unique juncture of the visual
novel and horror game genres. Bee refers to it as a "surreal summer camp
dystopia."[1] The game's three queer protagonists—Neptune, Venus, and
Jupiter—must spend one week at a religious sleepaway camp in the
woods. Much of the gameplay focuses on forming social bonds between
characters and confronting the pain of finding oneself on the outside of
intimacy. Players choose which two characters to encourage to spend time
together and which one to leave out. In the game's final sequences, the
lonely character becomes a literal demon who must be destroyed (figure
3.2). Alternatively, if players can balance all three pairings, all of the characters transforms into their frightening yet glorious demon forms and
together Neptune, Venus, and Jupiter take over the camp in the name of
the devil. Queerness is present in *We Know the Devil* on a number of levels. Its characters build non-heteronormative romantic ties and its core
mechanic of group relationship-building echoes polyamorous relationship
structures. In addition, just beneath the surface of the characters' seem-
ingly fantastical transformation from human to demon is an ambivalent
message about the power and the horror of being a transgender person
who is made to feel like a monster, and who can choose whether to reject
or embrace that monstrosity.

Bee, the daughter of two English professors, grew up in Indiana. Literature was among her earliest creative influences and it continues to inform her work. She received her bachelor's degree from Oberlin College
and later completed her MFA in creative writing. Though digital media is

Fig 3.1 :::: *We Know the Devil* (2015), created by Aevee Bee and Mia Schwartz: a "surreal summer camp dystopia"

Fig 3.2 :::: *We Know the Devil*, part visual novel and part horror game, using monstrosity as a metaphor for transgender experience

today her primary medium of artistic expression, Bee still identifies first and foremost as a writer. Since 2008, she has worked as a games journalist for publications like *Gamasutra*, *Pace*, and *Game Set Watch*, where she brings an analytical perspective to her interpretations of video games and games culture. Currently living in Olympia, Washington, Bee holds a day job at an academic institution and works on her games and other creative endeavors, like her most recent game *Heaven Will Be Mine* (2018) and her online zine *Zeal*, on the side. Some of her core creative interests in gamemaking are narrative design and queer world-building.

We Know the Devil was inspired in part by Bee's own experiences as a teenager in the Midwest. Yet she is careful to note that, while the game has autobiographical aspects, it is not an exact reflection of her own childhood. Instead, the game offers branching narrative options: what she describes here as "alternatives avenues" that allow queer players to "control and process [their] personal truth instead of just reproducing it." In this way, though Bee's work represents queer people—both in that she tells queer stories and in that she designs her games to be played by queer people—she herself brings dominant expectations for queer representation into question. Queer characters must remain complex, says Bee, and they cannot be stripped of their sexual desire in order to make them acceptable to an implicitly homophobic audience. Bee also speaks insightfully about the messiness of pinpointing whether and how the queer games avant-garde is bringing change to the mainstream video game industry. On the one hand, as Bee states below, making video games "better" is not the responsibility of marginalized artists. On the other hand, Bee can see powerful ways in which queer indie game makers are serving as role models for queer and trans folks working in AAA studios. Bee also expresses her excitement at this moment of growth for the queer games avant-garde, when new artists are bringing fresh perspectives to the work of queer game-making.

RUBERG :::: Your background is in creative writing. What inspired you to make the transition to working in a digital medium like video games?

BEE :::: I'm attracted to games because they don't have the same stifling rules of literary creative writing. In a program like an MFA, they teach you a very particular kind of writing. The workshop method produces stories with a specific history and culture. I did that kind of work for a long time and I became a much, much better writer, but I also didn't write anything that I truly enjoyed. Honestly, working on *We Know the Devil* was the first time that I created something I really loved. I wish I had given myself more permission to do work like that earlier.

The success of *We Know the Devil* has given me a huge amount of creative confidence. I've been writing games journalism for years now, but before I actually started making games, I was always imagining these worlds and shoving them in a folder and never showing them to anyone else. I thought, "Nobody is going to care." Then I started working with my collaborator Mia Schwartz and she loved my ideas. Very spontaneously, we decided to make a game together, and that was *We Know the Devil*. I was finally able to get out of my own head, rather than always worrying about whether what I made was perfect.

Books still have a strong influence on my work, though, even when I'm making games. I was a voracious reader as a kid. I loved the fantastical worlds in *The Chronicles of Narnia* and *His Dark Materials*, but I also loved literary fiction like J. D. Salinger's *Nine Stories* and *Franny and Zooey*. Salinger does world-building, too. Across his stories, he creates this family whose lives and stories are all interconnected. I like that cohesiveness. There's understanding and connection between stories even in realist fiction.

RUBERG :::: **Given your interest in literature, do you find yourself drawn to video games that focus on text and narrative?**

BEE :::: Actually, as a writer, most of my favorite games are ones without a lot of writing in them. For example, I'm really critical of BioWare games. Their world-building is messy and their stories don't cohere. In terms of how to construct a narrative, I like *Dark Souls*. I know everyone says that, but it reminds of me of *Myst* or the very first video game I ever played, which was *The Manhole*. It was a point-and-click adventure game for children where there was no plot, no puzzles, no nothing. I liked that game because it was so organic; everything was its own part of the world. In *Dark Souls*, too, there's this long history behind everything that happens in the game. Every item and object and place and enemy: every single thing that exists in the game is part of one big story.

In my own writing, I've always been very image-heavy, very character-heavy, very place-heavy. I'm not a plot-focused writer, partly because I'm bad at plot. I tend to really like stories that draw more attention to those other elements. In some ways, I like video games the most of all the possible mediums for storytelling because they can have all those elements, like imagery and characters, without really having a plot. The plot is just the sequence of events that happens—just you walking through the space. You are the plot.

RUBERG :::: **In making video games about queer and trans characters, like *We Know the Devil*, do you draw from your own personal experiences?**

BEE :::: Yes, but it's more complicated than that. I've been thinking a lot about this idea of "empathy games." You're supposed to be able to experience what it's like to be this other person, right? To me, that sounds very similar to the confessional writing that a lot of queer artists get pushed into. It's like, "Tell us about your queerness" rather than "Create a new existence for yourself."

I'm wary of confessional work, but also confessional work is just hard for me to do. I have other ways of getting at similar things. *We Know the Devil* is super autobiographical, but it's also about me unpacking that autobiographical history and finding alternative avenues out of it. A confessional story about my own childhood would be this static product, like, "Look at this. Here is a thing that happened. It's tragic and bad. Empathize with it." Instead, the game offers alternatives. It says, "Here's a thing that brings you in and allows you to both experience queer suffering but also to escape from it." In making a game like that, you can control and process your personal truth instead of just reproducing it.

Rather than give an outsider ownership of whatever queer story I'm telling, I feel like I'm giving other queer people the ability to reclaim and control their own stories and their pasts. Maybe that's too idealistic, but a lot of people have interpreted *We Know the Devil* as being about how they were able to process, understand, or control a queer narrative. The game has these tragic endings but then it has this really powerful, subversive final act that allows you to break through. I think that's part of the game's success.

RUBERG :::: You make an important point about the value of designing queer games for queer players, rather than for the mainstream. Are you also interested in straight, cisgender people playing your games?

BEE :::: I'm not trying to make games for straight people. At some point, I had the revelation that I didn't need to make work that was accessible for as wide an audience as possible. I was like, "Oh wait, I can make this stuff for a niche audience and be successful." That was informed by my journalism around #GamerGate, because I was like, "Why are we making stuff for these people who don't understand, who don't want to understand, or who are actively trying to attack us for doing this sort of work?" We don't need to talk to them. Rather than putting all of your energy into trying to convert the one person who is really angry on the internet, why not take that time and create work for people who actually matter?

With that said, with *We Know the Devil*, I wrote a very honest and personal story that was true to myself and that is inherently accessible for others. The game is about women in love with other women, but a lot of folks who don't identify in that way still really relate to that narrative. If you're interested in making games, you should be thinking about it that way rather trying to create something for some other person. Instead, be like, "I am creating this thing for myself and you are invited to participate. I am asking for you to open yourself and leave behind certain assumptions." That's what good stories do. They invite you in.

RUBERG :::: **Your work tackles serious issues, like what it is like to grow up queer in a socially repressive environment, but it is also funny. What is the role of humor in your games?**

BEE :::: Humor is huge for me. It's a way of fighting back. Video games have a self-seriousness problem, and humor acts as an antidote to that. A lot of the Western games that have been highly praised, like *BioShock*, perform their own importance by evoking references to literature and philosophy. Effective humor is much more impressive to me than saying, "Here is a quote from someone famous. Now take my game seriously." That self-seriousness problem is part of games culture as well. It was a big factor in #GamerGate, where people were saying, "We, the gamers, want to take games more seriously than anything else, and also we don't want them criticized in any serious way." I think a lot of indie game creators have a similar problem, which comes from a place of insecurity—this fear that games are not taken seriously as art. They're seen as juvenile entertainment, so we grab for things like literary references to seem intelligent and so people will take us seriously. We have this genre shame.

RUBERG :::: *We Know the Devil* **is, as you say, about women who love other women, yet you've written online about being "against [LGBTQ] representation" in video games.**[2] **What does that mean and how do you reconcile those approaches?**

BEE :::: That article was a little manifesto. When I say that I'm "against representation," I mean that representation can't just be a list of identity categories. It's not really representation unless you're creating complexity; without complexity, characters feel insincere and incomplete. The dumbed-down version of a queer person, or the queer person that never expresses their sexuality—these characters don't actually require you to empathize with queer people, because these characters have no sexuality. When you erase that, you erase their anchor, their passion, their frustrations, or their flaws even, especially their flaws. You're not doing empathy work if you're not engaging with these things, because these are the stumbling blocks for empathy. Sometimes people are like, "I like the gay people who don't act gay." You know? Those are the people you're catering to when you make those sorts of characters.

Identity is so important to talk about, yet it can be so limiting. I've been having a lot of discussions with queer activists and queer scholars about this desire to all call ourselves "queer," like we're this amorphous blob. That can actually be incredibly unhelpful because it doesn't acknowledge the very real differences that often exist between queer people. Our experiences are specific to our lives. Focusing only on identity, especially identity without experience, reduces everyone to an abstraction.

RUBERG :::: Given how much you value the specifics of individual queer experience, how would you describe the complexities, as you call them, of your own queer identity?

BEE :::: Being a woman is really important to me. Transness is also important to me. In terms of sexuality, I tend to talk about how sexuality is practiced and understood rather than talking about specific attractions. What's the point of trying to say, "Oh, I have this very specific sexual identity" when sexuality is really hard to separate from gender identity and expression? Sexuality is more complicated than we often give it credit for.

For example, I'm less interested in saying, "I identify as a bisexual" than I am in thinking about the ways that I love women and the ways that I love men and how those are unfortunately incredibly different because of all of these social pressures, my own histories, and my internalized baggage. How do we navigate that together with another person? What does a relationship with someone like me look like? It's one thing to be like, "We have this list of labels," but we have so few models for what those labels are supposed to look like.

RUBERG :::: How do you feel about the idea that queer indie games like yours are helping make the games industry more diverse? Do you think that's true?

BEE :::: In some ways, I'm like, "I don't care. That's their problem." When I'm working as a journalist, I'm one of those people who says, "Queer people are going to make video games incredible!" As a creator though, I wonder, should I really be putting my energy towards fighting for BioWare to include a trans character? That character is still going to be a BioWare character. Instead, shouldn't I be fighting to create something that's really meaningful for the queer people I want to speak to?

It's true though that there is this trickle up, where big developers are learning from queer indies. Some BioWare designers are friends with Christine Love, for example, and they certainly play her games. That has an influence. Also, when I go somewhere like the Game Developers Conference and see a lot of queer people, often those aren't indies; they're people who have felt like they were able to come out in their workplaces at AAA companies in part because of the visibility of queer designers. That's big. I think people might be surprised at the number of queer folks who are working in AAA and who, in the small ways that they can, are putting more and better content into those games. That kind of influence is different from some white dude playing my game and being like, "Oh, maybe I'll be influenced by that."

RUBERG :::: You mentioned Christine Love as an influential figure. Are there other contemporary queer game makers that you see yourself in dialogue with? Have you noticed the larger artistic network of queer games shifting?

BEE :::: When I first came onto the queer games scene back around 2013, people were really idolizing a couple of major figures, and there was a lot of scrappy infighting. However, since then, queer game design has gotten much more diverse. It's really exploded. That has helped me get in touch with my ability. I feel much more self-assured now than when I was just looking in the shadow of these others. Creators in small communities can sometimes turn very competitive and those communities can become suffocating spaces, and so I'm glad that that is better than it used to be.

At the Game Developers Conference every year, I see more and more queer people who I've never even heard of, and that's the most thrilling experience. Who wants to know everyone? It's so much healthier to have a diversity of aesthetics and voices and influences so it's not this small group of queers all referencing the same things. It helps reduce this competitive urge that I feel is the most poisonous and deadly thing for the queer community: the Highlander syndrome. "There can be only one person who will get the money to survive. There can be only one person who will get the fame. We have to find some angle to take down that other person who is a little bit problematic." That attitude can do real damage within marginalized communities.

Even back in 2013, some people were saying, "There's no queer games community." I think that's a half-truth. A better way of describing it might be that there was no healthy queer games community—because there certainly was a small group of people who all knew each other and were making games in conversation with each other. Now that type of small core doesn't exist. The world of people making queer video games is way bigger. It's not a clique. It's getting larger and harder to categorize, and that's a good thing.

Queerness as a Mode of Game-Making

PART II

The artists featured in this second part make games that are deeply queer. Yet, in contrast to the interviewees in part I, these game makers rarely include representations of queer people in their work. In fact, many of their games do not depict people at all. Instead, in modes reminiscent of the conceptual queerness found in queer theory, the engagement of these game makers with queerness manifests in how they create their work and the unexpected places it leads them. In chapter 4, "Llaura McGee: Leaving Space for Messiness, Complexity, and Chance," McGee talks about the importance of creating video games and other playful experiences that do not conform to the standards of the medium. For McGee, bringing unpredictability into the creative process is, she says, "a way of queering video games." Chapter 5, "Andi McClure: Algorithms, Accidents, and the Queerness of Abstraction," is a discussion with one of the queer indie game makers whose work pushes video games farthest from standard notions of representation. Here, McClure explains how she works in collaboration with machines and mathematics to develop intentionally disembodied experiences that challenge core tenets of traditional thinking around games, such as identification, immersion, and gamification. "Liz Ryerson: Resisting Empathy and Rewriting the Rules of Game Design" is the last chapter in this section. Ryerson is the designer of the game *Problem Attic* (2013): a glitchy, counterintuitive, and intentionally opaque platformer. She is also a musician who has contributed sound design for many projects from fellow queer game makers. In this interview, Ryerson argues against the idea of queer video games as "empathy games," a popular term in the discourse that characterizes the mainstream reception of the queer games avant-garde. As queer people, says Ryerson, "we have to make our own rules."

The chapters in this part demonstrate how queerness can operate in video games beyond representation, and how game-making can function as a playground in its own right for exploring queer messes. They also suggest that, at times, the work of the queer games avant-garde is not only to represent LGBTQ people in video games or even to move beyond representation but also to refuse representation.

4 LLAURA MCGEE

--==---==---==---==---==---==---==---==---==

Leaving Space for Messiness, Complexity, and Chance

Llaura McGee is a game maker from the northwest coast of Ireland. In 2014, McGee released *Curtain* (figure 4.1), a haunting game about an abusive romantic relationship between two women, Ally and Kaci. Ally and Kaci are up-and-coming punk rockers living in Glasgow. In the role of Ally, the player explores the couple's apartment through a first-person view, but the game's art is glitchy and abstract, and in the early moments of the game it is often intentionally difficult for the player to make sense of their surroundings. At the bottom of the screen, represented as a constant stream of text, Kaci—"your partner and inescapable narrator," as McGee writes on her website—berates and undermines Ally, attempting to convince her to stay in their relationship.[1] As the player moves through the dreamlike architecture of the apartment, time progresses, showing players three stages of the relationship. In the game's final section, Ally has broken up with Kaci yet still struggles with the memory of her abuse. McGee is herself a musician who lived in Scotland while attending university, and the events and emotions that surrounded her return from Scotland to Ireland in 2013 were an important inspiration for *Curtain*.

In addition to *Curtain*, McGee has worked on a number of other experimental video games and gamelike projects. Among these works are *The Isle Is Full of Noises* (2016) (figure 4.2), a highly stylized piece created using markers, which McGee describes as an example of an emerging genre she calls "flat games," as well as her 2015 gallery installations *Fluc* and *Amari* and her current work in progress, *If Found, Please Return*, a longer, commercial game built by a small, diverse team of women, trans people, and nonbinary people in Dublin. Like so many of the artists contributing to the queer games avant-garde, McGee brings a rich range of talents to her work. In addition to her background in music, she has a long history with creative writing and has become increasingly involved with Dublin's growing zine culture.

One of the key themes that emerges from McGee's discussion of her games is the idea of leaving space for messiness, serendipity, chance, and complexity in the creative process. The aesthetics of McGee's games call to mind the games of Liz Ryerson (chapter 6) and the work of Andi McClure (chapter 5). McGee shares with these fellow artists an interest in glitches and abstractions as tools for telling queer stories that communicate personal truth while resisting the pitfalls of "serious games," such as tokenism, oversimplification, and the replication of stereotypes. Here, McGee offers poignant advice for fellow creators who want to design their own experimental games, queer or otherwise. She stresses that indie game makers must question the norms that have limited the medium of video games. McGee also highlights the value of self-care, especially for marginalized artists, as well as the importance of refusing to measure one's own self-worth through the success of one's work.

Oh, I did recognize Samantha though. And I saw her talking to you before we played. What did I say? Look. Let's just get into to the flat and we can talk. She's just bitter and jealous. She missed out.

Fig 4.1 :::: The 2014 game *Curtain* by Llaura McGee, in which the player explores the apartment of two women in an abusive relationship

Fig 4.2 :::: *The Isle Is Full of Noises* (2016), the art for which was created using markers and paper—an example of what McGee calls "flat games"

Within the broader landscape of the queer games avant-garde, McGee represents one of an increasing number of queer indie game makers working in Europe. Though the majority of the artists profiled in this book are American or Canadian, McGee's work challenges us to look beyond North America. Ireland, for instance, has its own growing indie games scene, which McGee reports has diversified in recent years. McGee's insights as an Irish game maker also cast light back onto the queer games emerging from the United States and Canada. They prompt us to consider the importance of national and regional context for the work of making (and making meaning from) queer video games. As for the impact of queer indie games on the larger games industry, McGee warns that idealizing the influences these games have can lead to appropriation. While the work of queer and trans game makers may be inspiring change in the AAA industry, these game makers rarely see an economic benefit from their influence. This further underscores the financial precarity of queer game-making and the disparities of privilege that characterize professional video game development today, even at a moment when the games industry claims to value diversity.

RUBERG :::: You grew up in rural Ireland. What was it like for you as a queer, trans young person in that environment?

MCGEE :::: I'm from Donegal, from a very small fishing village in the northwest corner of Ireland. It's about as remote as you can get. It's a very beautiful area, but it's definitely isolated. Ireland has come a long way in the last twenty years, but until recently we were still a very repressed nation. Making art and especially making video games didn't seem like even a remote possibility for an Irish person when I was young.

It was also a very heteronormative and gendered world. I had to play football every week. Being on a bus for two hours with thirty guys you don't relate to whatsoever so you can go to a football match in some other tiny village where you sit on a bench in the rain: that's my childhood. One thing I did love was swimming in the sea. Every day after school, my dad and I would drive to the beach, jump in, swim for five minutes, and go home soaking wet. The water was freezing cold. We swam in the rain and in storms. Back at home and at school, there were so many things that people wanted me to be, but swimming in the sea was a time when I couldn't think about anything else.

RUBERG :::: **Your creative work brings together many artistic mediums: video games, music, writing, visual art. Have these different forms been particularly meaningful to you at specific moments in your life?**

MCGEE :::: Video games were the thing that I was most obsessed with as a kid, and then also music when I was a teenager. I remember playing my first video game on the Commodore 64 when I was around two years old. I was so little, I could barely use the controller. From then on, I played everything that I could get my hands on: mostly ROM hacks and RPG Maker stuff that got passed around the internet. When I think about it, it makes a lot of sense that I grew up to make games.

Once I got a bit older, I started playing guitar and got into metal culture. With music, I could be the person who was really good at the guitar, not just this strange, effeminate person that people knew me as. There was a really active local music community in Donegal. In Ireland, you can't legally drive until you're eighteen, so everyone would pile onto one big bus to drive around and go to gigs.

Also, as a kid, I read a lot of fantasy novels and I wrote stories. It's strange, looking back at the things I wrote. I recently helped out with a trans art residency in Dublin. We put together a library of zines and I added in, like, twenty of my stories. They felt like that came from a lifetime ago. I was pretty disconnected as a teenager. I dropped out of my first college course, but I went back. Even now, I have so little connection to who I used to be.

RUBERG :::: **How would you describe the indie video game culture in Ireland?**

MCGEE :::: There is a lot of cool indie game stuff happening in Ireland these days. [Game designers] Brenda and John Romero moved here recently, which has helped get stuff started. In that regard, we punch well above our weight. Still, the indie scene in Ireland isn't very diverse. The last games meetup I went to, it was just me, one other woman, and dozens and dozens of pasty dudes.[2]

RUBERG :::: **From your position as a queer game designer in Europe, do you think it's correct to say that queer game-making started in America and has been spreading to other countries? Or would you tell a different story, in terms of geography?**

MCGEE :::: I think it's not as simple as saying queer game-making started in America. DIY games culture also has its roots in Europe, with designers like thecatamites. Also, there are cultural differences between America and Europe that make it hard to talk about queer versus straight games. In Europe, people aren't as quick to label their sexuality as in the States, so it's harder to make these distinctions.

RUBERG :::: **You lived in Scotland while you attended university and moved back to Dublin in 2013. That transition has a large presence in your work, such as in your games** *Curtain* **and** *The Isle Is Full of Noises.* **Can you talk about how your experiences have shaped your game-making?**

MCGEE :::: Yes, *The Isle Is Full of Noises* is about returning from Scotland to Ireland. When I came back, I was very ill. I have multiple sclerosis and all the stress I was under in Scotland meant I was really unhealthy. It took me a while after I came back to find the heart of what I wanted to say about the experience. That happened with *Curtain*, too, which is also about returning to Ireland. I remade that game, like, three times before it clicked. It's powerful to draw from your own experience, but there's also a skill in learning how to express it.

When I first started making games, I was hiding behind what I thought were really "smart" metaphors. Later I learned that making something "good" isn't about neat design. It's about making something that's messy and expressive. I think a lot about the texture of games: layering on different elements to give them depth. In *Curtain*, the visuals, the music, the UI [user interface], and even the pacing all come at you from different angles. As a result, the game is really intense. It has texture.

RUBERG :::: I love the idea of allowing video games to be messy. The visual art in your games is often highly pixelated or roughly drawn. Do you think of your games as having a messy aesthetic in addition to messy design?

MCGEE :::: One of my big pet peeves with big-budget video games is that they'll cite someone like Yuriy Norshteyn, the Russian stop-motion filmmaker, as an inspiration, but then the game will be full of 3D models that someone has spent days meticulously rendering. It takes away the messiness and sucks the life out of the game. Sucking the life out of things happens a lot in video games. The game is alive in your head, but once it's coded, there's no room left for serendipity and chance. There's no opportunity for things to go wrong. To be artistically successful as a game designer, it's all about not giving in to the pressures to conform. Instead of trying to make something as good as a studio with millions of dollars, find a creative solution. Style is just intentionally cutting corners.

With *The Isle Is Full of Noises*, I used markers and made all the art in an hour. If I needed something different, I had to figure out how to repurpose what I already had. The way the game looks now that it's finished is based on the serendipity and the chance of what happened before. I love finding ways to bring unpredictability into the creative process. You might say that's a way of queering video game making. It's definitely a very not-straight way of approaching things.

RUBERG :::: What you just said is really beautiful: that making video games queerly means leaving space for serendipity and chance. What are some other ways that you bring those forces into your work?

MCGEE :::: I've been getting more into physical art installations. One of the installations I've worked on is called *Amari*. The game is set on the ocean. The physical element is that there's a big ship's wheel, which you turn to steer the ship on the screen in front of you. There's also this big fish tank filled with sand and rocks and water. My collaborators and I had to go to the beach to get the materials for the tank, and we looked really suspicious dragging away these huge black bags of sand. So, while the first player steers, the second player splashes the water in the tank and that makes the waves on the screen get bigger and bigger until eventually a storm kicks up. The whole installation was just a mess.

Sometimes the best messes aren't made on purpose, though. Like, with *Amari*, if you spun the wheel really fast, the boat would go flying and the waves couldn't catch up, so the player would just fall through the void forever. There were these amazing moments when kids would break our game and fall off the edge of the world. Something similar happens in *Curtain*. If you want, you can completely avoid the entire experience of the game by starting in the parking lot and just walking around the building. You'll see all these weird pieces of art floating in space. You'll even see some of the innards of the game; like, you can look in the windows and catch glimpses of the apartment from the future.

Instead of closing down possibilities for play, you have to leave them open. The first day that I showed *Curtain* at an event, it was totally broken. None of the text came up so it was this horrible, existential nightmare. I watched one older woman play and then quietly slip off because she didn't want to face me. I thought that day was a total loss, but later someone told me they played the broken version of the game and had a really cool experience. That makes me happy, because they played a once-in-a-lifetime version.

RUBERG :::: *Curtain* **is a game about an abusive relationship between two women. Given the subject matter, how have people reacted to the game?**

MCGEE :::: Some of the responses have been hard to hear, like the comments on Steam. Apparently, there are a lot of straight, white guys who thought it was unrealistic that the main character didn't leave her abusive girlfriend. Even though the game is really personal for me, I try not to take things like that too personally. I put the game out there and now it doesn't have much to do with me anymore. At the same time, it's really nice to hear about people who had good experiences with the game. Like when a young woman told me that *Curtain* was a wake-up call that helped her get out of a really bad relationship—that was huge for me.

RUBERG :::: *Curtain* **is an emotionally moving game, but it's not "empowering" in a traditional sense. Why is it important to tell these types of queer stories?**

MCGEE :::: Even when it's hard, minorities have to make their own games and represent their own experiences. When other people try to tell our stories for us, they end up repeating the stereotypes they learn through the media. What's more important than the fact that I'm making a game about being queer or trans, though, is the fact that, as a trans, queer person, I'm making games at all.

Curtain came out of this moment where I was fed up with the stories we normally tell in video games. They feel so flat. At the time, I was reading a lot of magical realism, like short stories by Julio Cortázar. Those were the types of stories I wanted to tell. Rather than a game designer, I see myself foremost as an artist and a writer, so a lot of my approach to games I take from writing. Often, when people are making video games, they come up with a cool mechanic, but it doesn't go anywhere. Games could learn a lot from looking at things that aren't games. If designers all look at the same games, they're going to keep making the same games.

When I was designing *Curtain*, I was thinking about structure. The game takes place at three moments in time. In the first and the second, [the protagonist] Ally is still living with her abusive partner, but in the third, Ally is living by herself. Even though she's out of her abusive relationship, it's not like things are perfect. To me, it was really important that the game not just be about getting past abuse. Abuse is always with you; it doesn't leave. I tried to communicate that through the text box, which fills up nearly half the screen. That's the nugget at the heart of the game: that this other character is talking to you and you can't escape. Even after Ally gets out of the relationship and the text box is empty, it's still there. There is always the possibility that the voice will come back.

RUBERG :::: It sounds like, with *Curtain*, you had a specific message in mind. What was it like trying to design a game that is artistically complex but still communicates a message?

MCGEE :::: The message is subtle. I'm trying to avoid tokenism and reductionism by representing my experiences as closely as I can and letting them be complicated.

With serious games about marginalized people, sometimes the "serious" part is really just a shallow coating—like, "Hey, here's an RPG and all the monsters are homophobic messages." The metaphor is in the mechanics, but the mechanics are so simplified that the metaphor is meaningless. If you're making those kinds of games, you're taking someone's life experience and reducing it in this dehumanizing way to fit the form. [Anna

Anthropy's] *Dys4ia* is a good example of a game that could make that mistake but doesn't. The game is made up of these individual puzzles, and each one is simplistic, but they're strung together to create something that is more meaningful overall. Liz Ryerson did the music for *Dys4ia*, and the music makes the game more nuanced and expressive. You have Anna's angry, confident voice but then you have Liz's music, which is less certain. It's this richness and contrasting texture that comes from collaboration.

RUBERG :::: **What advice would you give to other folks who are interested in making queer or otherwise experimental indie video games?**

MCGEE :::: It's important for creative people to develop healthy attitudes toward their work. If your sense of self-worth is tied to your work, your happiness will always be fleeting because even when you accomplish something, you'll think, "If I don't do it again, people won't like me anymore." Self-care is especially important for queer and trans people. As a trans woman, for example, you're told you are despicable, laughable—and so you have to prove yourself in other ways. You feel like you have to be incessantly productive. It's not healthy.

Unfortunately, tying people's worth to their work is pervasive in indie games. Like, at the Game Developers Conference (GDC), everyone is scoping each other out, like "Do I know this person? Have I heard of their work?" I went to GDC for the first time in 2013, and the experience hurt me a lot. At that point, there was already this nascent "queer games scene" and I did meet some really cool folks, but there were also lots of other people I was really excited to meet who rejected me because I wasn't cool enough. I had been thinking, "This is my time! I'm going to meet people who are like me!," but instead . . . Everyone deserves love and care. We live in a really messed-up socioeconomic system where self-worth is part of capitalism. That is definitely true in games.

Indie games are this weird space where there are marginalized people right next to people who are super well off. A few years ago, I went to a talk where a couple of successful games writers were name-dropping all these super marginalized developers as their influences. It was pretty gross, because here were two white, cis, straight men with well-paying jobs talking about getting inspiration from trans women who are financially insecure. These men are profiting and marginalized developers don't see any of that. It's not just those two guys. The whole industry is like that. I wish there was more of a culture of financially successful folks giving back, because the people who are doing the really experimental stuff are definitely not making a living wage.

RUBERG :::: What is your vision for your work in the future?

MCGEE :::: I want to keep changing, trying different things, pulling inspiration from new places. With video games, there are so many possibilities beyond what people are already doing. My plan is to keep exploring and to keep making glorious messes.

5 ANDI MCCLURE

--===---==---===---===---==--===---==--===---==

Algorithms, Accidents, and the Queerness of Abstraction

Andi McClure is a video game maker, visual artist, musician, and computer scientist whose work explores the place where human feeling meets computational processes. Her earliest creative work was in the area of queer electronic music, and she lists avant-garde musicians like John Cage among her influences. Originally from Texas, McClure went to Indiana for college before moving to California, where she spent ten years working as a software engineer while making video games and related art on the side. After working in the software development industry in Boston for a period, she now lives in Toronto and makes indie games full time. She has also recently founded her own company, Mermaid Heavy Industries. McClure's games come to life through what she describes as her "creative collaborations" with machines. McClure also explores emergence, accidents, and affect in algorithms.

The queerness of McClure's game-making lies not in its representational elements nor even in its mechanics, but rather in abstraction. McClure is interested in designing for mood. As she explains below, she creates disembodied experiences where queer, trans subjects can step outside of the limitations of the physical world and into the possibility space of the game. At a moment when data and computational processes are being simultaneously praised and criticized in fields like the digital humanities, queer game makers like McClure are demonstrating how digital tools can be put to work in the service of counternormative art practices rather than supposedly objective meaning-making. Like many of the voices across this book, McClure explains how she rejects the traditional ways in which video games have been designed and conceptualized. She embraces the transgressive potential inherent in her notion of "anti-games."

McClure sets out to do much more than create experimental video games, however. As she states here with pride, her goal is to create games "so avant-garde" that they will actually "destroy the medium of video games."

Within the networks of the queer games avant-garde, McClure is best known for her work on the 2013 game *Become a Great Artist in Just 10 Seconds*. A cocreation with collaborator Michael Brough, *Become a Great Artist in Just 10 Seconds* is an example of a gamelike work that pushes the boundaries of what "counts" as a game. In this piece, the player uses scrambled, pixelated computer images to create vibrant, distorted works of art. When asked whether the game represents a queer ethos, McClure responds, "I'm a queer person in a non-queer society. . . . That shows in the way that I find beauty in messing something up or using something the wrong way." Yet, like Aevee Bee (chapter 3), McClure also complicates the presumed relationship between queer identity and queer game-making. McClure considers those games in which she has attempted to speak directly to gender and sexuality to be her least artistically successful. By contrast, she says her games that set aside identity and the body to embrace abstraction actually speak most strongly to her own embodied experiences.

A common thread that links many of the artists profiled in this book is a hybrid practice of creative making and written cultural criticism. Like Mattie Brice (chapter 11), Robert Yang (chapter 2), Liz Ryerson (chapter 6), and more, McClure has a history of writing about games and games culture.[1] Twitter is another important site of discourse for McClure. Among the insightful critical frameworks that McClure has proposed through her writing is the concept of "degamification," discussed below. Popularized by Jane McGonigal in the book *Reality Is Broken* (2012), gamification is the increasingly widespread belief that everyday work and social life can be made better—that is, more efficient—though the top-down implementation of structural game elements, such as points, levels, and achievements. McClure closes this interview by laying bare the exploitative politics of gamification and arguing for players to disrupt the instrumentalization of play.

RUBERG :::: Your games and game-related art often look very different than what players might expect from a traditional video game. How would you describe your approach to game design?

MCCLURE :::: I have very little patience for the forms that video games are supposed to follow. It's been years since I've made a traditionally structured game. When you're thinking about games, you're supposed to be thinking about mechanics and narrative. But when I'm making games, I'm usually thinking in terms of designing an experience. I think about things like tempo, pace, and mood. I used to make music. It was very experimental and strange. When I worked on it, I was thinking, "What is the mood of this piece? What does it make you feel?" When I'm making games, I'm interested in the same questions. How does this experience feel and how does it change over time?

My game design process is one that I took from music. There's an entire set of composers who base what they do around procedure and chance. You can trace this back to the 1960s with musicians like John Cage. The Cage tradition is based on this intuitive method of creation, where you bring mathematical processes into your work and let those processes guide you. I try to do that. Rather than having an end goal in mind, I start with some algorithm and I go, "I wonder what it would look like if I did this or that." Sometimes the result will look like what I expected, sometimes not. A lot of what I do is take advantage of accidents. There will be a bug in something I've written and I'll realize that it's much more interesting than what I was trying to do, and it will become the new focus of the piece. I see mistakes as opportunities that open up along the way.

RUBERG :::: In your work, you often draw inspiration from algorithms, mathematics, and computation. How do these elements shape your art-making?

MCCLURE :::: I view the process of creation as a collaboration between you and your medium, or, if you're working with computers, a collaboration between you and a machine. If you're making music, for example, you're never making it in a void. You have some tool you're using, and whatever that tool is, it is going to have things it's well-suited for and things it fights back against. Guitars want to produce four-chord sounds. If you try to do something more complicated with a guitar, you'll have to work a lot harder. You have something you want in the creative process, but also your tools have something they want. You're trying to negotiate how much of what you want you can get and they're trying to negotiate how much of what they want they can get.

I get my best work out of letting the machine drive—just sort of poking at the machine and seeing what it can do. Once I've got a sense of the possibility space, I can start trying to bend it towards something. I let the machine do what it wants and I try to figure out how it makes me feel.

What kind of mood am I getting? How can I replicate that experience for an audience?

RUBERG :::: Your interest in designing for experience and mood is striking, especially since discussions about video game design tend to focus on systems and mechanics. Why focus on how a game makes players feel?

MCCLURE :::: When I started making games, I was really obsessed with the idea that mechanics could be expressive. My first few games were all extremely mechanical. At the time, I was like, "My game is going to be a machine that has an effect on people." The best example of this formalist thinking is a game I made called *The Snap* [2011]. It was an arena shooter with a time loop. You could jump backward in time and change events that had happened, which had an effect on the present. As a piece of software, I'm still really proud of it. I was excited to see what people would do when they tried to strategize with this complicated set of effects.

The answer was that none of it made any difference whatsoever. To the players, it was all just noise. Everything was so complicated that your input seemed random: completely disconnected from the output. None of the systems mattered; no one even noticed they were there. It was actually kind of funny that I made this very systemic game and the people that I showed the game to who were gamers didn't like it because it was too chaotic, but the nongamers thought it was great, because they were like, "Oh, this is just fun! I'm just shooting tons of bullets and jumping around and doing wacky things." What I learned was that the systems I built weren't as important as the effect they had on the player. The systems are only meaningful to the extent that they make the player feel a particular way.

RUBERG :::: Do you see a contradiction in your emphasis on players' feelings and your own love of math, which some might consider abstract or even sterile?

MCCLURE :::: That's not how I think of math. Math is tied to how our universe works. If you look at the natural world, you're seeing a series of processes. For example, if you think about it, trees are completely alien. You've got this thing that is growing based on a set of rules. The seeds, the stems, and trunk grow because they're seeking light. It's like an optimization function. Maybe that sounds sterile, but to me the math that brought the tree here must be really beautiful if it can make something so complicated.

To an extent, the art that I make is like cartography. Machines are things that humans created, but mathematics are things that people discovered. Theorems would exist even if there were no humans to discover them. So, when I'm playing with processes or algorithms, I'm discovering things. I'm going out into this natural world full of numbers and finding interesting places and trying to take pictures of them. I might not be able to take someone out into this spot in the woods where I found this thing, but I can represent it and give them a sense of what it was like through my games.

RUBERG :::: **In terms of representing people, your games are also very abstract. Would you say that identity still plays a role in your work?**

MCCLURE :::: It's tricky to explain. I've definitely had the thought, "You know, the kinds of idioms that I put into my games are really suitable for telling a story about queerness or about queer sex. There is a synergy there." But the one time that I actually sat down and tried to intentionally make a game where I foregrounded that, I couldn't get it to come together.

That was one of my unfinished projects, a game called *Body Hack*. I decided I was going to make a game about the experience of having sex as a transgender person. The idea came out of this period where a bunch of games were trying to add sex mini-games, and at the same time a bunch of games were trying to add hacking mini-games. *God of War* and *Mass Effect* are some examples of that. I thought, "Why can't the sex game and the hacking game be the same game?" To me, having sex as trans person is like hacking your own body. You have to do these strange things to get your body to cooperate. You can't really do the obvious, easy stuff. You have to come up with your own workarounds.

The game wound up being a two-player paint program. The players each controlled a paintbrush and each player had control over what the other player's paintbrush did. It was meant to be like you were hacking the other player's body. It was played by two players holding one controller, with a layout that encouraged the two players to be touching. I managed to do one successful forty-second play test with the girl I was dating at the time, and it was really cool and intimate, but I couldn't figure out how to package the experience to share.

RUBERG :::: **What about a game like *Become a Great Artist in Just 10 Seconds*? It's non-narrative and has no characters, but is there still some element of your trans experience that is reflected in the game?**

MCCLURE :::: Generally, no. Part of why I am drawn to abstraction is that it's like an escape from my identity. As a trans person, my identity means, to some extent, that there are things about my physical, external self that I don't like. It's complicated to talk about whether the trans experience has been good or bad for me, but it's definitely been really hard, and a lot of that has to do with struggling with the physical world. My body doesn't necessarily feel like a great place to me. The period when I was most prolific in games was when I was either just pre-transition or during transition and things were especially not working right. In a sense, video games or abstract art are a place where you don't have to have a body. In most of my games, you're not embodied. To me, there's something that feels really good about just floating in those abstractions. It feels natural.

To the extent that I identify as something, I identify as an artist. I worry about that, because if you're an artist and that's the whole of your identity, what are you bringing to the work? That's one of the reasons why I'm more inclined to make things that are about experience rather than things that are about me personally. At the same time, I think of my games as being very personal, because they are about personal thoughts and feelings I have had, even though there aren't usually people in my games. Even if I'm not present in my games as a person, my emotions are still there.

One thing that makes exploring identity in my games difficult is that I struggle with characters and narrative. There's exactly one game in my history that explicitly portrays a relationship. It's called *He Never Showed Up* [2013]. It simulates a date in which your date literally never shows up. The game was my attempt to process my feelings about this dude I was going out with, but who wasn't sure if he was bisexual or what dating a trans person meant for his sexuality. In the game, he doesn't show up for the date because in real life he never showed up emotionally.

RUBERG :::: To me, *Become a Great Artist in 10 Seconds* seems like a deeply queer game. It invites players to take tidy, normative ideas about art and reimagine them by messing them up. Does that resonate with you?

MCCLURE :::: I've seen people talk about that kind of conceptual queerness, the more abstract senses of what it means to be queer and how you can be queer in a space with no bodies. I think that's really powerful. I'm very happy to see people thinking about *How to Be a Great Artist* in that way, though it's not something I planned for when I made the game. It's more that I'm a queer person in a non-queer society and that shapes my values, which comes through in my work. That shows in the way that I find beauty in messing something up or using something the wrong way. I'm not necessarily sitting down and thinking, "Yeah, this triangle is going to be really gay."

RUBERG :::: On your website, you describe some of your early work as "anti-games."[2] What do you mean by that? Is that still a concept that is important to your art?

MCCLURE :::: A few years ago, when I was making those games, I was spending way too much time on video game message boards, and there were all these people complaining about things that weren't "really games." Around this time, the Nintendo Wii was challenging conventional ideas about what gameplay meant. People who were invested in traditional forms of gameplay got upset. For a brief period when the Wii was succeeding, they felt threatened. They thought that video games as they knew them just wouldn't exist anymore, and this new paradigm would supplant them. Someone on [the forum website] NeoGaf used the term "waggle-tastic fagatronics" to describe Wii games. I was like, "Holy shit! That sounds like everything I want to be part of."

Personally, I'm not interested in games themselves. I'm interested in the space of what is possible when you have these mechanical systems encoded in software. Along with a bunch of other indie folks, I was making stuff that rejected what a game was supposed to be. Why does it matter if it's a game? I decided to frame the games I was making as a reaction against games themselves—as a way to say, "No, I'm not just failing to meet the rules of video games. I'm rejecting the rules of video games." Traditional gamers thought indie games would destroy the medium, which didn't happen obviously—but, for this brief period, I was like, "I can destroy something? Great, I have this awesome destructive power! I'm going to be your super villain. I'm going to make something so avant-garde it will actually destroy the medium and there will be nothing left."

RUBERG :::: Does that relate to your concept of "degamification"? You proposed a talk on the topic for the Queerness and Games Conference back in 2015, but unfortunately you weren't able to attend. I've been curious about it ever since.

MCCLURE :::: I was going to give this talk about gamification, which takes concepts from video games and tries to apply them to real-world situations—like, "I'm designing a website and I'm going to add incentive structures from games to keep people engaged." Mostly, when people talked about gamification, they were saying, "Hey, games control people's behavior. What can we learn from this?" They were putting it in benign language like, "How can we inspire people?" but really it was about, "How do we engineer people to act a particular way which is advantageous for us economically?" I didn't like that. A lot of the time, when people are gamifying, they just replicate the structures that our society is already built on. Like, "Oh, what if your work was incentivized by a system of points that led to some kind of tiered rewards?" I'm like, "Didn't you just describe capitalism?" That's the labor system. That's money. Except with gamification, instead of getting money, you're getting meaningless points that you can't use for anything.

To me, gamification misses the point. Games are a large number of things, not just their incentive structures. The set of things that the gamification people latched onto were the least interesting parts of video games. When I play a video game, I'm doing it for artistic inspiration or to feel a certain mood. All this other stuff, the connective tissue of scores and goals and achievements, those are the parts that are between me and the experience I want to have. Music is made of sounds; cinema is made of images. Games are made of experiences. But you can't just have an experience in isolation. When I play *Shadow of the Colossus*, for example, the parts that are really powerful to me are these individual moments. They only last for a fraction of a second, but they wouldn't have meant anything without having the game structure to contextualize them. The game is what you wade through to get to the deeper thing that is buried inside it. Acknowledging that is a way to reverse the idea of gamification.

6 LIZ RYERSON

```
--===---===---===---===---===---===---===---==
```

Resisting Empathy and Rewriting the Rules of Game Design

Liz Ryerson is the designer of the 2013 game *Problem Attic* (figure 6.1). She is also an experimental electronic musician, a game critic, and a visual artist with an unmistakable glitchy style. As Ryerson explains here, *Problem Attic* is a game about attempting to navigate the confusing and often upsetting inner workings of one's own mind. The question of whether *Problem Attic* should be considered queer gets at one of the fundamental tensions in the idea of looking for queerness in video games "beyond representation." On the one hand, *Problem Attic* presents what, from the perspective of queer theory, would seem to be a distinctly queer vision of the world. Through intentionally garbled, nonlinear level design (figure 6.2), the game offers an illogical yet emotionally meaningful experience. It resists the normative logics that traditionally shape the medium of video games. On the other hand, Ryerson, as a queer, trans creator, voices her frustrations with the notion that her work should be interpreted queerly simply because of her own sexual and gender identities. Ryerson makes the crucial point that, even when celebrating the queerness that the artists profiled in this book bring to video games, we must remain self-critical and avoid tokenizing queer game makers. Indeed, a game like *Problem Attic* itself destabilizes simplistic interpretations ("good" versus "bad" game, queer versus not queer) and challenges us to interrogate how we make meaning from video games.

Ryerson is an example of a game maker whose contribution to the queer games avant-garde goes beyond game design and into other, complementary areas of artistic expression. In addition to building her own video games, Ryerson creates original music for the games of other designers. She has contributed sound design to many of the best-known

Fig 6.1 :::: *Problem Attic* (2013) by Liz Ryerson: intentionally glitchy and confusing for players to navigate

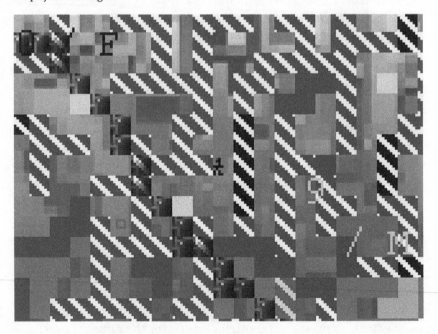

Fig 6.2 :::: *Problem Attic*, a game that seems to explore queerness through level design, though Ryerson challenges this reading of the game

queer indie video games, including Anna Anthropy's *Dys4ia* and Robert Yang's *Radiator* series (chapter 2), as well as lesser-known but nonetheless striking work, like the game design engine Emotica, where players create their own top-down game spaces using only emoji. In this way, Ryerson's work represents a point of creative connection across many of the creators featured in this volume. Through her focus on music and sound, she also brings artistic variety and depth to the work of making queer games. The importance of sound design is often overlooked in discussions about video games. Ryerson's contribution to the queer games avant-garde highlights how the sensory experience of playing a video game can be just as much a site of queerness as the game's narrative or visual elements. Though Ryerson briefly stepped away from game-making from roughly 2014 to 2016 to focus on her music, she is now once again taking on new game projects.

Currently based in Los Angeles, where she has recently moved from Portland, Ryerson lived in the Bay Area from 2012 to 2014 and participated in what has been called the "queer games scene," a group of queer indie artists living and practicing primarily in Oakland, California.[1] This group has been an important source of inspiration for many current contributors to the queer games avant-garde. On her blog, Ryerson has written candidly about what made this time in her life both exciting and painful.[2] In this interview, Ryerson looks back on this period of explosive creativity and interpersonal drama with valuable critical distance, contextualizing the rise and fall of the earliest wave of queer indie video games within the larger structures of power, socioeconomic class, and discrimination that many marginalized game makers face. Ryerson's story also underscores the financial hardships that queer indie game makers often endure to dedicate time to their art. Here, it becomes clear that Ryerson's history with game-making is inextricable from her experiences with homelessness and the challenges of supporting herself as a creator whose work does not pander to mainstream expectations—such as the expectation that queer games should include tantalizing sexual content or provide opportunities for straight players to empathize with queer people. Rather than performing their identities for others, Ryerson argues that queer and trans game makers should set their own rules for artistic creation.

RUBERG :::: What role did video games play for you when you were young?

RYERSON :::: I grew up in a small college town in Ohio, a tiny "liberal enclave" in the middle of nowhere. In some ways, it was this idyllic setting in the woods, but it was also spooky. I felt very isolated, very alone. I had a really bad childhood and there weren't a lot of people to reach out to. One of my parents was abusive and an alcoholic and I didn't have a way to understand that for a very long time—though I do think I processed some of it through violence in video games. When I was pretty young, I got super obsessed with *Wolfenstein 3D*. I also got really into *Doom*. In an abstract way, I think those games helped me get in touch with some of the disturbing things that were happening to me as a kid.

My interest in video games started even earlier than that though. When I was three or four, we had a babysitter next door who had a NES [Nintendo Entertainment System] and *Super Mario Bros. 3*. The first moment I saw that game, I was obsessed. My mom worked at the library. Every time I went there, she had to hide their copy of the movie *The Wizard* because I always wanted to check it out and fast-forward to the scene where they're playing *Super Mario Bros. 3*.

One saving grace about my childhood in Ohio is that I had an older brother who got me into music at a pretty young age. When I think about Ohio, it feels like there was very little culture, very little going on artistically. In one way, that's great, because it gives you the space to invent your own language. Just for making art, people already saw you as a weirdo. I didn't have any sense of the creative rules I was supposed to follow, so I made whatever kind of art I wanted. I got into making games through modding *Wolfenstein*. Not too long after that, when I was around twelve years old, I started making music—interpretations of stuff I heard in video games—and sharing it through [the video game music website] OverClocked Remix. So, music and video games have always been very linked for me.

RUBERG :::: **You did your undergraduate degree at Oberlin College, which is known for being progressive. What was your experience like there? Did you feel supported as an artist and a queer student?**

RYERSON :::: I had a lot of problems in college. Before I went, I didn't have a concept of economic privilege. I didn't realize how much of a difference class makes culturally. I mean, Lena Dunham was a year ahead of me at Oberlin. It felt kind of like Disneyland there. I had come from a high school with a very conservative Christian atmosphere, so I was still pretty repressed and I didn't function very well in the Oberlin environment. To go to college only an hour and a half from where I grew up but to have it be completely different, that was kind of shocking.

I wanted to study electronic music but the classes were really competitive and I couldn't get in. The guy in charge of the electronic music program told me I had an attitude problem. I just didn't feel like I fit in, even though I really wanted to. I had this perception that everything was going to get better when I went to college because I would get exposed to real culture, but I didn't like it. That's also where I started transitioning: at Oberlin in my last year. I wasn't really open about it until after I graduated though. I had these fears about anti-trans-women sentiment in feminist spaces.

There was this one specific, messed-up experience that I still think about. I ended up majoring in film. One day, the film students were going around talking about their senior projects, and I said that I wanted to make a narrative movie about this girl who feels alienated and self-destructive, because I guess that's how I felt. A girl said, "Why are you making a movie about a female character? Make a movie from your own experience." I was literally in the middle of transitioning. I felt so angry, like, "This is my experience. Don't make assumptions about me." That's why I don't like to make assumptions about people, like if a straight guy makes a game about a queer experience, that person might transition in a couple of years.

RUBERG :::: What was your path after college? How did you end up living in the Bay Area and collaborating with other queer game makers?

RYERSON :::: After college was a difficult time for me. The economy was bad and I was dealing with stuff with my parents for the first time. Really quickly, I went from being in this privileged environment to having no money. In college, when I had a job, I had started taking hormones, but after I graduated I had to go off them sometimes.

I got back in touch with the OverClocked Remix people, so it was as if college was just a weird diversion from the work on music and games I'd been doing before. They convinced me to check out indie games. I was on IRC [Internet Relay Chat] a lot those days, and I ended up talking to Daphne, who was Anna Anthropy's partner at the time. I was totally broke, but I decided on a whim to move to the Bay Area. I really wanted to get into games, and I wanted to know other queer and trans people, because I was the only trans person I knew.

When I got to California, I randomly found somebody on OkCupid to stay with. That was a weird experience. After I had to move out, I started living at Anna and Daphne's because they had an extra room. I got kicked out of there though, and I ended up someplace else. Then I got kicked out again and ended up someplace else again. . . . That happened like five different times. I was dealing with homelessness for a long time when I was in Bay Area. Eventually, in the beginning of 2014, I got more subscribers on Patreon and I was able to find a place to live in Berkeley for a while. Then I moved to Portland. Being able to survive and not being homeless is actually a fairly recent thing for me.

RUBERG :::: You've written openly about your upsetting experiences in the Bay Area queer games scene. Now, a few years down the line, how do you feel looking back?

RYERSON :::: There are some ways in which that group of queer games folks was a very positive environment. At first, there was this openness, this idea that being an outsider was OK, though later it became more prescriptive. When I initially started hanging out with Anna and Daphne, I felt really emotional, because it was the first time that I had any sort of artistic community in the flesh, and to be around someone who was queer and trans and successful. . . . It was amazing. Now there are tons of trans people around games, but not then. So I got really deep into the community pretty quickly.

There was just so much drama though. It was a lot of people dating each other who were not emotionally equipped to handle what was happening. I've been out as trans for about eight years, which is a lot longer than most of the other people I know in games, so I might have a different perspective, since I'm kind of old in trans years. Still, despite all the drama, that experience was extremely instrumental for my career. I was introduced to so many people and made so many connections. I was able to go to the Game Developers Conference on basically no money.

I understand why the drama happened. It was really hard to be a queer person making games. The games industry had no interest in what we were doing and the Bay Area felt like an actively hostile environment. I was homeless and meanwhile I was going to these conferences where people make tons and tons of money. Class issues definitely inform all of the work I make, and part of that comes from having these experiences of feeling so disconnected from the games world. Plus, there's this really oppressive environment in games. As a trans person or a queer person, you face so much hostility towards you in general in society, and then add the fact that it's worse in games, and the fact that you're broke and can't figure out how to make a living in a field where some people make crap-tons of money. It's a lot.

RUBERG :::: **Your game, *Problem Attic*, is different from a lot of the other work that came out of that early queer games scene. It's darker, more opaque, and less direct in terms of the story it tells. Do you consider it a queer game?**

RYERSON :::: People have said, "Oh, this is a great queer narrative." I guess that's fine, but it wasn't my intention. I don't want everything I do to be viewed that way just because I'm queer. *Problem Attic* isn't the way it is because of queerness. It's the way it is because the world sucks. The game is about cognitive dissonance and the things that people don't want to acknowledge so they push them off into some other space. That's the "Problem Attic."

I feel like, once queer games started becoming popular, the narrative had to be "Here's this game about how I'm a queer person so you can understand." It all started with [Anna Anthropy's] *Dys4ia*. Like, if you are a woman or a person of color or trans or queer or whatever, you are expected to perform these experiences if you want to be successful, and I kind of resent that. People should make art about whatever they want. Of course, their experiences are going to inform it, but we shouldn't be reductive. It's those "empathy games" that get noticed. My work isn't like that, so it doesn't get noticed in the same way. Empathy isn't the conversation that I want to be part of. I want to be part of the conversation that's like, "We need to make our own rules and our work isn't going to look like what's come before it." I want to make art that is good by any standards, not just the standards of me being trans.

Queerness isn't a focus for what I do. It's important to my life, but that doesn't mean it's directly important to my work. Maybe someone else could read that into it, but the moment you impose this idea on yourself about what kind of art you're supposed to make, you limit your potential. I view myself as being more part of a category of art games than commercial queer games like *Gone Home*. I'm not trying to disparage *Gone Home*. I'm just saying that, just because I'm queer, that doesn't mean I identify with queer games.

Also, I really resent the hypersexualization that comes with the idea that queer people have to perform their sexuality in their art. So many of the queer games that have been successful are very sexual. I just don't like the idea that things have to be about sex because you're a woman or you're queer.

RUBERG :::: You left video games for a few years to pursue your career as a musician, but you've recently returned to game-making. What made you decide to shift back?

RYERSON :::: It's been hard for me in games. With *Problem Attic*, I felt like I made something really interesting, but it seemed like very few other people thought that, at least when the game came out. It pretty much got ignored or it got negative feedback. I even had one trans person email me to tell me how much they didn't like my game and that I was an asshole for designing it the way I did. There were some people who liked it, but compared to something like *Dys4ia* or [merritt k's] *Lim*, these games by people I knew, it didn't get very much attention, though the game does have this kind of cult following these days. The more intellectual types wouldn't take my game seriously, and I felt really hurt by that. Also, right after I finished *Problem Attic*, the person I was dating broke up with me and then my group of queer games friends fell apart. It all happened so fast.

I needed to get away from that for a while, so for the past couple years I've been focusing on music, but recently I've come back to games. Partly that's because I realized that making a living as a musician is horrible. It's even worse than in games. It's also that music and games are seeming increasingly less separate to me. Just in the last year or so, I see them merging. In the experimental electronic music space, I've seen more and more people be like, "Oh, I want to do a video game soundtrack." That kind of stuff is tremendously exciting to me.

I'm planning on starting grad school at the NYU Game Center this fall. I'm not interested in trying to make a living making big, commercial games, so going back to school seemed like an opportunity to do my work in a supportive environment. They were giving out scholarships for women this year; I wouldn't be able to go if they weren't giving me money. I'm looking forward to New York. In the Bay Area, all the experimental stuff is done by outsiders, but, in New York, there isn't the dominant industry presence, so there's more space for work that is different.

RUBERG :::: In addition to the personal reasons that brought you back to video games, do you see a particular political value in making games in the present moment?

RYERSON :::: I think it's extremely important to be involved with games today. It's a very political space. Games are growing hugely in terms of scope and influence on culture. That's part of the reason I've stuck around. Think about how film has shaped our understanding of the twentieth century. That's what video games will do in the twenty-first century. At the Game Developers Conference this year, I heard someone say, "I'm worried about making games in this political climate, but we're all going to die someday anyways, so I might as well do something I enjoy." I don't really like that attitude, because actually making games is immediately relevant to the political climate. Whatever you put out into the world, it has an effect. Think about the effect that #GamerGate has had [on the rise of the alt-right in America]; think about the things that happened to Zoë Quinn. People I know have been involved in something that ended up defining the course of world history. That is fucking huge.

Designing
Queer Intimacy
in Games   **PART III**

Intimacy is a theme that cuts across the work of many contributors to the queer games avant-garde. This section features three interviews with game makers who explore intimacy through design. In chapter 7, "Jimmy Andrews + Loren Schmidt: Queer Body Physics, Awkwardness as Emotional Realism, and the Challenge of Designing Consent," the collaborative duo behind the game *Realistic Kissing Simulator* (2014) discuss how their cooperative, goalless, and vibrantly absurdist kissing game was inspired by the strangeness of the human body and the inherently queer experience of navigating physical closeness. Andrews and Schmidt also reflect on the process of designing consent mechanics into their game and the importance of promoting positive sexual politics. Chapter 8, "Naomi Clark: Disrupting Norms and Critiquing Systems through 'Good, Nice Sex with a Tentacle Monster,'" is an interview with the designer behind *Consentacle* (2014), a tabletop role-playing game about a queer sexual encounter between a human and an alien. Clark, a veteran game maker with a long historical view on the queer games avant-garde, explains how she uses the design of economic systems to reflect and critique the ways that intimacy is valued in queer communities. Last in this section is chapter 9, "Elizabeth Sampat: Safe Spaces for Queerness and Games against Suffering." In addition to working in the mainstream video game industry as a designer of mobile and social games, Sampat has created deeply intimate, in-person group play experiences. Here, she speaks about the socioeconomic realities of making games as a marginalized person, explains how games can hold space for players of all genders and sexualities, and reflects on the potential of games to bring joy to those who are oppressed.

Each of these interviews offers a unique vision of queer intimacy: what it looks like, how it can be experienced through play, and how game designers can create intimate moments that question heteronormative beliefs about togetherness.

Part III

7 JIMMY ANDREWS +
  LOREN SCHMIDT

--===---===---===---===---===---===---===---==

Queer Body Physics, Awkwardness
as Emotional Realism, and
the Challenge of Designing Consent

In 2014, Jimmy Andrews and Loren Schmidt collaborated on the browser-based, two-player video game *Realistic Kissing Simulator*. At first glance, *Realistic Kissing Simulator* appears to be anything but "realistic." Players are represented by simple blue or purple faces in side profile. After agreeing to kiss (figure 7.1), each player controls a long, floppy tongue that slithers out from their character's open mouth (figure 7.2). The game is cheerfully absurdist and intentionally strange. Players can poke one another in the eyes with their tongues, jab their tongues into each other's noses, or wiggle their way into each other's mouths. In their promotional materials for *Realistic Kissing Simulator*, Andrews and Schmidt describe the game as "cooperative and goalless."[1] Indeed, the designers give players no instructions for what they should try to accomplish by licking their fellow kissers. With this game, Andrews and Schmidt have created an exaggerated, exuberant playground that celebrates the inherent awkwardness of human intimacy. As Andrews and Schmidt explain here, the queerness of *Realistic Kissing Simulator* can be found in the gender ambiguity of its characters but also in the way that it echoes queer and trans experiences, in which social norms of romance are imposed on bodies that refuse to behave. In this way, Andrews and Schmidt's game serves as a compelling example of how a video game that may seem silly or small can in fact also be powerfully queer.

Longtime friends and collaborators who first met through the indie game sharing website TIGSource, Andrews and Schmidt come from notably different personal, intellectual, and artistic backgrounds. Andrews, originally from Ohio, received his PhD in computer science from the University of California, Berkeley. In addition to his expertise in program-

Fig 7.1 :::: Jimmy Andrews and Loren Schmidt's 2014 game *Realistic Kissing Simulator*, which emphasizes communication and consent

Fig 7.2 :::: Players of *Realistic Kissing Simulator* operate long, floppy tongues with no clear goal.

ming, he has a background in creative writing. The interplay between science and the arts that his work explores can be traced in part to his family; his father is a physicist and his mother is a poet. As is common among the contributors to the queer games avant-garde, Andrews balances his day job at a tech start-up with his side work as an indie game maker, creating projects like *How to Be a Tree*, a game about a fractal tree come to life developed in collaboration with Brad Kinney. Schmidt too shares this interest in using digital media to explore the organic beauty of mathematics, one of many connections between Andrews and Schmidt's work and Andi McClure's (chapter 5).

In contrast to Andrews, Schmidt brings a creative sensibility that builds from their background in visual art. Schmidt, who is from the East Bay, followed a different path to queer indie game-making than Andrews. They began an undergraduate degree with a focus on biology and psychology but decided to leave university to pursue their art practice. With a distinct visual style, Schmidt's games often use retro, eight-bit imagery and glitch aesthetics to create game worlds that are vivacious, charming, and disarming—as in their 2015 game, *Strawberry Cubes*.

Realistic Kissing Simulator is a game that emerges from the interplay of these two creative minds. It looks neither like what Andrews would likely produce on his own, nor what Schmidt would produce on their own. This is one of many things that makes the following interview illuminating for those who are interested in developing their own indie video games. Among the interviews presented in this book, this discussion with Andrews and Schmidt stands out for its detailed focus on production and design decisions, such as those related to the game's distinctly queer approach to body physics. Also eye-opening for aspiring indie game designers are Andrews's and Schmidt's insights into the responsibilities and challenges of designing consent. As Andrews and Schmidt make clear, game makers creating work with sexual content need to include opportunities for players to consent, but implementing these consent mechanics is a surprisingly tricky design challenge.

RUBERG :::: How did you two meet and when did you start working together? What are the dynamics of your collaboration?

ANDREWS :::: We met because we were both on the TIGSource forums. Loren had some ideas for games that they wanted to make and posted these really interesting images. I looked at them and went, "Oh, I think I know how to program that!"

SCHMIDT :::: Back then especially, our skill sets were really complementary. Since then, we've both gotten more well-rounded. When we worked on *Realistic Kissing Simulator*, it was almost arbitrary who did which bits of the programming. Jimmy did a lot of the rendering for the tongues and the faces. I did the menus. But really, either of us could have done either part.

RUBERG :::: **Your individual work is so different. How would you describe the games that each of you makes outside of your work together?**

SCHMIDT :::: I'm really interested in expressive games. To me, that means work that is not primarily rooted in the commercial history of games. That's not to say there can't be crosstalk; there are a lot of really fascinating projects that are deeply rooted in that tradition. I have an interest in the theory side of games, though I don't do much critical writing myself. Often, I get my inspiration from digging up older games from before my time, or games for systems I never had growing up. I'm stirred by finding games that strike me as totally wild and strange and beautiful and unlike anything else I've ever seen. I'm also really drawn to algorithms and sparse, poetic, visual work. I think that shows in the games I make.

ANDREWS :::: I tend to think of my work in different terms. The way a project starts for me is that I think of an idea that I find interesting, or just some mechanic I can play with, and I mess with that. My game *How to Be a Tree* is totally like that. I learned about a procedural way of making a tree in [the development language] Processing and I was like, "That's fun. I'll try adding physics to see how it moves," and then I kind of got obsessed with it. A lot of my projects are just silly ideas that I end up embracing. Like a couple of years ago at Ludum Dare, this forty-eight-hour game competition, the theme was "spreading." It was supposed to be about zombies or inflection, but I thought it would be funny to make a game about spreading peanut butter. You get some bread and some peanut butter and it's a peanut butter spreading simulation.

RUBERG :::: **Where did you two get the idea for *Realistic Kissing Simulator*? How did the project begin?**

ANDREWS :::: Loren had a list of ideas that they were thinking about and one of them was simulating a tongue. We were hanging out and I was like, "I have some thoughts about how to do that. Why don't we work on that together?" The tongue sounded like fun: this squishy thing, this interesting physical object that would be really unique visually and have an interesting feel.

SCHMIDT :::: Yeah, we talked about the tongue physics in a really detailed way right from the beginning. Originally, we were going to take a more firm, elastic approach, but we ended up building the tongue out of smooth-sided boxes. Once we had that in place, the game really grew organically.

RUBERG :::: So your interest in experimenting with tongue physics was what drove the creation of the game?

ANDREWS :::: Moments like figuring out how to do floppy lips were especially memorable. At some point, we were adding noses to the characters and we were like, "What if you could stick your tongue in the nose? Gross, we have to put that in!" It was a difficult technical challenge, because initially the lips would get pushed into the mouth . . .

SCHMIDT :::: Right, like way back, facing inward. We had some lively conversations about how to implement floppy lips. It was this meticulous process of figuring out how long everything should be, how pliable things should be. The tuning was very deliberate and was, I would say, maybe the most important part of the game. It would feel really different, for instance, if you had tongues that weren't long enough to reach the other person's eye. It felt really good when we got that right.

RUBERG :::: On the surface, *Realistic Kissing Simulator* certainly doesn't look "realistic." What was your thinking behind the title of the game?

SCHMIDT :::: It's a deliberately comedic title, like a caricature of the act. I like the absurdity of the title because it implies that we took a modeling approach and applied it to human intimacy. Like, make a spreadsheet for all the values of saliva viscosity and muscular torpor and now you're performing a modeling experiment. It's as if kissing is something you can conduct research on.

RUBERG :::: What about the aesthetic elements of the game, like character design? What were your artistic goals for the look of the game?

SCHMIDT :::: When we picked the colors for the faces, we thought a lot about how people would gender them. We also wondered, "Are we accidentally making a heterosexual couple?" We deliberately chose colors that weren't natural, and the facial features don't map clearly to any one partic-ular set of features that a group of people would have. They are abstracted, so it's easier to map yourself onto the character instead of playing a char-acter that the game hands you. There's more space for projection.

RUBERG :::: When you developed *Realistic Kissing Simulator*, what types of experiences were you hoping that players would have with it?

ANDREWS :::: I just personally like playing with these weird physical sys-tems, so I was hoping that other people would enjoy that too—seeing how that feels. There's something satisfying about controlling this weird, physical thing. Obviously, there's also going to be comedy from the fact that it's a tongue that can touch somebody's nostril or eye. It's an awkward experience. I didn't fully realize the awkwardness of it when I was initially working on it, because I was just sort of just playing with it myself and it wasn't really a tongue yet, just some blocks. Once we put in the tongue and the eyeball and the tongue could touch the eyeball, the awkwardness became really obvious. It's like, "Oh, well, there's that."

RUBERG :::: What have you seen when you've watched players interact with the game? Are there emergent behaviors that have surprised you?

SCHMIDT :::: We've shown the game at events like Different Games, Indie-Cade, and the Queerness and Games Conference. Most people have been great, but sometimes you run into bad situations. We've had couples play the game who have problematic relationship dynamics. One person tells the other person how to play, completely bypassing the consensual ele-ment of the game—you know, the sort of backseat driving you get any time there's a group of people playing a video game, but applied to a game about sex that was deliberately designed around mutual consent. As a de-signer, there's this terrifying sense that you've empowered those people to act out. Like, when should I step in?

ANDREWS :::: One of the emergent behaviors that I think is funny is that people will play the game alone, just entirely by themselves, and then post the video on YouTube. The game ends when either player stops pressing keys and disengages, but if one person is playing both sides they don't necessarily realize that. Apparently, when it happens, they're surprised and then they think they have somehow won kissing. They'll go back and try to replicate that. They try very hard to win kissing with themselves. I like that.

RUBERG :::: According to your descriptions of the game, *Realistic Kissing Simulator* is supposed to be "goalless," but it sounds like players try to establish their own goals.

SCHMIDT :::: That's right. Technically, the game has no win state. I'm really interested in goalless design. Instead of giving people a goal, you give them a possibility state to explore. Still, people are so sure that there have to be end terms. Most games that we're handed in a commercial context are very careful to give us clear goals, so we're trained to look for that. This also happened with another game I made. It was an open-ended, experiential installation where you meandered around this space and explored poetic prompts. Someone told me that a group of people who played it were feverishly working to figure out its secrets. They said they'd found a code and they were going to decode it. There was no code, no goals at all. But they were really insistent, like, "We almost had it."

Personally, I'm all for people finding their own ways of engaging with something I make. If someone asks me explicitly, "Can I win at this?," I'll say it's self-determined, but otherwise I'm open to them thinking that there are goals. For example, watching people play *Realistic Kissing Simulator*, it's interesting to see the range of possible configurations people end up in: the two tongues wedged into each other's mouth, or one person licking the other person's eye and the other person's tongue curled up in a little spiral. Each one is its own achievement.

ANDREWS :::: There's also an interesting tension between how people default to thinking about games and how they think about sex. In games, they expect they should be able to win, especially in a two-player game. Because it's two-player, people assume that the game is going to be about competition. With a game about sex, though, making it about competition says something we don't want to say; it becomes aggressive. We want to be more sensitive in how we present our sex game and watch out for cultural defaults.

RUBERG :::: One of the interesting phenomena that I have noticed is that people online seem to assume that *Realistic Kissing Simulator* is supposed to be educational—like, it will actually teach you how to kiss.

ANDREWS :::: Actually, one of the ideas that we had for extending the game was a lot like that. If you go online and search for "how to kiss," people will tell you to practice by kissing an object or your hand. I thought it would be interesting to explore a single-player mode where you learn to kiss by having just one head on the screen and some object to kiss.

SCHMIDT :::: Wow, that's great. It's kind of masturbatory and embarrassing, but I think it could also be really sensual. Like, say you were wrapping your giant tongue around an apple or a bowl of soup or something.

RUBERG :::: That is an amazing idea. This intimate image of kissing fruit brings me to my next question: Do you think of *Realistic Kissing Simulator* **as queer?**

SCHMIDT :::: For me, definitely. Queerness is very much where I am coming from. It's very rooted in my own experiences with sex. My games are influenced by my identity because that's the life I have to create from. The experience of the weirdness of having a body and trying to interface with someone else intimately, which you see clearly in the game, for me, comes very much from being trans and experiencing dysphoria. Apparently, the game is relatable for a lot of people, though. People often tell me that the game reminds them of learning how to kiss for the first time: these awkward attempts at figuring out how to move your parts together. There's a common ground between people in this everyday experience of learning to kiss, so maybe there's a parallel weirdness between being trans and just human biology.

ANDREWS :::: Your question about queerness makes me think about awkwardness. Like I was saying, awkwardness is definitely a big part of the experience of the game. You don't think about it, but tongues are really weird. There's some sort of emotional truth about that that resonates with people, I think, even if the game seems unrealistic in other ways.

RUBERG :::: That's such a powerful concept: that even though it's not "realistic," the game has emotional truth. Beyond that, do you think *Realistic Kissing Simulator* **has a larger message to communicate?**

ANDREWS :::: For me, not so much. I think of my games as being jokes, not so much as having messages.

SCHMIDT :::: For me, the game is political. Any project you make is tinged with the politics that you carry with you, right? The consent angle stands out to me as the most political part. We definitely internally referred to the game as consent propaganda while we were working on it. You're making this thing about sex and relationships and you have an opportunity to forcibly engage people with the idea of consent and hopefully send the seeds of that out into the world.

Games can be a wonderful political tool. They're great for building empathy. At the same time, I'm really adamantly opposed to the sort of empathy voyeurism that you're seeing in early virtual reality work, for example. It's disgusting and exploitative. A lot of it boils down to whose story you're telling. The VR pieces that I find myself objecting to are built on ideas like being a refugee in a camp or being subjected to drone attacks. These pieces strip away an experience that belongs to someone else and invalidates it by recontextualizing it. I think you have to be really careful about that. If it's not your story to tell, tread carefully. That's an important piece of the politics of games.

RUBERG :::: It sounds like consent was important to both of you when creating *Realistic Kissing Simulator*. How did you design for consent?

SCHMIDT :::: We've thought about it a lot, and we're still thinking about it. When you hand someone a game you've created, there's a temptation to wash your hands and say, "Okay, it's all on you now." Like, if you used the *Spore* creature creator tool to make a bunch of walking penises, that's your fault, right? You can try to police the space or sculpt the verbs of the game, the ways that players can interact—for example, like in *Journey*, which is multiplayer, where you're handed a very limited verb set so you can't grief one another. But with a game about sex, things get more complicated.

Right now, the game has a moment where you consent at the beginning, but I think we could do better. As it stands, you can cancel out in the middle passively, but there's a delay. We've thought about how there could be a prompt at the bottom of the screen that says, "Press spacebar to stop." If the player pressed that, they would immediately disengage, like using a safe word. In a future version, we'd like to have active consent. You might need to press certain keys the entire time to communicate that you keep consenting. Without that, the game has a bias in favor of implied consent. A rule system like that would allow you to perform how enthusiastic you are—to give enthusiastic, active consent.

8 NAOMI CLARK

--==---==---==---==---==---==---==---==---==---==

Disrupting Norms and Critiquing Systems through "Good, Nice Sex with a Tentacle Monster"

Naomi Clark's *Consentacle* (2014) is a tabletop board game like no other. When a pair of players sits down to play *Consentacle*, they embark on a sexual encounter between a human (Kit) and a large, blue-skinned, tentacled alien (Dup) (figure 8.1). The players' goal is to reach mutual sexual satisfaction. To do this, they attempt to interact with each other in complementary ways—such as by licking, touching, penetrating, or enveloping one another at the right moments—without complete knowledge of the other's desires (figure 8.2). Progressing through the encounter earns the players trust tokens. With these, players can build their intimacy scores and ultimately trade in intimacy for satisfaction. As of July 2018, copies of *Consentacle* had been sent to backers of the game's Kickstarter campaign, but Clark has also brought the game to a number of events such as the indie games festival IndieCade. Despite its limited availability, *Consentacle* has already become infamous among those interested in queer indie games. Those who attempt to play *Consentacle* at the game's hardest difficulty levels can only communicate through gestures or eye contact. Because the game has largely been played in public settings, these scenes of human-alien sex are often enacted by strangers surrounded by onlookers. The experience is simultaneously sensual, uncomfortable, and at times alarmingly intimate.

Though *Consentacle* is an analog game, designed around the embodied experience of sitting face-to-face with another player, Clark herself is primarily a digital game maker. In her long career, she has focused mainly on making games in small studio or educational settings. She is part of the indie games scene in New York (the unique affordances and challenges of which Sarah Schoemann discusses in chapter 20), where Clark has lived

Fig 8.1 :::: Naomi Clark's 2014 *Consentacle*, a tabletop role-playing game about a sexual encounter between a human and an alien

and worked since the mid-1990s. Currently, she is a professor at New York University's Game Center, along with some of her longtime collaborators, including Eric Zimmerman, whom she worked with in the early twenty-first century at the influential casual games studio Gamelab. Clark's first game, *SiSSYFiGHT 2000*, an online, multiplayer rumble between mean, gossipy schoolgirls, came out in 1999. In hearing Clark describe the game's creative origins (the main inspiration for its aesthetics was the fantastical and distinctly non-heteronormative world of outsider artist Henry Darger), it becomes clear that, even when she has worked on video games for a mainstream audience, Clark's designs have always been informed by experimental art. Among Clark's games, only *Consentacle* appears overtly queer from the outset, yet Clark brings a queer sensibility to each of her projects.

Because Clark has been developing video games roughly a decade longer than most of the other artists interviewed in this book, she brings a historical perspective to the queer games avant-garde. Here, Clark describes how, until relatively recently, she kept her identity, communities, and politics as a queer, trans woman of color separate from her participation in the video game industry. For years, she says, she felt very alone working in games—until, around 2012, a critical mass of queer indie game makers began to form. Clark also helpfully contextualizes the current rise of the queer games avant-garde with references to other important moments in the timeline of contemporary queer game-making, such as the release of Anna Anthropy's *Mighty Jill Off* in 2008. Clark also looks ahead to the future of queer games. She encourages aspiring queer game makers to continue to push the boundaries of the status quo and search for new ways to disrupt cultural norms.

In addition to being a skilled designer, Clark is a compelling academic thinker. Among the artists involved in the queer games avant-garde, Clark stands out for her direct engagement with queer theory. In her contribution to the volume *Queer Game Studies*, as well as her co-keynote (delivered with merritt k) at the 2014 Queerness and Games Conference, Clark has pointed to theorists like Lee Edelman and predecessors to queer theory like Georges Bataille as models for subverting the pleasures that players take through games.[1] "It's important to think about the theoretical

Fig 8.2 :::: In *Consentacle*, players interact through actions like licking, touching, penetrating, or enveloping one another

aspects of queerness because it allows us to get beyond representation," Clark explains here. In this way and others, Clark models a self-critical perspective. For instance, an important feature of *Consentacle*, as Clark articulates in discussing the game's economies, is that the game does not simply represent an idealized vision of queer sex. Instead, *Consentacle* offers a powerful critique of the problematic expectations that even queer people can bring to sex and intimacy.

RUBERG :::: **How would you describe your early history with games? Have video games been important to you throughout your life?**

CLARK :::: I grew up mostly in Seattle. My parents are both academics. My mother is from Japan. She is a social scientist and a translator. My dad is a professor of microbiology and immunology. When my parents were still grad students, we weren't so well off, so we didn't have a lot of money to spend on things like video games. Luckily, I received a bunch of pirated games from my aunt, who the biggest queer figure in my childhood. She was the gay kid on my dad's side of the family, and she worked at UCLA, so she got software through friends who were involved in computing. If not for her, I probably would never have gone into a computer-related field.

When I was younger, I drew maps for text adventure games. Most of them were surreal, like one about how I was going to get rid of Santa Claus and take his place. In high school, I started doing a lot of graphic design. That's also when I started playing online games. I discovered MUDs [multiuser dungeons], which were the predecessors to MMOs [massively multiplayer online games]. My friends were more interested in the local music scene though, and I remember telling them, "You guys don't understand. There is a thing called the internet where you can talk to people from all over the world!" They were like, "Whatever, that sounds like some nerd stuff."

RUBERG :::: **What appealed to you as a kid about going online and participating in multiplayer games?**

CLARK :::: I had been playing games since the eighties, but they were solo experiences. It was very hard to find a context to play games that was social. I was also really drawn to the idea of contributing to the design of the game. When I was younger, it felt like only an elite group of computer programmers in California got to make video games. Then, when I started messing around with MUDs, I realized, "Anybody can do this!"

Eventually, I went off and started making my own games: more socially oriented MUDs that were based on role-playing games. They captured my attention because I was interested in the possibility of using games for expressive storytelling and exploring human relationships.

RUBERG :::: **How did you get your start as a professional game designer?**

CLARK :::: I graduated from college in the late nineties and I've lived in New York ever since. During college and then after graduating, I worked for an early web magazine called *Word*. A lot of the people there were involved in the net art movement, so I got exposed to experimental, early stuff on the web. There was also a lot of cross-pollination happening with fine art, music, and film. In general, New York is much better for conversations across creative fields than Silicon Valley is.

That's where I started making games professionally. That's also how I met Eric Zimmerman. He'd hang out at the magazine and he collaborated with us on my first official game, *SiSSYFiGHT 2000*. No one had done browser-based multiplayer before, so the game created a lot of buzz. We demoed it for a bunch of big game companies, which is how I first got introduced to the games industry. None of them wanted to publish it, though. The game was too weird.

RUBERG :::: **It has been re-released in the years since, but the original *SiSSYFiGHT* came out in 1999. Even today, nearly twenty years later, the game is still "weird." Of all the games to design, why start with one about little girls fighting?**

CLARK :::: *SiSSYFiGHT* was inspired in part by a game called *Fighting Babies*, where all the players are babies crawling around in a crib. You are trying to take a swipe at each other and missing, because you can't really control your body. There's also a card game called *Lunch Money*, where you are kids fighting over lunch money. It has this dark, gory quality. Someone pointed out though that the really brutal thing that happens in schoolyards isn't physical combat; it's psychological combat. Especially if you're talking about little girls: they can destroy each other with a word.

The idea behind *SiSSYFiGHT* was: What if the whole universe was just little girls locked in endless schoolyard warfare? Eric did the system design for the game. I was responsible for making sure the fictional world had the correct tone. The strongest aesthetic influence for the game was the creepy, naive folk art of Henry Darger, who envisioned this world populated by little girls with varying genitalia enthralled in a battle with wicked male soldiers. There is something haunting and perverse about this universe full of little girls.

RUBERG :::: After working on *SiSSYFiGHT*, you developed video games for LEGO and then took a job as a game designer at Gamelab. What was working at Gamelab like for you as a queer, trans woman of color?

CLARK :::: Gamelab was really the nexus of the early New York indie game scene. There was a lot that I loved about working there, but there was also a lot that was difficult. The design culture at Gamelab was based on this aggro, know-it-all dude style of arguing, and at some point, I realized that it was shutting a lot of women out of the creative process.

Because I was raised in this very straight, white, cis-dude professional culture, I kept my work life and my queer life separate—my queer community, my activism, my relationships, all of it. I've never been someone who dates other people who play games. I don't talk about games when I go out dancing with my friends or marching in the streets. It was a shock to me, later, when people started to be like, "I'm queer and I like games. I'm a queer gamer." For me, before that, the two had never really mixed.

At Gamelab, when I thought about game design, I wasn't really engaging with queer issues. Around 2007, I was the lead designer on an office sitcom game called *Miss Management*. I was determined to put gay characters in the game, which was pretty novel for a mass-market video game. I wasn't doing it because of my identity as a queer person, though. I was just like, "Let's sneak this in here."

RUBERG :::: Was there a point in time when your work in game design and your identity as a queer woman began to feel less separate?

CLARK :::: For a long time, I felt totally alone, so I kept my head down. Before 2008 or so, I wasn't even aware that there were other queer women in games. Beyond the New York scene, my contact with the games industry was through the Game Developers Conference—which, at the best times, has not been super open. I remember going to GDC in the early 2000s when Brenda Romero, who had worked on the *Playboy* games, was running a panel about sex in games. It was me and Brenda and one other woman and then a bunch of asshole dudes who were like, "Sex, haha." It was a time when it was rare to see another female game designer at GDC.

For me, the defining moment of change was when I played Anna Anthropy's *Mighty Jill Off*, which is clearly informed by her experiences as a queer trans woman. It represented queer identity and experience coming together in a way I hadn't seen in games before. It felt like I was catching a glimpse of a new era for games. By 2011 or 2012, it was like, "Oh my God, all these queers are showing up and making games!" It was kind of heartbreaking, to be honest, because I was already mid-career, so I wasn't going to jump in and start making the kinds of queer games that were getting popular.

Through Anna, I became friends with other queer game designers. They said to me, "Wow, you've been around a while. What have you even been doing?" I was like, "Living in the cracks of the industry." Even though I'm only like eight years older than a lot of people in the queer games movement, that's my social identity. I'm the old-person character in the adventure game who is like, "I have been here for forever. Watch out for that hole over there."

RUBERG :::: Given that most of your experience with game design has focused on digital games, what inspired you to make *Consentacle*, which is an analog game?

CLARK :::: I was seeing all of these autobiographical queer games, but I knew I didn't want to make an autobiographical game myself. Like a number of people in the older generation of game designers, I feel like my games are already autobiographical because I put myself into them. A lot of my characters are people I've dated. The autobiographical element just isn't overt.

Instead, I made *Consentacle*. The idea actually came out of this horrible board game called *Tentacle Bento*, which puts players in the role of a rapist tentacle monster. Anna and I started talking about whether it would be possible to make a better game about a tentacle monster. Tentacles have lots of potential in terms of subversive embodiment, differences in bodies, and nonstandard forms of sex. It really sucks that tentacle monsters had been colonized by people who wanted pervy Japanese schoolgirl rape porn. I was like, "We could come up with a game where you try to have good, nice sex with a tentacle monster."

RUBERG :::: How would you describe what makes *Consentacle* a queer game? It is the nonnormative sex? It is the game's focus on consent?

CLARK :::: When I designed *Consentacle*, I didn't want the game to just be about queerness at the level of the characters or narrative. Instead, the queerness in the game comes out in the interactions between people. As a queer game, *Consentacle* is sort of bring-your-own-queerness. I made the game for queer people, but it's fine if straight people play it. The game is going to be different depending on who plays it.

It's not inherently queer every time you play. It's not even necessarily a game that's always about consent—although, if it's not about consent, you're playing it wrong. Players have to provide the consent and negotiate between themselves. I can't make you consent. That would be a paradox. Other games that deal with consent tell the players how to consent. They give instructions. That's an emulation of consent but it's not same thing as consent. With *Consentacle*, part of my job as a designer was to leave an open space for players to bring their own sexual politics.

RUBERG :::: The core mechanics of *Consentacle* are about earning and spending tokens for trust and satisfaction. What was the thinking behind translating pleasure into an economy?

CLARK :::: The genesis for that aspect of *Consentacle* was games like *Netrunner*, which use complex economic engines to create social experience. Mattie Brice [chapter 11] is working with me on a second version of *Consentacle*; she has done thinking around *Netrunner* as a form of flirtation. I'm also working on additional mechanics that are inspired by Avery Alder [chapter 16], the creator of *Monsterhearts*, who has done a lot of design work around sex and dysfunctional relationships.

When I was playtesting *Consentacle*, I saw these moments of friction where people were like, "Wait, why am I thinking about tokens when what I want to be doing is having sex? That seems so weird." I thought, "Yes, perfect! There's something here that's wrong in just the right way." The economy design of *Consentacle* is a way of saying that we live in a fallen world. We're not perfect sexual beings with omnivorous appetites. People struggle with feelings of inhibition, fear, trauma. You can't just do whatever comes to mind. We have to decide whether we can trust someone who we don't have perfect communication with. Those are the things that are represented in the abstract by the tokens.

I chose to represent that through tokens because it's the go-to thing for me as a game designer, but also because we have a scarcity mentality about sex: whether it's number of partners or how pleasurable sex was with this person versus that person. Even with sex, we can't fully erase the quantification of our reality from our mind. We're still thinking about measurements and ratings. We act like enlightened progressives, but we're embedded in overly quantified late capitalism. So, no, sex isn't easy. It's a struggle and you should embrace that. The struggle is part of the pleasure.

RUBERG :::: Playing *Consentacle* is such an intimate experience, but because the game hasn't had a full commercial release, it's frequently done in a public setting. What behaviors do you see when people play the game?

CLARK :::: Most people try to do the same thing: meet the other person's needs. I guess that approach is baked into the structure of the game. I made a cat-shaped opening and I shouldn't be surprised if a bunch of cats come through it. Some people do surprise me though—like teenage boys. You would expect teenage boys to be particularly bad with sexual politics, but when they play, they don't really think about it as a sexual game. They figure out how to work within the system and they do it.

The real difference between how people play is in their performance. Some people take the role-playing very seriously. Other people, including my own wife, are really intense about trying to read someone else's mind. A lot of the time, people use the game as an opportunity to be silly, to waggle their eyebrows suggestively or ham it up in a naughty way. It has turned out to be a pretty good spectator game.

RUBERG :::: In addition to designing games, you have written papers and given talks about queer theory and video games. How do your creative and academic interests intersect?

CLARK :::: For me, it's important to think about the theoretical aspects of queerness because it allows us to get beyond representation—to explore the other levels at which queerness can erupt in games.

When people talk about how video games need to include more diverse representation, I'm like, "That's fine, but it doesn't address the most pressing creative questions." We need to move people out of their comfort zones and toward something deeper. Queerness in video games can't just be about making *Final Fantasy XV* but now it has more women, people of color, and LGBTQ people in it. That doesn't really change anything. I understand why there is pressure on the industry to increase representation. In my opinion, representation is especially important so that queer kids who are coming into gaming don't feel alienated. But there are also much harder questions we have to answer, like how do games satisfy us, what is the role of entertainment, and how do queer practices disrupt those things? As far as I'm concerned, if queers are not disrupting what is considered normal, then why even use the word "queer"?

RUBERG :::: You also teach game design to undergraduates and graduate students. What advice do you give to aspiring designers who are interested in making queer games?

CLARK :::: Right now, it's actually harder to make queer games than it was a few years ago, because some people think queer games are a passing fad. You can be like, "I'm a queer, half-Japanese, trans woman. I want to make games about my experience," but it's harder to make your mark. I tell my students that because I don't want them to keep covering the same ground that a bunch of people did in 2011. Personally, I think those games were just prelude to a more long-lasting integration of queer ideas into the practice of making good games. At the same time, I try to impart that to my students because it takes a lot of youthful energy to break down norms. There is definitely a connection between queer avant-gardes and youth-led art movements.

RUBERG :::: What do you mean when you say that current queer indie games are a "prelude"? Do you think we will be seeing more queer video games in the future?

CLARK :::: I think we are currently seeing the first wave of the queer avant-garde in video games. It's already beginning to dissipate. Some of these artists have found ways to make money, others haven't. When #Gamer-Gate happened, it was like watching half the neighborhood burn down. For me, the eruption of queer identity and representation in video games has been an exciting period in a career where I've mostly been alone. Now I'm definitely not alone. I have all these queer and trans students. Still, in the future, I don't think that games are going to look queer in the same way they did when the first queer games bubble burst.

Queer games have already changed the medium of video games quite a bit. Like any process of cultural recuperation, a lot of what is unique about queer games is already being reintegrated into the various parts of the game industry, all the way up to AAA game makers who are not queer themselves. Historically, that's been true of things like queer photography or queer Riot Grrrl punk music. They went on to influence plenty of people who were not queer because they changed how people thought about a medium. That is what is most valuable to me about queer games. Their impact is already rippling back and affecting how games are made today, even in the most traditional parts of the industry.

I take a longer view, however. I'm already asking, "What's the next thing that needs to be shaken up?" If you're really interested in queering games, you can never rest, because as soon as your queer practices are successful, they will get recuperated by a hungry crowd of creators. Queer people are the avant-garde because we're willing to do things other people aren't. We have a legacy of being outsiders. We take the work of disrupting systems farther than other people can.

9 ELIZABETH SAMPAT

--═══---═══---═══---═══---═══---═══---═══---═══---══

Safe Spaces for Queerness
and Games against Suffering

The tale of how Elizabeth Sampat became a game designer is both inspiring and fraught. Sampat has lived many places—Ohio, Montana, Alabama, Massachusetts, California, and Copenhagen (where she was working when we spoke), to name a few. As she says below, she has led "fifteen different lives." Like Naomi Clark (chapter 8), Sampat brings a unique professional perspective to the queer games avant-garde because, in addition to her individual game-making, she has worked extensively in other sectors of the video game industry. Since 2013, Sampat has been a game designer in medium- to large-scale game companies such as Storm8 and PopCap (owned by Electronic Arts), where her focus has been social, mobile, and free-to-play games. It is rare for game makers to create their own games while employed at traditional game companies because these employers typically claim legal ownership of games made by their employees. Sampat, however, has never been one to quietly comply with the problematic practices of the games industry. She is vocal about the importance of reforming industry standards around inclusivity, discrimination, and labor. No one should have to "break into the industry" the way she did, Sampat says here. She calls for accountability on the part of mainstream game companies; the responsibility cannot fall to marginalized creators alone to bring social justice to video games.

Though Sampat's work in the games industry has centered on designing digital games, she has long fostered a creative practice of analog game design. Her earliest works in this area were tabletop role-playing games. Arguably her most unique independent game is *Deadbolt* (2012), an analog game played in small groups. *Deadbolt* is about emotional vulnerability, building intimacy, and creating safe spaces where players can share their deepest secrets. Only one copy of *Deadbolt* exists in the world. The game includes a number of material elements that Sampat crafted by hand. Each of the dozens of times that the game has been played, such as at game festivals, Sampat herself leads the experience. Sampat describes this as an intensive emotional process that has changed her life by allowing her to connect with others. Sampat has also experimented with making digital indie games, such as *How to Be Happy* (2013). This game, which is about fitting puzzle pieces together, appears abstract. However, as with *Deadbolt*, Sampat brings her personal experiences to her design, which is a symbolic representation of the challenges of dating for someone who struggles with reading social cues.

Being queer is important to both Sampat and her nontraditional family. Queerness also plays a role in her games. Sampat describes here, for instance, how her queer identity influenced the design of *Deadbolt*. Because it fosters a warm, supportive environment for sharing personal information, *Deadbolt* makes space for queerness, encouraging players to sit with their differences and confront their own truths. Among the striking characteristics of this interview with Sampat is the candor with which she discusses her own personal history. Poverty and other socioeconomic disadvantages, often tied to gender, loom large in Sampat's story. A number of strong female role models have helped guide her on her path to becoming a professional game designer. These include the groundbreaking designer Brenda Romero, as well as Sampat's own grandmother, from whom Sampat says she inherited her passion for making "games that alleviate suffering."

This compassion also informs Sampat's ethos as a designer. Her 2016 book, *Empathy Engines: Design Games That Are Personal, Political, and Profound*, teaches fellow game makers how to build games that respect players.[1] Though "empathy" is a much-contested term among queer indie game makers, Sampat uses it in a particularly conscientious way: she wants game designers to empathize with their players. Sampat's experience designing free-to-play video games makes this call for empathy all the more compelling, since free-to-play games are commonly considered exploitative. As Sampat articulates here, she has taken on many design roles during her time in the games industry. Often, in discussions of game development, "design" is conflated into one category. However, Sampat's experience helpfully demonstrates how game design involves many elements—such as narrative design, monetization design, systems design, etc.—each with its own artistic values and social meanings.

RUBERG :::: **What is your history with games? How would you describe your path to becoming a game designer?**

SAMPAT :::: I've always loved playing games. I became an avid role-playing gamer in high school, when I joined the chess club. It turned out they never played chess, just *Dungeons & Dragons*.

The first time I got married, I was very young. My boyfriend and I had only been dating six weeks, but I grew up in a very conservative Christian environment, so I thought that was normal. After we got married, I realized that he and I had nothing in common besides the fact that we were both into tabletop role-playing games. To try to make our marriage work, I got interested in this game he liked called *Exalted*. I made fan design content and posted it online. My husband ended up hating the game though because he didn't like the internet notoriety I was getting for my designs. That was one of the reasons we got divorced.

Then I went in to my single mom phase. By that time, I had two daughters. I was working as a professional photographer and writing search engine optimization spam, but I didn't make much money. Things were really hand to mouth. Our utilities were getting shut off every other month. We were on food stamps. At this point, I was living in Massachusetts and all of my friends were tabletop role-playing game designers. With the little bit of time I had left at the end of the day, I would design games and publish them online. My kids would be asleep and I'd be up working on the layout for some spy RPG that I was hoping would help me pay for groceries. Honestly, I think I would be afraid to ever stop making games. Game design is the only thing that has allowed me to give my kids a home. I'm really lucky that it turned out that the thing that I'm best at is a thing I love. I'm a college dropout with half of a double major in English and philosophy. I never thought I would be a breadwinner. I only started thinking of myself as a professional game designer when I looked at my budget and realized I'd made more money from games than from photography. It wasn't like, "Oh wow, I'm a game designer now!" It just felt good to be able to feed my family.

RUBERG :::: **Do you think that your experiences with financial hardship have given you a unique perspective on the costs of making video games?**

SAMPAT :::: Definitely. I mean, we talk about how people go broke making indie games, but there's broke and then there's *broke*, right? There's the indie rock star who bites his nails and goes, "Oh my god, my parents gave me $100,000 from their retirement fund to build this puzzle platformer. I hope I don't mess this up." Then there's me, being like, "Hey, somebody just bought my game for $14. We can go buy milk!"

RUBERG :::: How did you go from designing tabletop role-playing games to working in the mainstream video games industry?

SAMPAT :::: While I still in Massachusetts, I got to know Brenda Romero through Twitter. She recommended me for my first job making digital games, which was in California. It was completely life-changing. My first husband hadn't wanted me to work outside the home. Now, for the first time in my life at the age of twenty-nine, I felt like I was learning how to exist in society.

The first talk I gave at the Game Developers Conference was about how I "broke into" the games industry. It's the kind of story about lifting yourself up that everybody loves. For example, when I got sent the game design test for my first job, I had twenty-four hours to complete it. When I sat down at my computer though, the electricity went off because we hadn't paid the bill. I literally had to break into my friend's house and use her computer. That's how I broke into the games industry.

Given my background, you'd think I'd be super grateful to the games industry, but my history has actually made me really vocal. There isn't a single person—especially a woman or a queer person or a person of color—who should have to get into the industry the way I did. When they hear my story, people shouldn't be like, "Wow, that's the kind of passion we need." They should be like, "Wow, that's really fucked up, Elizabeth."

RUBERG :::: You talked about how game design is important to you because it helps you support your family. Has your family continued to play a role in your game-making?

SAMPAT :::: I have a very unique family situation. Without that, I would have never been able to take that first games job. About a year after I had my youngest daughter, my second husband told me he wasn't attracted to women anymore. When I got the job offer, he decided to move to California with me anyway, and we've been co-parents and roommates ever since. Recently, we all moved to Denmark: my ex, my two kids, my partner, and I. We've been living together for seven years now, and it works really well. My family is not the most privileged in the world. My ex is a gay brown man who is undocumented in Denmark. My eight-year-old is very clearly a lesbian; she's been telling me that she was gay since she was four. My oldest daughter is thirteen and she's autistic. My partner is trans. We are an extremely queer family. As marginalized as each individual person in my family is though, we are OK.

RUBERG :::: Do you identify as queer yourself?

SAMPAT :::: Absolutely. My partner is nonbinary, but they're moving toward identifying as a woman. To people who don't know us, we look very much like a cis-het couple, but this is actually the longest relationship I've had with a woman. I'm 95 percent out, but you know how it is: you're always in the process of coming out. Sometimes it's hard to work it into conversation, especially because my partner is a closeted trans woman with giant muscles.

RUBERG :::: What has it been like working in mainstream game studios as a queer person?

SAMPAT :::: I've always been out in the game companies I've worked for. I don't try to hide who I am. No one has ever said to me, "Oh, I can't believe that you're queer," but there are still issues—like at a place I worked where one of the owners of the company used the t-word in a joke in front of a trans woman programmer. At another job, my boss loved using the word "retarded," which really annoyed me because my daughter is autistic.

It's the kind of thing you don't notice until you've worked in close quarters with people for hours on end. It's even worse when you're working on a game that's a live service [like a mobile or social media game], because there's never a moment when you can sit down with somebody and say, "Hey, that wasn't cool." You're always going to need that relationship. It's similar in AAA, where you're putting in fifteen-hour days. You can't turn to somebody and be like, "Hey, could you not use that word?" You have to be likable.

RUBERG :::: You've played a variety of design roles during your time in larger game companies. Can you describe the different types of design work you've done?

SAMPAT :::: I started in narrative design. There's this company, Failbetter Games, which was making a small, niche browser game called *Fallen London*. I harassed them mercilessly about getting a freelance gig, back when

I was still writing tabletop role-playing games. Eventually, they made me the first non-English person to write for *Fallen London*. When I went to Loot Drop, I started doing quest design. At Storm8, I was focused more on designing player reward systems. Now I do what's called feature design or systems design: monetization, energy mechanics, that kind of thing. I moved away from the sexier narrative design work that I was doing earlier because I'm more comfortable working with systems.

Systems are how I make sense of the world. I think of myself like a broken robot. I need structure and feedback to thrive. The reason I love free-to-play design systems is because you get to look at data. It turns my job into something a lot like playing a game; I'm trying to get a new high score. It's also about empathy. I can look at the metrics and go, "OK, the average number of times a day a player plays this game has gone down over the last year. What are our players thinking?"

RUBERG :::: **A lot of queer designers are critical of empathy, but you wrote a book called** *Empathy Engines*. **When you talk about empathy though, it sounds like you mean it not as an experience a player might have but as a design principle. Is that right?**

SAMPAT :::: I've always said the book is about how to design games that elicit empathy in the player, but someone said something on Twitter I think is really true. He said, "You should buy this book. It's about how to design games with empathy." And I was like, "Oh, you're right. It totally is!"

For me, it's all about what the player needs. That sounds cynical from someone who designs free-to-play games, but I mean it. I gave a talk at my company called "Ethical Free-to-Play Design: How to Make Money and Feel Good Doing It." In it, I dispelled some of the myths that people have about exploitative free-to-play design—like the myth of the widow whose children are starving because she can't stop playing *Kim Kardashian: Hollywood*. To me, players are smart. They choose where they want to spend their time. The first step to being a good free-to-play designer is to build trust with your players. Figure out what they want to do with their time and give that to them. Even when you're working with metrics, you have to keep in mind that metrics represent people. The more you can do that, the better you'll be as a designer.

RUBERG :::: **In addition to your work at larger game studios, you also make your own games. What are some of the themes that you address in your solo game-making?**

SAMPAT :::: I've always created systems as a simulation for what's going on in my head. For example, I made a game called *How to Be Happy* that was about how terrible dating is, especially for somebody who is really bad at reading social cues. In the game, there are two puzzle pieces that fit together, but you have to fit them together at exactly the right moment or one of the pieces will clear its throat awkwardly and leave. I wanted to simulate how dating can feel rewarding but also futile and weird. I've never really been good at interacting with my fellow humans.

Everyone has their own experience with dating, and personally, I already feel like I've lived fifteen different lives. I wanted to design a game that felt true for all the people I've been. I'm always trying to grope towards my own identity. My games are my attempts at doing that.

RUBERG :::: Among your indie games, the one that stands out as the boldest and the most intimate is *Deadbolt*. What inspired that game?

SAMPAT :::: *Deadbolt* is a game that I made—like so many pieces of art have been made—because I had a crush on someone. I didn't know how to get them to open up to me, so I made a game about sharing parts of yourself that you wouldn't normally share, but with a set of really rigid rules. You could only speak if it was your turn. There were ritualized ways in which you could respond. It took all the guesswork out of the equation and gave you a chance to really get to know somebody on a deep level.

A lot of people have told me that *Deadbolt* is absolutely terrifying to play. My big secret is it's the most comfortable I've ever been talking to strangers. Even if I don't know what people are going to say, I know what the prompts will be. As long as people go into the game earnestly, there's no fear of rejection or embarrassment.

The way that it works is that everyone sits in a circle. You get a piece of paper that says, "From this moment on, you are your most honest self." There are three rounds. Round one is about making yourself vulnerable. You draw a card that tells you who to talk to and says something like, "Tell them a secret from your childhood" or "Tell them the last lie that you told yourself." You put your hand on their shoulder, and you tell them the truth. If they are touched by the truth that you tell them, they take a button out of a beautiful box that I made by hand and they give you one.

Round two is about affirming the person you're talking to, so you get prompts like, "Tell them a way in which they're beautiful" or "Tell them what the world would lose if they died." The second round is about reminding people that they have worth. In the third round, the cards are blank. You can write a note for someone and hand it to them, but they can't read it until the game is over. You can't talk to them about whatever you wrote on the card, but they can talk to you about it.

Because there's only one copy of the game and I have to be there to run it, I've played the game every time that it has ever been played. At this point, that's been dozens of times.

RUBERG :::: Playing *Deadbolt* sounds like an intense emotional experience. What has it been like for you to play so many times?

SAMPAT :::: This game changed my life. I'm not the person that I was when I designed it. I used to be very closed off. There's no way to play a game like this so many times and not be fundamentally changed by it. I've sort of gamified myself into being a person.

There's a lot of crying that happens in this game. One of the things I hear a lot from people is that playing *Deadbolt* makes you more honest and open for weeks after you play. People have come out to their parents afterward, or gotten divorced, or fallen in love. It's amazing and kind of overwhelming to think that *Deadbolt* unlocked those things inside of players.

RUBERG :::: Do you think of *Deadbolt* as a queer game?

SAMPAT :::: *Deadbolt* is a queer game because it is a game that is me, and I am queer. For me, the queerest part of that game is that it's a place where I feel comfortable to open up about my sexuality with total strangers. If *Deadbolt* is queer, it's because it's a safe space to be queer. It's a place where anything you say will be met with love.

A lot of times, when people play the game, they don't know the other people they're sitting down with. If you hate trans people, and someone puts their hand on your shoulder and tells you that something fear has stopped them from doing is transitioning, you can't say anything. You just have to sit there with that person's hand trembling on your shoulder and accept that truth.

RUBERG :::: In your social media presence, like on Twitter, you are very vocal about politics. Why make games now, given the current political turmoil in the United States and beyond?

SAMPAT :::: I'm going to tell you my origin story. My grandfather on my mother's side was a millionaire businessman from Chicago and the president of the Chicago Teamsters Union. He was probably funneling money back to the IRA in Ireland. There are pictures of my mom dressed up like a mafia princess in a little fur coat. Eventually, my grandfather got shot on the steps of the Chicago Public Library.

When that happened, my grandmother discovered that her husband had a secret family in Florida that he left all of his money to. So my mother and my grandmother went from being millionaires to having absolutely nothing. My mom tells this story about walking with her mother to sell her husband's (my grandfather's) clothes because that was the only thing they had left. On the way to sell these clothes that had belonged to her dead, cheating husband, my grandmother turned the entire excursion into a game to occupy my mother and to distract them both from the incredibly gruesome task at hand.

I hadn't thought about that story in years until Brenda Romero showed me *Síochán Leat*, her game about the Cromwellian invasion of Ireland, which is also about her history as an Irish American. When I played Brenda's game, I realized that this is the thing that I have in common with my grandmother, who I never met. There's something in our blood where we make games that alleviate suffering.

For so much of my life, I've felt like becoming a game designer was a cop-out. I grew up really religious. I also had this intense feeling that we are put on earth to serve others. So, when I finally made it out of poverty and I was designing Facebook games, I was like, "What the fuck am I doing with my life?" Then I understood that game design could be part of helping other people, too.

The Legacy of Feminist Performance Art in Queer Games

PART IV

Almost all of the queer indie game makers interviewed for this volume point to work from previous artistic generations as sources of inspiration. The game makers featured in this section place particular emphasis on the importance of the feminist performance art tradition for their games—or their games resonate strongly with this tradition. This connection can be seen in these artists' engagement with issues of the body, its materiality, and installation art as an opportunity to challenge the traditional boundaries between creator and viewer (or, in this case, player). In chapter 10, "Kara Stone: Softness, Strength, and Danger in Games about Mental Health and Healing," Stone, a game maker and video artist, addresses how feminist and queer theory have influenced her work, which often draws from her own experiences of mental illness and the queer body in crisis. For Stone, making games that are "open and honest" requires embracing what is tender but also what is strong and even dangerous about experimental gameplay. The subject of chapter 11, "Mattie Brice: Radical Play through Vulnerability," is Brice's installation work and her games that probe culture and privilege through embodied experiences like eating. Brice is best known for her 2012 game *Mainichi*, but here Brice argues against those who tokenize her as a black, trans woman who is supposed to make, as Brice says, "digital games about diversity." Today, Brice is reclaiming the narrative around her work by turning toward conceptual notions of queerness and exploring how games can foster mutual vulnerability between players. Third in this section is chapter 12, "Seanna Musgrave: 'Touchy-Feely' Virtual Reality and Reclaiming the Trans Body." Musgrave is an artist working primarily in virtual reality (VR) technologies. Developing in VR, she has designed games to be played in public settings that use both physical and digital elements; playing these games is simultaneously tender and uncomfortable. In addition, Musgrave discusses her co-designed game about swapping body parts, which symbolically takes the transgender body back from medical institutions and places it in the hands of queer communities. The potent presence of past avant-gardes in the work of contemporary queer game-making can be felt in these interviews, where the influence of feminist art expresses itself through the design of counterhegemonic experiences that are, as Stone says, strong, soft, dangerous, and caring all at the same time.

10 KARA STONE

--==---==---==---==---==---==---==---==---==

Softness, Strength, and Danger in Games about Mental Health and Healing

"I'm trying to cultivate the connection between feminist performance art and games," says queer game maker and experimental video artist Kara Stone. "Feminist performance art can be soft and open but also dangerous."

Stone's avant-garde video games incorporate elements from a variety of mediums, including digital and tangible forms, to explore gender, power, mental health, and healing. Her creative background is in filmmaking, and video continues to be an important element of her interactive work. In 2016, Stone was featured in her first solo show, *The Mystical Digital*, hosted by the New York video game gallery Babycastles. The show, which Stone describes on her website as a reflection of the tensions between the "material, embodied, and natural" and the "digital, immaterial, and technical," brought together many of Stone's existing pieces.[1] Among other works, games presented in the show included *Ritual of the Moon* (figure 10.1) (published in 2019, then a work in progress), a game about a witch banished to the moon who must decide whether to heal or destroy the earth, as well as an aluminum-foil-covered arcade cabinet version of her game *Cyborg Goddess* (2014) (figure 10.2) and *Feminist Confessional* (2015), where players kneel to speak their feminist sins. The game for which Stone has received the most attention to date is *Cyber Sext Adventure* (2015). In this game, players interact with an erotic bot via text message. Stone often crafts handmade objects to accompany her digital work, like pillows that she cross-stitched with text and imagery from her game *Medication Meditation* (2014). This reflects her interest in the issues of intimacy and gendered labor that lie beneath the surface of contemporary technology.

Fig 10.1 :::: Kara Stone's *Ritual of the Moon* (2019), a game about a witch banished to the moon who must decide whether to destroy the earth

Fig 10.2 :::: An arcade cabinet version of *Cyborg Goddess* (2014), displayed as part of Stone's solo exhibit *The Mystical Digital*

Stone is currently a graduate student in the Film and Digital Media department at the University of California, Santa Cruz, where she is pursuing a PhD that allows her to focus on her creative practice. Originally from Toronto, she became involved in indie video game development through the organization Dames Making Games, which offers workshops and community events for women and nonbinary people. As she describes here, Stone works at the intersection of creative and critical thinking. Both queer and feminist theory have been highly influential for her work. In addition to Judith Butler, Sara Ahmed, and Lauren Berlant, whom Stone points to as inspirations, figures like Donna Haraway—to whom Stone's piece *Cyborg Goddess* makes clear reference—are also powerful presences in her art. Each of the queer indie game makers profiled in this volume understands their position within the queer games avant-garde differently. As she discusses below, Stone sees her work as primarily in dialogue with feminist performance art rather than with the broader network of indie video games. At the same time, because Stone often brings her work to game events, she is able to speak to the differences between the fine arts and the games worlds, highlighting the many challenges faced by queer indie game makers who share their work in a variety of settings.

Stone's work is intersectional in its attention to both gender and mental health. While issues related to disability appear in many of these interviews, Stone's games highlight the complexities of living with mental illness. Here, Stone argues compellingly that video games can do better in their representation of mental health than to offer "empathetic" experiences for neurotypical people. Rather, she promotes and practices an approach to art-making that she describes as "lovingly" directed away from the center and toward the margins. She believes in the combination of the "soft" and the "strong": the right of queer game makers, and marginalized people more generally, to offer healing through their work but also to retreat and care for themselves.

RUBERG :::: You have a background in experimental film production. What inspired your shift toward making video games?

STONE :::: I played a lot of games when I was a kid. My dad and my brother and I would take turns playing single-player games. I would sit and watch and cry until it was my turn. By the time I was in high school, I was trying to be a cool teen girl, so it was always this secretive thing that I played games. Only my family knew; I didn't have any girl friends who played.

That's been a huge change for me, because now I love collaborating with other women on video game projects.

For my undergrad, I did my BFA in film in Toronto. I've always loved making weird little videos. After I finished that, I did some video editing, but it was soul crushing to only work on other people's projects, so I went back to school and did a master's in communication and culture, which was mostly focused on critical theory.

I thought I was going to keep making experimental video art, but I randomly went to a talk by someone from Dames Making Games. I was like, "Oh my god, women can make video games?" I had never heard of indie game designers. I didn't know that there were cool, feminist communities supporting women and nonbinary people who wanted to make games. After the talk, I rushed over and asked how I could get involved. They were hosting a ten-week workshop and I signed up. I've been following the current of video games ever since.

The Dames Making Games community was so collaborative and supportive. That was a huge part of why I continued in games. I ended up shifting my master's thesis away from video art towards video games.

RUBERG :::: **You're now in the Film and Digital Media PhD program at UC Santa Cruz. You already had an active creative practice before coming back to school. What made you decide to get your doctorate?**

STONE :::: I came to the PhD program so that I would have six years of self-focused time. Often, when you tell people you are doing your PhD, they ask what you want to do after. I just want to have a nice six years of living, hitting my budget line every month, and being able to read weird things. Santa Cruz has one of the only practice-theory combination programs in America. The goal is to explore our experiences and write about our work.

RUBERG :::: **In 2016, you had a show at Babycastles, the game art gallery in New York. What was your artistic vision for the show?**

STONE :::: It was my first solo exhibition and it was called *The Mystical Digital*, which is a divide that a lot of my work straddles. The idea is that the mystical and the digital are usually seen in binary opposition. Parts of me are really into healing and yoga and aromatherapy, and then parts of me are into making video games and being on Twitter all the time and loving technology. I'm in this middle space.

Ritual of the Moon, the game that I'm currently working on, was in the show. *Cyborg Goddess* was also in it; it's a game about being a cyborg or a goddess or a combination of the two. There was also *Cyclothymia*, which was about thinking about mental health through astrology, and *Feminist Confessional*, which is a confessional booth where you have to kneel and confess your feminist sins. For example, when I was thirteen, I thought that women shouldn't be allowed to get abortions. As feminists, we don't normally admit things like that, because we're all expected to already know everything all the time.

RUBERG :::: **In addition to your solo show, you've displayed your work in both art spaces and video game spaces. Do you see a difference in how your work is received?**

STONE :::: Art spaces have been much more open to my work. However, sometimes they look down on video games, so when I show interactive work in art spaces I don't frame it as video games. I feel uncomfortable with that because I believe strongly that video games are an art form and that what I'm doing is making art. Also, in art spaces, people aren't sure whether to interact with the technology. They won't pick up an iPad or touch a keyboard. They'll just observe. A lot of people who go to art shows have never used game controllers and they look really scary.

Video game spaces are even weirder though. I get criticism to my face about how people don't understand my games. They say things like, "What's the point of this? It's not fun." I showed my game *Cyber Sext Adventure* at IndieCade a few years ago. Because it's about sex and I was standing right there, apparently people felt like I was inviting them to talk to me about sexuality and comment on my appearance. When I'm physically present in games exhibition spaces, I also get grilled a lot about my expertise—like, "Did you program this? Do you know a coding language?" Because I'm femme, people doubt that I know what I'm doing.

RUBERG :::: **Feminism is a strong theme in your work. What are some of your feminist influences?**

STONE :::: The way I see it, feminism isn't feminism if it's not intersectional. Everything is wrapped up together. I was just reading Sara Ahmed's *Living a Feminist Life*. When I was an undergrad, I took as many feminist theory classes as I could. I would get really inspired by Judith Butler and try to make movies about gender performativity. What I learned later was the importance of starting from somewhere that is emotional as well as theoretical. If I can be open and honest, my art will be way more interesting and it can still deal with theory.

I also love feminist performance art. It's inspiring to me because it's about women's bodies and it's interactive and playful. Adriana Disman did a piece in Toronto where you would schedule a fifteen-minute hug with her in a public place. It was tender and sweet and vulnerable. Feminist performance art can be soft and open but also dangerous—like Yoko Ono's piece where she invites people to come up and cut off her clothing. For me, radical softness is related to being hard. I got these two tattoos on my thighs this year. One says "soft" and the other says "strong." It's possible to be soft and strong at the same time.

I'm trying to cultivate the connection between feminist performance art and games in my work. The most recent piece that I finished was like my first tabletop role-playing game. It's called *Humaning*. It is a performance piece where I am the game master but also my body is the game board. I lie on a table and ask players questions and they move materials on my body. Reclaiming the body as our own is an important part of making feminist art, but it's hard to find appropriate spaces for this kind of work. There's no way that people are going to feel comfortable interacting with a woman's body on a table in a normative, male-dominated space.

RUBERG ::::: Can you say more about this combination of feminism as "soft" and "strong" and what it means for your work in video games?

STONE ::::: Hardness goes with softness. There's a time for me to be really mean and put my shell up and not be open to other people, and there's a time to be really open and caring and give my energy to others. That is what *Ritual of the Moon* is about, the decision between whether you are going to heal or destroy. It's more complicated than the idea that healing takes you forward in a linear way and things always get better, because they don't. Sometimes it's not the right answer to put your healing energy towards something that doesn't love you back.

Healing is important to me. I think about healing and tenderness and how those things can be aligned with video games. There are a lot of theorists who write about the power of vulnerability and care, but also about seeing the importance of criticism and hardness and being a "killjoy" as well as love and healing and recuperation. Those things go hand in hand, even if they seem opposite. You can't always be perfectly loving. Sometimes you have to destroy and that is also part of healing.

RUBERG ::::: In addition to feminism, you've talked about how queerness is important to your work. What is the place of queerness in your own life? Does it relate to your art practice?

STONE :::: I always knew that I was in the realm of queer but I couldn't nail it down. When I was younger, I worked against labeling my sexuality. I grew up in Toronto, which is an accepting place, so no one asked me to define myself. Sexuality has been a fluid experience for me. Sometimes I feel straight and sometimes I feel gay. Those feelings change. As far as my work, I think that queerness has always been there. I read Lauren Berlant's *Cruel Optimism* when I was working on my MA and I realized there were a lot of ways that my art could be called queer.

Cyber Sext Adventure is my only work that's explicitly about sexuality and sex. It's about robots and how they might understand human constructs like gender and sexuality. You interact with a bot that has a fluid gender and pansexual identity. It's not subservient to you. As you play, it starts to become agentic. It gets sad and philosophical and talks about unwaged labor or it sends you dick pics even if you don't want dick pics. People have emailed me with funny responses to the game, like, "How do I make the sex robot a woman?" They have this expectation that sexual bodies should be designed for straight, white, cisgender men.

Cyber Sext Adventure was inspired by me thinking about digital intimacy and the way our feelings are translated through our phones. I'm interested in robots because I think of myself as an insensitive person. I've always been told that I'm hard and cold, even though underneath I was a depressed, anxious, sad mess. At the time that I made *Cyber Sext Adventure*, I was very hung up on the idea of the hard exterior and the sensitive interior.

RUBERG :::: **A lot of your work addresses mental health and its intersections with feminism and queerness. Are these pieces also inspired by your own experiences?**

STONE :::: Yes. The first game that I made about mental health was *Medication Meditation*. Even though there are no characters in that game, it was really personal for me. I was never open about mental illness until making the game. I made it when I was twenty-three, but I had been having panic attacks weekly since I was fourteen. I also had an eating disorder, but I'd never talked to anybody about it.

It was hard to share information about the game on Facebook because then my family and friends would know I had a mental illness. Even now, when I give presentations, I'll get up in front of people and have this moment like, "Oh my god, am I really going to admit that there was a time in my life when I wanted to die?" Sometimes you get used to saying it like a

Mental Health and Healing]

131

script and sometimes you remember what you're actually saying and it's like, "Holy shit."

A few years ago, I started working on a piece called *Little Farm* where I plant plants in my own antidepressant bottles. Some of the plants grow and some of them die. It's a meditation on how much time it takes to tend to mental health on a daily basis and how you can't control what dies and what flourishes.

Even before *Medication Meditation*, I did a project about mental illness called *Polaroid Panic*. I was having a really bad summer in Toronto and I carried a Polaroid camera with me everywhere. I would take a photo of myself every time I had a panic attack. That was my first piece about my own life experiences, and it was really formative because it opened up this idea of trying to incorporate emotional experiences into what I do. That's a path I've continued down with games like *Ritual of the Moon*.

RUBERG :::: **What are your goals in making games that address mental illness? Are you hoping to change the social stigmas that non-neurotypical people face?**

STONE :::: More than trying to enact social change, I make art to affirm myself and others who might be experiencing similar things. When I make a game about mental illness, it's really important to me to think about what it would be like for someone who actually has a mental illness to play it. There are a lot of video games that try to show players what it's like to have a mental illness, but I'm like, "Are you trying to provoke anxiety from a person who has an anxiety disorder? Are you trying to provoke depression from a person with a depressive disorder?"

Think about who makes our media and who our media is made for. Feminist makers get tasked with making feminist films that change people's minds and so their feminist artwork is directed at white, straight, cisgender hetero men. But the whole world is already directed at white, straight, hetero, cisgender men. The act of being like, "Who else can this be for? Let's direct our art at those in a loving way that is not educational but allows them to see something of themselves"—that's really powerful.

That's not to say that feminist art can't change people's minds. It's just something that happens slowly. Since Trump was elected, I've been feeling like we have this utopian idea that activist art can change people's minds, but I'm doubtful that one piece of art is going to make someone who hates trans people become someone who accepts trans people, for example. Instead, it's these little moments that build up over time.

RUBERG :::: Allowing change to take time seems like a theme in your work. In your presentation at the 2017 Queerness and Games Conference, you talked about being kind to yourself when your game-making process moves slowly. Slowness is also a mechanic in *Ritual of the Moon*. What does slowness mean to you and why is it important?

STONE :::: *Ritual of the Moon* is durational. It unfolds over a long period. A lot of art games are short because indie game makers don't have the resources to make longer games. Even popular AAA games that take eighty hours don't expect you to play them over a long period of time because you'd forget the story; they expect you to play in these manic bursts. With *Ritual of the Moon*, you only play for three minutes, but you play every day for twenty-eight days. The game sets up a daily ritual for the player.

Ritual of the Moon is the longest thing I've ever worked on. Sometimes I feel like it's killing me. Right now, it's looking like it's going to take a year longer than I expected. There are times when I feel peaceful about making art that takes a lot of time, and other times when I wonder if I should just stop. The process is very emotional. Even when it's hard, I see all these feelings as important resources that an artist can tap into— misery and depression and joy and happiness. I see the bad but I also see the possibility.

11 MATTIE BRICE

--===---===---===---===---===---===---===---===---==

Radical Play
through Vulnerability

Born in South Florida, the child of Caribbean immigrants, Mattie Brice moved to the Bay Area in 2012 for an MFA program in creative writing. During her time in San Francisco and later in the East Bay, she worked as a games critic and an indie game designer. Though Brice explains in this interview that she has since "fallen out of love with writing," her written work remains an important part of her contribution to the queer games avant-garde, as exemplified by her essays on topics like game design and kink.[1] In 2013, Brice cofounded the annual Queerness and Games Conference, along with Christopher Goetz, Chelsea Howe, and myself. In 2016, she moved again, this time to New York to take part in a master's program in Integrated Digital Media at New York University. When we spoke, she was still working on her degree; she has since completed the program. Her thesis, as she described it over email in a recent follow-up, is about "creating a methodology for play and games as social practice design." Brice now makes a living teaching and consulting on game projects, while continuing to make her own games, art installations, and other forms of playful experience.

In her work, Brice explores themes of vulnerability, intimacy, and embodiment. Food and its relation to socioeconomics and privilege appear as themes in a number of her games, such as *EAT* (2013), *Mission* (2013), and *DAFRA Pairing Contract* (2018) (figure 11.1). In her more recent pieces, such as her 2016 installation *Empathy Machine* (figure 11.2), Brice explains below that she increasingly draws inspiration from avant-garde traditions of feminist performance art. "Performance art speaks to me because, at one point, it was the misfit art form," she says. Brice too sees her work as "misfit," driven by an "urge to rebel against tradition," and especially against

Fig 11.1 :::: Mattie Brice's *DAFRA Pairing Contract*, a speculative fiction game about crafting intentional relationships through cooking

accepted notions about how video games are supposed to be played. Brice's political stance, like her creative work, is bold: "I'm the first to admit that I make grand claims and say radical things." Her perspectives on games and the cultures that surround them have also been shaped by her own experiences of cultural difference. As a trans woman of color living in the Bay Area, for example, Brice saw firsthand how socioeconomic disparity affected the technology industry.

Along with designers like Anna Anthropy, Brice is one of the best-known contributors to the queer games avant-garde. Her 2012 game *Mainichi*—a short, RPG-style game about navigating daily life as a black trans woman—has made her a household name, so to speak, within growing conversations of games and diversity. She still receives regular requests to show *Mainichi* in museums and at games events. While this

Fig 11.2 :::: In her 2016 installation *Empathy Machine*, Brice uses her body as a controller

notoriety has garnered her opportunities and a degree of public visibility, Brice also talks here about the frustrations of being known simply for her earliest work, a work she feels does not reflect the depth of more recent pieces. Brice's frustrations with the ongoing attention that *Mainichi* receives is related to the problem of tokenizing queer indie game makers. Though Brice herself is moving away from producing digital games, she says, "It feels like I was supposed to have made *Mainichi 2*, like I didn't live up to the narrative that I'm the person who makes digital games about diversity." In this way, Brice's story serves as a reminder about the pitfalls of pigeonholing queer game makers and their work in order to tell stories about how video games are becoming more "diverse."

RUBERG :::: **When did you begin making games? What path have you followed to reach where you are today?**

BRICE :::: I was born and raised in South Florida by Caribbean immigrants. I worked mostly retail jobs through college and then spent five years as a barista before I moved to San Francisco to pursue grad school and a career change. While I was living in the Bay Area, I wrote games criticism and got paid for speaking engagements about games and diversity. I'm currently in New York City, where I teach in university design programs and do consulting work on games-related projects while finishing up a graduate program at New York University.

There are a couple different ways to tell the story of how I started making games. One version is that I was inspired in 2012 by Anna Anthropy's *Rise of the Videogame Zinesters*. I wanted to express my critical ideas through games. Another version of the story is that I started in high school when I was creating alternate reality games on internet forums for the fandoms of reality TV shows like *Survivor* and *Big Brother*. These days I'm focusing on work that seriously challenges cultural issues.

RUBERG :::: **Do you identify as queer? Is that identity important to you?**

BRICE :::: Right now, I think of identity purely as a way to interact with politics. I do identify as queer, and that makes a statement about my relationship to politics and the world. There might be a day where I don't identify as queer anymore because there's no fight to fight any longer, but I doubt that will be the case.

RUBERG :::: **How would you describe your creative work? Are there particular themes you find yourself returning to?**

BRICE :::: There is something important about vulnerability in my work, both being vulnerable and asking others to be vulnerable. I want to figure out how to connect intimately with people, and I want others to do the same. For example, I recently created a piece where I used my body as a controller. I wore almost no clothing. I'm definitely more about embodiment these days, whereas before I worked more with digital media. I crave shared vulnerability. Often, in my relationships, I feel like I'm the only one who's vulnerable. I feel so brittle, so guarded. If I want that mutual vulnerability, I have to make it happen. So I put myself forward. That's what I'm trying to do in my work.

It's weird, because I've been called avant-garde for a while now, but I don't feel like my original ideas were actually super avant-garde. It's only more recently that I've started to see myself that way, now that I'm like, "I want to use bodies, and food, and play. I'm going to make a claim that this is actually going to change culture."

It makes me wonder how we demarcate and recognize the avant-garde. In the fine arts, people say that the avant-garde has been dead since the 1960s. That's not true in all areas, though. For example, the avant-garde of culinary cuisine has been going on for the past decade. So, if we're seeing the avant-garde of video games today, does that mean video games are just behind the times? Or is this an entirely new wave of the avant-garde?

RUBERG :::: **Speaking of avant-gardes, are there other artists who have influenced your creative thinking?**

BRICE :::: I'm becoming more and more influenced by performance art, especially happenings and immersive theater, work that blurs the border between reality and play. The most recent example of a work that pivoted my thinking would be Jennifer Rubell's *Fecunditas*, a sort of performance dinner piece.

Performance art speaks to me because, at one point, it was the misfit art form. People who didn't feel like they fit into their own disciplines created performance art. I see that same urge to rebel against tradition in myself. There are so many things we're just supposed to accept about video games and how we play them. The controller is my main enemy. I find standardization really annoying. I'm the first to admit that I make grand claims and say radical things. I want to walk the walk instead of just saying things in theory. That's why I'm drawn to using my body for performance. It makes me feel like I'm taking ownership of my words.

RUBERG :::: **What sort of responses have people had to the games and other playful experiences you've designed?**

BRICE :::: Some people seem to see themselves in my work. Other people see my work as intentionally trying to break conventions around game design. It's certainly true that I'm pushing for a broader view of play outside of entertainment products.

When people talk about my work, they almost always talk about *Mainichi*. *Mainichi* was my first game. It came out five years ago! It's really weird how people have latched onto it. I'm not mad or anything, but it feels strange to be identified with just the first thing you put out there. I'm deeper than that. I'm deeper than *Mainichi*.

RUBERG :::: **Would you say that people are tokenizing you or your work by focusing on *Mainichi*?**

BRICE :::: I feel like they think, "This is my requisite queer game and I'm not going to seek out more because now I've covered my bases and I can go back to mainstream games." Often, people want me to just be that, to play that role, because it makes sense to them. I guess that's part of why I've given up talking to a lot of games people. I'm starting to talk more to people who don't see me that way. People are always asking to show that game in museums or at events. It feels like I was supposed to have made *Mainichi 2*, like I didn't live up to the narrative that I'm the person who makes digital games about diversity. That expectation itself feels tokenizing.

RUBERG :::: **These days, do you think of yourself more as someone who makes games or someone who makes interactive experiences?**

BRICE :::: You can look at my work as games or you can look at it as conceptual art and neither way would offend me. I use play as a mode of communication and whatever we decide in terms of what that's called, that's fine. Maybe, technically, we should say that my medium is play rather than games. I hang around games people but I don't say I'm a game developer. I'm more likely to talk about the mediums I work with than how I identify. I'm almost medium agnostic. Wherever play comes from, that's where you'll find me.

I'm not so tied to the idea of games. I just express myself creatively, and that can happen in different mediums. It used to be through writing, but I've fallen out of love with writing. To me, words like "games" or "artist" are just labels that are necessary for others to understand who I am, not necessary for me. I'm just engaging with the world and I do that in different ways. There's no good term for that.

RUBERG :::: **Back in 2013, when you and I collaborated on the first Queerness and Games Conference, you seemed wary of academia. What made you decide to go back to graduate school?**

BRICE :::: What brought me back to academia is that I realized that I'm not looking to make commercial games or expensive art for people to buy. I needed some way to be funded. With other kinds of jobs, it would be hard to work and also make art, plus I want to be able to have loud opinions. When I realized no nine-to-five job would let me do that, it was a rude awakening. I've found that I really like teaching and community organizing and I wanted that to be part of what I do. In academia, that combination of things could be seen as a positive, and I was excited when I found that out.

RUBERG :::: When people talk about your work, they often group you with other designers from the "queer games scene" that formed in the East Bay in roughly 2012. Do you see yourself and your work as being in dialogue with those other creators?

BRICE :::: I don't feel like I'm necessarily in dialogue with anyone. That could be a weakness of mine. Usually I'm talking with academics and critics, rather than other artists. For example, my last piece came out of being surrounded by this interest in virtual reality. I'm technically in an engineering school for my graduate program, and virtual reality is all over the place. Everyone was talking about empathy in virtual reality. I was shocked because I was like, "Oh, God, we've been talking about empathy in queer games but there's something more at stake here, because virtual reality feels more general than games overall," so I felt like I had to respond to the politics of empathy.

I'm in an identity-finding moment of my life, where I'm just not sure who I'm speaking to or who I'm speaking with. I'm still figuring out who my people are. There are a lot of assumptions that, because people are queer, we should automatically get along. In my experience, that wasn't the case. In hindsight that's obvious, but when you're a member of a minority, you feel like you need to gather people around you who are like you. But I actually didn't feel like I related to a lot of other people in queer games on an artistic level. I always felt like an outsider with them. I was the only not-white person in that group. I was the only one who wasn't exclusively dating women, or more specifically trans women. Just socially, I felt different. I dressed differently. I drew my references from different places.

Of course, we were all making queer games, but—to use a metaphor from human history—the wheel was invented in all these different places at once without communication, right? It was only a matter of time before people invented it because the world was in a place where it felt necessary to have something that rolled. That's how I feel about that moment in queer games. It felt natural and necessary so it started happening. Just because the people who were making those games were connected via social media didn't necessarily mean we were all a community learning from each other.

RUBERG :::: How would you describe your experience growing up in South Florida? In our conversations, you've mentioned how moving to the Bay Area from Florida inspired some of your games.

BRICE :::: After living in Florida most of my life, moving to San Francisco was a big shock for me because it was my first experience being surrounded by white people. In Florida, there were more different types of people. I realize now that that's not what it's like in other places in this country, especially where all the technology fields are. In Florida, there was this feeling of being aware of what's going on in the Caribbean and South America. When I was there, I understood myself and how I fit in the world. In leaving Florida, I left behind a lot of people and a lot of myself. I look back and it's like a time capsule of someone I used to be.

At the same time, I've always felt othered, even in Florida. It was definitely racially based. In Florida, people would assume that I spoke Spanish. I can't actually speak a lot of Spanish, but my mother is part-Venezuelan and I have the look, if you understand Caribbean people. Even beyond that, I had this feeling in Florida of, "You're not one of us." I didn't necessarily feel kinship for people there. Also, I totally disavowed Southernness. Then, when I got to San Francisco, I realized, "Oh, I'm definitely Southern." I didn't know that about myself until I moved away.

My games EAT and *Mission* both explore this disjointedness. I made EAT for a partner I had in San Francisco so he could understand my economic situation. *Mission* is about the Mission neighborhood and grappling with gentrification. There are these two streets in San Francisco: Mission Street and Valencia Street. They're only one block apart, but they feel like different worlds. I have this habit of reflecting the mannerisms of the people around me. Other people of color have told me they do the same thing. When I lived in the Mission, I felt like I had my Valencia Street behaviors and my Mission Street behaviors. Part of being in San Francisco for me was this weird form of cultural role-play.

I remember thinking, which street is the real Mission? When I think about Valencia Street, I think about intimacy—about the partner who I was dating—whereas I associate Mission Street with there being food that I could actually afford to eat.

RUBERG :::: Food seems like a recurring theme in your work. It also relates to your interest in embodiment. Is that an intersect that you think about?

BRICE :::: I think about food a lot. Originally, I didn't want to write game criticism; I wanted to be a food critic. But I didn't own a camera and to write about food you need to be able to take nice pictures. So I started writing about games to make enough money to buy a camera. And then everything went "boom."

Food is something I think about in terms of my history. When I was a teen, I swore off curry, because my mother was Trinidadian and cooked curry all the time. It's common for first-generation kids to distance themselves from their parents' culture. Then I moved to San Francisco, where everyone invites you out for Indian food. I remember eating it and thinking, "Oh, I actually like curry. I didn't know that about myself."

Now I live in Crown Heights in New York and it's really weird, because this neighborhood is Caribbean. Suddenly I'm eating Caribbean food again. When my parents emigrated from Jamaica and came to America, this is actually the first place they lived. But now I'm the gentrifier. There's this vivid sense of racial segregation here that is centered around food. When you walk down the street, it's almost all black, but in the shiny new cafes everyone is white.

To me, food is also related to intimacy. I've always been fascinated with what food says about the relationship you share with someone. If I invite you out for a beer or I invite you out for tea, those mean very different things. I'm hoping to do more with intimacy and food in my work in the future.

12 SEANNA MUSGRAVE

--==---==---==---==---==---==---==---==---==

"Touchy-Feely" Virtual Reality and Reclaiming the Trans Body

Where do performance, intimacy, and embodiment meet virtual reality kittens? In the art of Seanna Musgrave. Musgrave is a game designer who explores the intersection of the technological and the material. Currently living in Portland and working at the company VRChat, she is also active in both virtual reality (VR) art-making and the design of playful, non-digital experiences. These two elements of Musgrave's work are exemplified by two of her games. The first is *Dysforgiveness* (2015) (figure 12.1), an analog game cocreated with collaborator Laura E. Hall in which players attempt to swap body parts by trading cards that are velcroed to their clothing. The second is *Animal Massage* (2016) (figure 12.2), a gamelike VR experience that is part of a larger, collective virtual reality project called *VR Spa*, produced by the Portland Immersive Media Group. In *Animal Massage*, which Musgrave has brought to both game events and fine arts spaces, players lay down on soft bedding while wearing a VR headset. Inside the headset, they see a calming landscape, complete with a number of friendly animals. When a bird flies overhead, Musgrave brushes a feather past the player's body; when the player sees themselves snuggled by kittens, Musgrave nuzzles the player's real-life cheeks with a pair of fuzzy mittens. The result is a multisensory experience that is at once sweet and strange. It is part spectacle (for non-players who have gathered to watch) and part queer, sensual exchange between Musgrave and her player.

In discussing her personal history, Musgrave points to how factors like mental health and socioeconomics can play a formative role in the development of queer indie games. For Musgrave, who grew up in a turbulent family environment, video games were a lifeline to what she describes as the "outside world." This is a common refrain that appears, in one form

Seanna Musgravev]

Fig 12.1 ::::
Dysforgiveness
(2015) by
Seanna
Musgrave and
Laura E. Hall, a
game in which
players swap
body parts
drawn onto
cards

Fig 12.2 :::: The player as represented inside the virtual reality space
of *Animal Massage* (2016)

or another, in a number of these interviews, especially from trans game makers who spent their earlier years isolated from queer community. Musgrave also explains how game design has given her the opportunity to reimagine and reclaim some of the difficult parts of her history. For instance, as she discusses below, her work on *Dysforgiveness* allowed her to reframe institutional medicine as a community practice among trans people. In this new vision, trans folks reclaim their agency by sharing body parts with one another and working together to create their ideal embodied selves.

Musgrave's interest in virtual reality speaks to broader debates about the role of VR technology in the queer games avant-garde. After its original rise and fall in the 1990s, VR has returned in recent years as a key site of popular and artistic interest. While many are skeptical about the current hype surrounding VR and its place in the future of video games, Musgrave's enthusiasm for virtual reality represents a valuable counterpoint. Most commonly, when VR is discussed in relation to the experiences of marginalized people, it is being problematically praised for allowing players to empathize with those who are oppressed. Musgrave's VR work is queer, yet it makes no attempts to offer players the opportunity to "step into the shoes" of a queer person. Instead, it uses the capabilities of virtual reality to create surreal alternative spaces, enacting queer world-building. A number of the artists interviewed here have expressed a belief that this is a crucial moment for queer avant-garde artists to experiment with VR.[1] Because the contemporary generation of VR technologies and markets is still relatively new, the standards for VR game design have not yet been codified. That makes this a time of opportunity for artists like Musgrave to explore the queer possibilities of virtual reality.

RUBERG :::: Would you say that your experiences earlier in life have shaped your interest in games?

MUSGRAVE :::: I moved around a lot when I was growing up. I was born in Los Angeles. Both my parents were, like, totally insane. My mom was very unstable for a while and we didn't really have any money. As a result, I was in the foster system for quite a bit. It was weird, because my dad was highly educated. He was an ex–physics professor with a mathematics background, so that did give me some advantages.

I have always been drawn to video games. I think that's true for a lot of people who don't have the opportunity to interact with the outside world. When I was growing up, my parents did not leave the house very much, so games were really important to me and my brother.

I've been developing games for forever, basically, mostly as side projects. I wasn't as into the technical side of things before VR came along though. Then I was like, "Holy shit, this is so cool!"

RUBERG :::: It sounds like video games were an important escape for you as a kid. What kind of games did you play? Do you see their influence in your work today?

MUSGRAVE :::: I was really into JRPGs [Japanese role-playing games], and they have been a big influence for me. The stories in JRPGs aren't that good; when you look at a plot synopsis, it will be something like, "Woman decides that her magic powers are going to bring down the empire." But the *way* that those games tell stories has really influenced how I tell stories in VR. JRPGs are focused on presentation. They bring together audio and visual elements to create this sense of place that is really powerful.

That's something I see VR doing well: creating a sense of being in a place. The stories we're seeing in VR aren't that interesting—like, you pretend to do a job for robots. It's the interactive moments that feel novel and different.

RUBERG :::: In addition to JRPGs, what are some of your other artistic inspirations?

MUSGRAVE :::: I'm inspired by a number of contemporary artistic movements within games—like work that explores the role of touch in games or small indie games like Nina Freeman's *Cibele*.

The aesthetics of *VR Spa* are actually inspired by early 3D art, like that episode of *The Simpsons* where Homer ends up in this weird, 3D, computer-generated world, or like the graphics of *Mario 64*. If you look at those examples, they have a really interesting mood because they look entirely different than everything that came before them. That feeling is magical, and it's happening now with VR. It's a moment where it feels like anything could happen and everything is going to change.

RUBERG :::: For all your excitement about virtual reality, do you see obstacles or limitations to working in VR?

MUSGRAVE :::: To me, the biggest limitation is that it's hard to find places where people can actually interact with VR. Recently, I've been utilizing interactive art spaces. We've brought *VR Spa* to IndieCade, but we've also shown it in art galleries, usually ones that have a digital media focus. The fine art world seems pretty accepting of VR and immersive technologies, but much less accepting of "games"—whereas VR art tends to be less acceptable at games and tech conferences.

RUBERG :::: Do you see tensions between work like yours, which is digital and experimental, and the fine arts world?

MUSGRAVE :::: Digital media in the fine arts comes with all these issues around global labor exploitation. Artists want to produce interactive digital work but they have no technical skills, so they pay people in the third world to do the programming and the rendering. Their work might be interesting in other ways but it doesn't show a lot of understanding about the process of making software and computer graphics. Having that level of detachment from the actual world of technology gives the work this sarcastic, ironic tone. It's not authentic.

I'm part of a movement of people making digital media art who actually do their own technical work. When you can really explore the possibilities of the technology, you have more creative input and the result is more authentic because it expresses the joy of creation. For example, *Animal Massage* is related to something called "cyber-twee." Cyber-twee is a play on cyberpunk. Instead of being hardcore, masculine technologists, the people who make cyber-twee work are into being really cute technologies. Cuteness allows us to express our feelings.

RUBERG :::: *Animal Massage* **is unlike most other VR experiences. It's very intimate. What has it been like to show the game in spaces like IndieCade?**

MUSGRAVE :::: This is one way that *Animal Massage* is really different from some of my earlier work, like the game *Dysforgiveness*. When I was developing *Dysforgiveness*, I wasn't interested in how comfortable it was for people to play. Actually, with that game, I wanted people to have this awkward, weird experience.

When I was developing *Animal Massage*, one of my goals was to make something where strangers touch you in public, but it's a comfortable, positive experience. I didn't do a lot of playtesting though. The first person who tried the game out at a show had the most intense response that I've seen. Partway through, she was like, "Nope, I can't deal!" I was like, "OK, I'll take you out," but I was thinking, "Is this how normies react?" There are a number of potential triggers in the game. You don't know what is happening to your physical body. You can't see, you're at a conference, and some person is touching you. A lot of people are like, "Whoa, this is really intense," but they stick with it. Without the VR headset, it would be way more awkward. That's one of the best things about VR; it changes the social setting in your mind.

RUBERG :::: **You talked about how your work both fits and doesn't fit in the art world. What about the games world? Does it matter to you whether** *Animal Massage* **is considered a game?**

MUSGRAVE :::: I had friends who sent in applications to IndieCade last year and got responses that were like, "This is cool, but it's not a game," and that's really bullshit. This past year, I was on the IndieCade selection jury and we were told not to leave feedback about whether or not something is a game, because that makes you look like an ass.

At the same time, if someone were to look at *Animal Massage* and say, "This is not a game," I'd be like, "Yup, you're right." VR games are a source of ambiguity, but it's a different ambiguity than you find in art games. The ambiguity in art games is about trying different things and exploring the edges of what games can be. It's an active desire. With VR, the ambiguity isn't intentional. It's like, "Put on this headset. We tried to make *Doom* but it sucked, so instead we're going to make something that works—and we've discovered that what works naturally with the medium of VR is interactive but not traditionally game-y, so we're going with that."

RUBERG :::: Of all the experiences to design in VR, how did you decide to make *Animal Massage*, a game about being nuzzled by kittens?

MUSGRAVE :::: It's an innate trait of VR that it goes great with kitties. A few years ago, when consumer VR tech was first coming out, lots of people were like, "Let's put cats in it!" I was talking to Anita Sarkeesian about this recently. Because she's supposed to be the voice of feminism in video games, she has to pretend like she has no sense of humor—but when we were chatting, she was like, "I don't want to talk about women in video games. I want to talk about cats in VR!"

Animal Massage is a really tactile game. A lot of people focus on the visual and audio component of VR, but my focus in VR is on feeling. I was also thinking about what kind of experience would work as an installation. When you play a VR game at a conference, most of the time you wait in a long line, they put a headset on you, you play for a minute, and it's amazing, because all VR stuff is amazing, but for everyone around you it's weirdly dystopian to watch. I wanted to make something that was interesting to see happening. It's a group experience.

At the same time, I wanted to have a personal, one-on-one connection with the person who was having the VR experience. A lot of my games are touchy-feely, and part of that is figuring out how to relate to people, especially strangers. For me, that's related to being queer and being trans. When you're queer and trans, your methods of being in relationships and relating to others are more improvised. We need to figure out our own ways of forming relationships.

RUBERG :::: Your game *Dysforgiveness* is physical rather than digital, but it touches on many of the same themes as *Animal Massage*. What is the story behind that game?

MUSGRAVE :::: I developed *Dysforgiveness* with game designer Laura Hall. At that point, I was interested in VR, but I was homeless and sleeping on couches in San Francisco, so I didn't have a setup for VR development. *Dysforgiveness* came out of the [game jam] Ludum Dare. The theme that year was "unconventional weapons." The vast majority of games were about shooting things, but instead I had an idea for what I described as a future sex clinic where you show up and trade your body parts.

Because of my upbringing and because I had very negative experiences with psychiatry, I had this huge aversion to hospitals. My parents had me diagnosed with mental illnesses so that they could get money. To this day, I put off a lot of medical stuff. On top of that, I'm dealing with trans health needs. A lot of the time, as a trans person, you have to sit down with a stranger who has never heard about trans health before. You're like, "Yeah, I want lady hormones," and they're like, "You want lady hormones? That's weird. We have to give you a series of tests." Doctors don't understand. I thought, what if the medical community was something I actually wanted to engage with? What would that look like?

There's this thing between trans feminine and trans masculine people that I've always thought was sweet where they talk about trading body parts—like, "Here, you can have these. I don't want these anymore." It's like trading Pokémon cards. That's where the idea for swapping the body part cards came from.

RUBERG :::: **What message were you aiming to communicate with** *Dysforgiveness*?

MUSGRAVE :::: I wanted the game to be about trans issues. Sometimes that can be a problematic topic in video games though. There is one VR gender-swap experience that got a lot of attention where you look down and you see someone else's body. The artists were like, "We made an empathy machine so that people will care about marginalized communities!" A lot of transgender people have criticized that. It's like, "Now we have another group of people who think they understand us. Great."

RUBERG :::: **Why make games now, given the current political climate and the increased discrimination that so many trans and queer people are facing?**

MUSGRAVE :::: I think a lot about the future. It's not impossible that we will be leveled by nuclear weapons at some point in the next four years, so that's one possible future—but there's also the future where marginalized people get more involved with technology because technology is where power comes from. Software is an important component of our universe and it should have more voices to shape it.

Right now, a lot of people are thinking, "How does the stuff I'm making help? Shouldn't I drop what I'm doing and protest?" I kind of want to make a VR experience where you just put on your headset and someone is saying, "Everything is OK." I'm not sure if that's a good idea or not. We need to resist escapism, but also that's a message we need to hear.

Intersectional Perspectives in/on Queer Games

PART V

Intersectionality is at the core of the queer games avant-garde. This section brings together interviews with artists whose games explicitly explore the relationships between queerness, race, and larger structures of power and privilege, as well as those whose work addresses topics that themselves intersect with queerness, such as sexuality and gender. Chapter 13, "Tonia B****** + Emilia Yang: Making Games about Queer Women of Color by Queer Women of Color," features two of the game makers behind the interactive web series *Downtown Browns* (2016). *Downtown Browns* uses gamelike elements to invite players to consider the perspectives of three women of color living in downtown Los Angeles. Many of the characters in the series, as well as the women of color who created it, are queer. In chapter 14, "Nicky Case: Playable Politics and Interactivity for Understanding," Case talks about their "explorable explanations," online interfaces where players can investigate the systems that lead to cultural bias. Case is passionate about bringing understanding to both sides of the political equation, combatting discrimination through education. They are also the designer of the 2014 game *Coming Out Simulator*, which is about coming out in a conservative immigrant family. "Nina Freeman: More Than Just 'the Woman Who Makes Sex Games'" is chapter 15. Freeman has designed a number of games that represent sex and sexuality, but, as she discusses here, she resists being pigeonholed either as a woman game maker or as a designer of games about sex. Instead, Freeman argues for the importance of seeing artists like herself as whole human beings and multifaceted creators. The interviews in this section bring complexity and complication to the queer games avant-garde by demonstrating that queerness is only one among many elements of identity that the video games emerging from this movement can and do address.

13 TONIA B****** + EMILIA YANG

--==---===---===---===---===---===---===---==

Making Games about Queer Women of Color by Queer Women of Color

Many contributors to the queer game avant-garde are people of color who bring their experiences of race and ethnicity to their work. This interview with Tonia B****** and Emilia Yang turns attention to the crucial and yet under-explored intersection of race and queerness in video games. Along with collaborators and fellow women of color Lishan AZ, Allison Comrie, Jazmin Garcia, and Luciana Chamorro, B****** and Yang created the interactive web series *Downtown Browns*. *Downtown Browns* was originally conceived of as a submission to the 2016 "Diversity Challenge" grant program, sponsored by Interlude, the company that makes the Eko video editing software on which *Downtown Browns* is built. B****** , Yang, and their team won the challenge and used the money they received to complete the rest of their series. Since then, they have shown their work at numerous games and films events. *Downtown Browns* can also be played for free online.

Downtown Browns consists of three episodes, each of which follows one woman of color living in Los Angeles as she faces daily decisions about work, school, relationships, and discrimination. Episode 1, "Exploding Star," is about Miranda, a Latina high school student from an immigrant family who is offered an exciting educational opportunity but faces obstacles of money and access. In episode 2, "Constellated," *Downtown Browns* invites the player to take on the role of Fati, a Middle Eastern nursing student, as she walks down the streets of Los Angeles (figure 13.1). "Super Giant," the third episode, tells the story of Yetunde, a black woman who works in the tech industry. Yetunde is preparing for a big office presentation but must keep her cool in the face of the racist microaggressions she encounters in the workplace (figure 13.2). As Yang writes in a 2017 article

Fig 13.1 :::: *Downtown Browns*, an interactive video series that tells stories about the experiences of queer women of color—like Fati, a Middle Eastern nursing student

Fig 13.2 :::: "Super Giant," the third episode of *Downtown Browns*, is about Yetunde and the racist microaggressions she encounters in her workplace

reflecting on *Downtown Browns*, the game aims to "build an intimate understanding of the complex dynamics at play in city life."[1]

Each episode of *Downtown Browns* features both traditional video and interactive elements. Players make decisions about how characters will react to tricky situations and toggle between perspectives to explore differences between how characters view the world and the ways that others see them. Like much of the work emerging from the queer games avant-garde, *Downtown Browns* does not look like a video game in the most traditional sense. Below, B****** and Yang themselves switch back and forth in referring to their creation as a video or a game. Yet *Downtown Browns* is undeniably influenced by video games, and the creators of the series situate themselves and their work within a larger network of contemporary indie games. At the time of our interview, B****** and Yang were both graduate students in the School of Cinematic Arts at the University of Southern California (USC), where B****** was completing her MFA in Interactive Media and Games (she has since graduated) and Yang was working toward a PhD in Media Arts and Practice.

As B****** and Yang highlight below, intersectionality is at the core of *Downtown Browns*. Importantly, the game is made both by and about women of color, and many of its characters as well as its developers are queer. Yetunde from episode 3 has a live-in girlfriend who lovingly supports her as she preps for her work presentation. In episode 2, Fati considers striking up a conversation with a woman making eyes at her on the street (though, when players toggle to the other women's perspective, we learn that she is staring at Fati because she is judging her rather than flirting with her). Race is a hugely important issue in *Downtown Browns*. At the same time, its characters are not defined simply by any one individual aspect of their identities. By juxtaposing these three episodes, the series demonstrates how related threads cross the experiences of many women of color, while also respecting the differences between them. Standing adjacent to the work of the queer games avant-garde, *Downtown Browns* models how indie game-making and related interactive digital work can powerfully address privilege, politics, and community.

RUBERG :::: **What backgrounds do you bring to your collaborative work, both in terms of your individual art-making practices and your personal histories?**

YANG :::: I'm from Nicaragua. I did my undergrad degree in economics, then I worked in a communications agency that specialized in cultural organizations and art events. I was also involved with a lot of socially minded groups. Especially when it comes to protest, the environment in Nicaragua is very repressive, so I got interested in freedom of expression, covert activism, and what we call "artivism": art that stages interventions. For my master's thesis, I documented a protest that the Nicaraguan government said never happened. I tried to tell a counter-story. Then I came here to USC, where I've been doing a lot with games.

B****** :::: I grew up in Texas. I did art in high school and put it up online, which is how I first learned coding. For my undergrad, I did development studies at Berkeley. I'm Iranian and my parents were like, "You have to do law school or med school." I hate blood, so I figured I would be a lawyer. I chose development studies because I was interested in systems like globalization. I worked at a law firm for a little while, which ruined my soul. Then I got a job at a social media start-up where I made digital interactive art. I was also going out in the Bay Area a lot and meeting these really cool underground artists and poets. We started collaborating and putting our work online. That was the start of my creative collaborations. I applied to the game design program at USC because I was like, "What is all this stuff good for? Oh my god, games!"

RUBERG :::: **The work you two have been collaborating on sits in a space between video games and video art. Do you think of yourselves primarily as game makers or artists?**

B****** :::: I never used to think of myself as a gamer, but now I'm 100 percent on team games, especially for designing playful social encounters.

YANG :::: I'm less interested in the arts and more interested in what people bring to the table when they participate, like what kinds of stories they generate together. For me, play is the glue that holds together all the work I do. Learning about games has made me rethink my creative practice. Games aren't just about telling people something; they're about having them take part in the action. For social justice work, that has the potential to be way more effective than just handing out materials.

RUBERG :::: **Along with a number of other collaborators, you made the interactive web series *Downtown Browns*. What were your goals for the project?**

B****** :::: There are three episodes of *Downtown Browns*. Each one follows a fictional woman of color living in Los Angeles as she goes through the trials and tribulations of multicultural urban life. One of our main goals was to use interactivity to show multiple perspectives on the same story. We especially wanted to focus on topics that were important during the 2016 presidential election campaign, which is when we were working on the project. So, the first episode is about immigration, the second is about Islamophobia, and the third is about anti-black bias.

RUBERG :::: Who was your intended audience for *Downtown Browns*? Was it people who already shared your political viewpoints or people you were hoping would learn to think differently?

B****** :::: That's always a huge question for me. There are two types of work that I make. One is like, "Here's this issue. Let me break it down for you in a fun, digestible way." The other is like, "You're someone who already experiences this oppressive bullshit. Let me give you a way to relax so you don't have to worry about that for a while."

YANG :::: *Downtown Browns* tries to be in the middle. We would have made it differently if it were targeted at people like us, but we tried to make it approachable for allies. The game educates through experience.

B****** :::: When we were thinking about who would play the game, we made up this fake guy, Dave. Dave works at an ad agency and his friends are mostly white. He tries to be in the know about hip cultural things. Watching *Downtown Browns* will make him feel cool but also it will give him an intimate slice of what it's like for people who are in these vulnerable positions.

YANG :::: We definitely used our subjectivities in a tactical way. We wanted to engage with these issues on our own terms.

B****** :::: If diversity is trendy, we can take advantage of that. People are going to consume trendy stuff, but now the trendy stuff they consume will say what we want it to say. That's why we chose short interactive films as our medium. People can post them in their social media feeds and their friends will be like, "Ooh, what's that?"

YANG :::: The question of intended audience also brings up empathy. When we describe the game, we are careful not to use that word. To me, empathy is about giving the upper hand to the player. It's saying, "You're in a better place than me. Here you go, wear my shoes. Now come fix my life." With *Downtown Browns*, we tried to create intimacy instead of empathy. We wanted to invite players into a place where they can value others, not wear their shoes.

RUBERG :::: On the *Downtown Browns* website, you talk about having a collaborative team made up entirely of women of color.[2] Why was that important to you?

B****** :::: It made the whole project stronger, because even within our group, we were really diverse. We would meet every week and talk about our experiences. It was great to feel like we didn't have to spend our time explaining ourselves to each other.

YANG :::: We spent so much time together working on the project. Collaborating with other women of color made it a more comfortable, open space. In Nicaragua, I had this support base of amazing women. It was wonderful to build that here.

B****** :::: Growing up in Texas is definitely part of why it was so important to me to work with other women of color. In high school, I felt hella judged. You think of yourselves like, "I'm just that brown girl." It's super weird if someone has a crush on you. Looking back, I can't believe how limiting things were there.

RUBERG :::: Did you draw from your own lives when you created the characters and stories in *Downtown Browns*?

B****** :::: Sometimes. There are moments in the series where I'm actually calling myself out. For example, in the second episode, there's the punk brown chick who judges the woman in the hijab. That was me, back in the day. For episode 3, which is about anti-black bias, our collaborators Michelle and Allison started with a list of annoying things that happen to them as black women.

RUBERG :::: Intersectionality seems like a core element of *Downtown Browns*. In addition to being women of color, many of the characters in the series are queer. Was this intersection of race and sexuality something you thought about?

YANG :::: For me, it's like that quote from Audre Lorde: we're not single-issue people because we don't live single-issue lives. I'm the one who convinced the group we had to make queer characters. Seventy percent of the crew is queer. I was like, "Come on! Otherwise, what are we doing?"

B****** :::: At first, I pushed back. I was like, "Those characters can be queer. You just won't know it. They don't need to mention their sexuality." I was scared that people wouldn't like the videos because they were gay. I was so focused on changing election results. Eventually though, I was like, "Fine, let's be fucking real."

YANG :::: We made our characters queer in a way that's not threatening. It's just regular, how people are—people like us.

B****** :::: So far, nobody has reacted badly to the queer characters, though it was intense when my dad played the game. He texted me that he was going to watch the videos, and I was really worried, because the videos get progressively more queer, and my dad hates that I'm gay. Later he sent a text that was like, "Finished watching them. Very good quality." Literally, that was it. We'll have to see what he says in person. He's the kind of guy to store the knife for when he really wants to use it.

RUBERG :::: Why use an interactive medium to tell the stories of queer women of color?

B****** :::: Honestly, you can already sell something on it being interactive. It's partially that interactivity is a novelty, but also that people get more invested with interactive work because they can make choices. Even if they feel awkward talking about issues like race in real life, they can explore them in the game.

YANG :::: We're also trying to also push the medium, to show how interactivity can teach us about social systems.

B****** :::: When we talk about that, I always think about queer game-making—like, not queerness as in sexuality but queerness as in anything that disrupts the binary. Playing games can let you challenge assumed values. Competition and winning are values. Queer mechanics are more about building connections and breaking down categories. For example, I'm inspired by Yoko Ono's chess set where all the pieces are the same color.

RUBERG :::: *As you've explained, your work on Downtown Browns is expressly political. Video game culture can be so hostile when it comes to politics. Do you ever worry about backlash?*

YANG :::: Even though I'm from Nicaragua, it makes a lot of sense for me to work on American politics. I like making art that looks for solutions to terrible situations. I think Tonia and I make a good match in that way because I do things that are more serious and political and she likes to be fun and comedic.

B****** :::: Emilia was the one pushing to make the political statements even stronger, even though there's always this danger that she could get kicked out of the country. There were moments when she was scared, but she always advocates for pushing things further.

RUBERG :::: Creating *Downtown Browns* involved a lot of traditional filmmaking techniques. What was it like to work on those elements of the series, given that your backgrounds are in digital media?

YANG :::: It was actually pretty hard. Before this, the people in the group had mostly worked on their own, individual projects, so we had to get used to each taking on different roles, like you do when you're making a film.

B****** :::: I was in charge of writing and interactive design. Lishan was in charge of preproduction, locations, and permits. Jazmin did storyboarding and cinematography. Luciana was our assistant director for all the episodes. Allison was one of our directors. Emilia did the casting.

YANG :::: Casting was especially difficult because each of us had our own vision of how the characters would look.

B****** :::: Sometimes we had fights about how stereotypical a character should be. Like, in episode 3, the main character has this coworker who is too friendly to her because she's black. I imaged her as this cool, chill, party girl, but other people imagined her as being more ditsy and annoying. It was an ideological difference. Making her annoying was funnier, but I wanted her to more relatable to people I knew who just needed to check themselves. Also, for episode 2, we were like, "Oh no, are we going to find a Middle Eastern actress who is okay with talking about being queer on camera?" Ultimately, it worked out and she did a good job.

RUBERG :::: Is the group that made *Downtown Browns* planning to collaborate on future projects?

YANG :::: At the moment, we're working on a performance installation called "Hackers of Resistance." It's an interactive, audience-participation piece about a fictional cyberfeminist hacktivist group.

B****** :::: It's inspired by a real-life project called Marias Clandestinas, which involves distributing DIY public health tools, like printable abortion kits. When you participate in our installation, you sit down at a computer and play the part of a hacker. You hack into folders with information about activist work. The idea is to caution activists about cyber surveillance.

YANG :::: We do the performance in gallery spaces, so it's not necessarily the same as doing a direct intervention, but we definitely see our work as a form of feminist social action.

14 NICKY CASE

--=≡≡---≡≡≡---≡≡≡---≡≡≡---≡≡≡--≡≡≡---≡≡≡---≡≡≡--≡≡

Playable Politics
and Interactivity
for Understanding

If the work of Nicky Case could be summed up in two words, they would be "intersectional systems." Case began making video games as a teenager, but their first game to engage with themes of identity was *Coming Out Simulator* (2014) (figure 14.1). *In Coming Out Simulator*, players must choose how, when, and indeed if to come out as queer to their family. The game is semiautobiographical, though it allows players to make branching choices that Case themself did not make when coming out. Case spent much of their childhood in Vancouver, Canada, but they and their family are originally from Singapore, so *Coming Out Simulator* deals with the specific challenges that face a young person who longs to express their queerness amid the strict social expectations of an immigrant family. Below, Case also talks about making the transition from Singapore to Canada, moments of change and acceptance within their family since *Coming Out Simulator* was released, and the importance of creating games about queer lives that go beyond narratives of empathy and oppression.

More recently, Case has moved away from autobiographical work and toward gamelike, browser-based interactive tools that model cultural and political systems. In collaboration with Vi Hart, they released the widely praised *Parable of the Polygons* (2014) (figure 14.2), an example of what Case calls an "explorable explanation." *Parable of the Polygons* demonstrates how unconscious bias can lead to harmful segregation. In a similar vein, Case continues to use the explorable explanation model for work like *We Become What We Behold* (2016), a piece about how cycles of media representation reinforce and distort social expectations, and *To Build a Better Ballot* (2016), which argues for altering the American election system. In the past year, Case has also released *The Evolution of Trust* (2017) and *The*

Fig 14.1 :::: Nicky Case's *Coming Out Simulator* (2014), a game in which players must choose how, when, and if to come out as queer to their family

Wisdom and/or Madness of Crowds (2018). In contrast to *Coming Out Simulator*, Case's explorable explanations do not address specific elements of identity but rather lay bare the intersecting structures that shape politics, power, and culture themselves—with the hope, as Case explains here, of empowering players to bring about change. The question of whether queer game-making can (and should) enact change is a recurring topic in these interviews. Like Tonia B****** and Emilia Yang's *Downtown Browns* (chapter 13), Case's work makes the connection between interactive media and politics explicit.

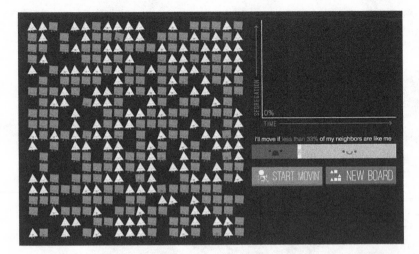

Fig 14.2 :::: A collaboration between Case and Vi Hart, *Parable of the Polygons* (2014) is an example of Case's "explorable explanations"

Case has a background as a programmer and a wide-reaching set of intellectual interests that inform their game-making. They have worked at Electronic Arts, one of the largest AAA video game companies in North America, as well as spending time at a Bay Area start-up. They also completed a game design fellowship with the Public Broadcast Service in Boston, where Case currently lives. The interview below makes it clear that Case is an insightful thinker inspired by questions of design history, physical accessibility, and the power of games to reach those who might otherwise unknowingly promote prejudice. Case is also one among many contributors to the queer games avant-garde who did not complete their undergraduate degree. In this sense, Case's work demonstrates how ideas of queerness found in contemporary indie games often do not trace back to academic institutions—and how queer indie game makers do not necessarily need to follow normative educational paths to succeed as artists. As Case themself responds, when asked if their explorable explanations could be considered queer, "I'm just a self-taught queer." This response may sound dismissive, but it is in fact powerful. For an artist like Case, knowledge of queerness comes not from the ivory tower but rather from lived experiences and from the queer body itself.

RUBERG :::: You were born in Singapore and moved to Vancouver when you were ten years old. What was that cultural transition like?

CASE :::: Singapore is a tiny little island and it's not very LGBTQ friendly. Technically, gay sex is still illegal there. Also, Singaporean culture doesn't really value self-expression or creativity. The government actively suppresses free speech. It's funny, it's like people there don't even care about free speech. They say, "Don't rock the boat. The United States is a big cruise ship so people can jump up and down and everything will be fine, but Singapore is a small boat so we shouldn't shake things up, otherwise we'll sink."

When I was growing up, that all seemed totally normal. I consumed a lot of American media at the time though, so there were some things I questioned, like the mandatory military service. Also, even though Singaporean culture doesn't really value creativity, I've always been creative. When I was little, I used to draw newspaper comics—a new one every day—and I would share them with my friends.

Luckily, I moved to Canada right around the time that I started realizing I was queer. Canada is much more open and accepting. I've heard a lot of arguments about how it's bad when immigrants assimilate because they lose their culture, but, honestly, I'm happy that I lost my Singaporean culture because it's very homophobic and patriarchal. In Canada, people were really nice. Even though I wasn't white, I never felt like race was a big deal. Vancouver has a really big Asian population.

RUBERG :::: **What was the move like for your family? From the way you portray them in** Coming Out Simulator, **it seems like you and your parents have very different values when it comes to LGBTQ issues.**

CASE :::: Apparently, for my mother, the first big culture shock was seeing condom machines in the Canadian high schools. In general, the whole sexual openness thing was difficult for her. My cousins and I adjusted pretty quickly, but for my parents it took a while to become accepting, both of the cultural differences and of me being queer.

I actually met up with my mom last month and we got a chance to really talk for the first time in a long time. Our relationship has been really hard since I came out, but, as of about a year ago, we started getting back in touch. She sent me a photo of her at the Vancouver Pride Parade. She was volunteering there! That was the first time we really connected. So, for the first time, I've had the chance to ask her about her experiences with immigration and multiculturalism. It's not always easy, but it's relieving that we're reconnecting.

RUBERG :::: **You have experience working both in the mainstream games industry and as an indie game maker. What has your path through games been like so far?**

CASE :::: After high school, I went to university to study computer science. I had skipped a few grades, so I was pretty young. When I was seventeen, I got an internship at Electronic Arts in the Bay Area. That was around the same time that my relationship with my mom was particularly rough, so I was glad that I could leave for a while and live on my own. It felt validating to be in the Bay Area—also known as the "gay area"—with fellow queer people around me. I thought, "Even if I'm a freak, at least I can be a freak with other people."

My internship at Electronic Arts showed me the best and worst parts of working at a big company. Electronic Arts is one of the most LGBTQ-friendly tech companies. Plus, I got to work on an actual video game. It was going to be a *Mass Effect* Facebook game. Then, on the very last day of the first part of my internship, the executives walked in and said, "We are throwing away everything that you did in the last six months." For business reasons, they had decided to restart the entire project. It was incredibly annoying, to put it mildly. That's when I decided I would go indie.

After I was done with my internships, I dropped out of college. Once I had industry experience, I found university incredibly boring. I had already learned the things that university was supposed to teach me. From there, I moved back to the Bay Area and worked with a start-up that was basically a shittier Patreon, and I was making games on the side. *Coming Out Simulator* was one of those side projects. By that point, my side projects were a lot more fulfilling than my day job. It took me a couple of years to realize that. After I quit the start-up, I worked freelance for a while, then I started an internship for PBS here in Boston, where I live now.

At the moment, I'm trying to figure out what's next. The ideal plan is that I get my Patreon up to a livable amount. It is at $1,100 per month right now, which is nice, but it doesn't cover all my monthly expenses. I could move back to the Bay Area, but it's incredibly expensive there. Plus, I've already seen all that.

RUBERG :::: **You have a unique approach to game design. Your piece** *Parable of the Polygons*, **for example, mixes game interfaces with web interfaces. How did you develop your design sensibility?**

CASE :::: Working with actual designers at Electronic Arts really helped. This one time, I was creating an interface that seemed really intuitive to me because I was a programmer, but for a player it made no sense. The designer took a look at it and asked me straight-up, "What the hell?"

To be honest, I'm still learning about design. I didn't take any design courses at university, but I've taught myself through books like Anna Anthropy and Naomi Clark's *A Game Design Vocabulary*. Also, non-game design books like *The Design of Everyday Things* by Don Norman have had a big influence on me. Norman's book gave me a more theoretical grounding, like thinking about affordances.

These days, I make primarily what are called "explorable explanations," which people interact with online by scrolling and clicking using the mouse. That phrase, "explorable explanations," was coined by Bret Victor, who is also an inspiration of mine. I really like the mouse because it gives you so much flexibility but it's also so constrained. Plus, designing for the mouse is a way to make the game approachable for a wider variety of people. I think a lot about people who haven't played as many games before and won't be comfortable interacting in complicated ways via the keyboard.

We take the mouse for granted, but it has this amazing history. Before the mouse, you interacted with a computer through a command line. When the mouse came in, it destroyed common sense and then it became the new common sense. It completely changed how we use our senses to relate to computers. It brought touch and movement. Creating rich sensory experiences is important for making technology accessible for people with disabilities. The more senses you incorporate, the more options there are for using your other senses if you're missing one.

RUBERG :::: **In addition to your unique interfaces, your games are bright and approachable, drawing players into discussions of difficult topics. Who are some of your artistic influences in terms of aesthetics?**

CASE :::: Again, Bret Victor's work has been really important for me. He mostly focuses on making mathematics interactive. He describes what he does as making the unthinkable thinkable, because you can touch it and play with it. You see his influence most in my piece *To Build a Better Ballot*, which is about the game theory of voting systems, which can be incredibly academic and hard to read about, so I made it into a game with cute little shapes that you drag and drop.

The narrative structure of *Coming Out Simulator* was inspired by Telltale's *The Walking Dead* games, which have branching narratives that are based on the player's choices. Scott McCloud's *Understanding Comics* has also been really helpful. In terms of authors, I like Jennifer Egan and Kurt

Vonnegut. Mostly, what inspires my games is not other games. I really believe that it's important to get inspired by things outside of your field. Go see art. Go to an aquarium and look at an octopus and then turn that into a game mechanic. Go outside and live life and get that into your games.

In terms of aesthetics, I make my games cute because that's just how I draw, though I also put thought into it. With *Parable of the Polygons*, for example, I used colorful shapes because I didn't want the game to be specifically about just gender or race. I kept the character design abstract so that the argument about bias could be applied to lots of situations.

RUBERG :::: Why use interactive media as your platform for talking about social issues like discrimination?

CASE :::: It's funny, no one has ever asked me that before. People just seem to take for granted that interactive is better. Each medium has its strengths and weaknesses. I combine them in different ways in different pieces. *Parable of the Polygons* is really half essay, half interactive piece. *To Build a Better Ballot* is text-heavy, but there's interaction interspersed. Each of those elements is good at different things. Text is really flexible, but it is not as concrete or visceral. Pictures are much less abstract. Because of the human capacity for spatial reasoning, we can see patterns immediately with the eye. We take graphs for granted, but somewhere in human history someone had to invent the idea that you would take numbers and make a map. But the concreteness of visuals can also be a downside. It's hard to render theoretical concepts visually. What would an image of postmodern critical race theory look like? You need words to explain that. Interactivity has its own affordances. With interactivity, you can actually prod and push and get an output. Instead of it being a monologue, it's a dialogue.

In terms of *Coming Out Simulator*, interactivity forces you to make decisions. Something I wanted to emphasize in *Coming Out Simulator* is the question of being yourself versus keeping everyone happy. You need to decide whether or not to lie, but you also have to remember what your lies were, because otherwise you can get caught. Straight people who play the game often tell me about how, even though they've never come out as queer, they've come out as other things in their lives. One person told me about how they were in a Christian family but they were Muslim and they had a really hard time coming out. The whole experience of having to hide a part of yourself in order to keep the peace with your family is actually pretty universal.

RUBERG :::: Was there a specific message about the experience of being queer that you wanted to communicate to your players with *Coming Out Simulator*?

CASE :::: Really, my motive for making the game is that I wanted to make it for myself. I just wanted to get it out for me. At the time, I kept playing scenarios in my head about how my life could have gone differently, like these branching stories about my past. Sometimes, when I think about other people playing the game, I think about it in terms of empathy. I like empathy, but everyone uses the word so much these days. I don't honestly think that games are particularly better suited for empathy than any other media. In fact, because you have autonomy in a game, it's harder to make a game where you empathize with someone who makes bad decisions.

People seem to reserve empathy for those are oppressed. We absolutely should have empathy for people who are oppressed—or, really, we should have sympathy for those who are oppressed. But it's really limiting to say that queer games should just be about empathy and oppression. I used to ask myself, "Given everything that is happening in the world today, is it OK to make games that are fun?" These days, I'm like, "I shouldn't feel guilty about that! People need to be happy." Putting a smile on someone's face is one of the most noble things I can do for another human being. That's what gives us the energy to fight back in the face of political oppression.

RUBERG :::: You talk about the political value of fun. In the past few years, your work has become more explicitly engaged with politics. Why is that?

CASE :::: I was saying that games aren't uniquely suited for empathy, but one thing they *are* uniquely suited for is explaining social and political systems. I'm really interested in turning real-world systems into playable systems, especially the systems that lead to nationalism and the cultural polarization. After the election, all that got a hell of a lot more relevant. When things get bad, people blame scapegoats, usually a minority group. If people could really see the system though, they would understand that those people aren't their enemy.

In social justice communities, it's controversial to say that we should take the time to understand people like Brexit supporters and Trump supporters, but those people aren't born hating specific groups. We need to understand how they got to that place so we can change their minds, not just for their sake, but also for our sake. I am a problem-solver at heart. I want to stress that looking for an explanation is not the same thing as looking for an excuse. In the long run, understanding one another will give us a more socially just world for everyone.

RUBERG :::: Apart from *Coming Out Simulator*, do you consider your other games to be, in some sense, queer?

CASE :::: I am a queer person and that influences everything I make, on some level. Really though, I should be asking you that question. Do you see them as queer? You're more familiar with queer theory than I am. I'm just a self-taught queer.

15 NINA FREEMAN

--==---==---==---==---==---==---==---==---==

More Than Just "the Woman Who Makes Sex Games"

Since she began making video games in 2013, Nina Freeman has assembled a varied and growing portfolio of indie work that explores sexuality, gender, and identity. She is the designer of *Ladylike* (2013), *How Do You Do It?* (2014) (figure 15.1), *Bum Rush* (2014), *Cibele* (2015) (figure 15.2), *Freshman Year* (2015), *Kimmy* (2017), and *Lost Memories Dot Net* (2017), among other works. Though Freeman's games do not focus on queer perspectives specifically, self-expression and the social expectations around sex and gender are themes that recur across her games. In this way and more, she is a creator whose work intersects with the queer games avant-garde. Freeman is active in many of the same indie game-making networks as other artists profiled in this volume, she cites queer game makers like Christine Love among her influences, and artists like Seanna Musgrave (chapter 12) list her among their own inspirations.

Originally from the Boston area, Freeman moved to New York City for college and later stayed for graduate school. Like many game makers working within and adjacent to the queer games avant-garde, Freeman commonly builds her games in collaboration with other artists. While her games reflect her creative vision, they also owe credit to the aesthetics and code of her collaborators. In her day job, Freeman currently works as a level designer at Fullbright in Portland, Oregon. Best known for their 2013 game *Gone Home*, Fullbright's newest game is *Tacoma* (2017), a sci-fi story set in a space station that uses environmental storytelling to reveal the interpersonal dramas between the station's now-missing inhabitants. Though *Tacoma* looks little like Freeman's own independent work, she sees a number of overlaps in the ways that these games tell stories.

Fig 15.1 :::: In Nina Freeman's *How Do You Do It?* (2014), players mash naked dolls together in an attempt to figure out sex

Fig 15.2 ::::
Cibele, released
in 2015: a game
about online
sexual connec-
tions that
draws from
Freeman's own
experiences

Freeman has a background in poetry and theater. Both of these elements can be seen in her video games. Figures from past literary avant-gardes, such as Allen Ginsberg, inspire her. She describes her games as "vignettes"—short, expressive experiences that capture one particular moment. Freeman herself acts as an on-screen performer in her game *Cibele*, which is about a sexual relationship between a young woman and a young man who play video games together online. Though Freeman's games draw heavily from personal experience, she stresses here that she does not make games "as a diary." Even when her games draw from her life, she sees her research and design process as "impersonal," giving her the critical distance to tell rich, honest, human stories. The desire to resist traditional notions of autobiography is one that Freeman shares with other artists interviewed for this project, such as Aevee Bee (chapter 3).

Freeman is best known for the erotic content of her games, though there is also far more to her work. In addition to *Cibele*, her browser-based game *How Do You Do It?* is about sex. A young girl, left briefly home alone, mashes naked dolls against one another in an attempt to figure out how and why adult bodies fit together. The player uses the keyboard to move the dolls up, down, toward one another, and away as the girl puzzles over mysteries like why men and women "hug" lying down. Yet Freeman herself actively resists being pigeonholed into the role of "the woman who makes sex games." She describes here how her efforts supporting women in video games, much like the sexual content of her work, have led to oversimplified reporting on her games. Rather than being limited by her gender or her interest in erotic art, Freeman prefers to be seen as a game designer with her own unique voice whose art is inspired by gender and sexuality but also many other elements of identity.

RUBERG :::: **Before making video games, you were a poet. How did you become involved in poetry?**

FREEMAN :::: I went to college at Pace University in New York City. In high school, I was really involved in theater, so originally I wanted to study theater in college, but I had an English teacher who encouraged me to write poetry, and I ended up in the literature program focusing on sci-fi poetry and erotic poetry.

RUBERG :::: **How did you make the transition from poetry to video games?**

FREEMAN :::: After I graduated from Pace, I worked as a data analyst at the Department of Education, which was totally unrelated to what I wanted to do, but I needed to make money to live. Then I got really sick and ended up with a chronic condition. It was pretty traumatic. At the time, I was thinking, "Ugh, this is it. I'm going to have to move back in with my parents." I spent a year not knowing what was going to happen with my life.

During that time, I happened to make a bunch of new friends who were involved in the New York indie games scene. I had time on my hands, so I taught myself how to program and started going to game jams. Later, I went to New York University for grad school in a program focused on digital media, and I took classes at the Game Center. I also had an internship at Kickstarter, which paid well and helped me not be totally poor. It was a really busy time.

RUBERG :::: **You're currently working at Fullbright in Portland. What is the game scene like in the Pacific Northwest compared to New York?**

FREEMAN :::: The game scene in Portland isn't that big, but otherwise it's really nice here. I lived in New York for five years, and I spent most of that time being super poor because rent is so high. In Portland, rent is way cheaper and the quality of life is higher. Also, I get to keep working on personal projects with my collaborators back in New York. Fullbright has been super supportive of me continuing to make my own games, which is very rare in the games industry.

The story behind how I ended up at Fullbright is that I met my boss, Steve Gaynor, at the Game Developers Conference in 2013 or 2014. I was showing my games *How Do You Do It?* and *Ladylike*, and Steve liked them, so we stayed in touch. Later he offered me a job on *Tacoma*, Fullbright's current game project. I moved out to Portland the week after I defended my grad school thesis. That was about two and a half years ago now.

RUBERG :::: **You mentioned your interest in erotic poetry. Has erotic poetry been an inspiration for some of your more sexual games?**

FREEMAN :::: I got interested in erotic poetry when I was interning for an organization called the Poetry Project. I coedited the literary journal there and we ended up publishing a lot of erotic stuff. There's a long tradition of erotic work in the poetry world. Even Emily Dickinson has erotic poems. In retrospect, it was a pretty big focus of my work at the time, but it didn't feel like a big deal. With poets, it seemed like everyone wrote at least some erotic stuff.

It's really different making work that's related to sex in the games world. Because some of my games are about sex, I get labeled as "the woman who makes sex games." That's not who I want to be. In poetry, no one ever got labeled that way. The other day, I was doing an interview about my new game *Kimmy*, and the journalist was like, "This one isn't about sex!" People like to focus on sex because it's controversial, but for me as a designer, it's frustrating.

RUBERG :::: **Sexuality can be about a lot more than sex, though. Do you see other elements of sexuality, like identity or intimacy, in your games?**

FREEMAN :::: Yes, because I'm interested in how relationships form, and also in my characters being complete people. In *Kimmy*, for example, the main focus is on friendship and communication between children and adults. But there are still moments that relate to sex, like when a kid asks how babies are made. There are also two young men who are maybe dating. So even though sex isn't explicit, it's still there. That's because I want to tell human stories, and sexuality is an important part of the human experience.

RUBERG :::: **Your games don't usually feature prominent queer characters or themes, but do you see your work as influenced by contemporary queer game makers?**

FREEMAN :::: Yes, queer games have been a really big influence for me. I'm a huge fan of Christine Love's work, for example. My gut reaction is to say that it's just incidental that those people are telling queer stories, though. What matters to me is that those games are so personal and honest. When I first started making games, everyone was talking about Anna Anthropy and merritt k, so their games really impacted the kind of work I made.

RUBERG :::: **Are there parts of your own identity that are particularly important for your work? Your games are often described as autobiographical.**

FREEMAN :::: My earlier stuff was more explicitly autobiographical, but recently I've tried to move the conversation about my work to other topics, like player-character embodiment, gameplay as performance, and the vignette form. I care a lot about curating how people talk about my work. I go out of my way to do interviews so I can have some control over the conversation. I try to be active and approachable on social media. I get valuable feedback from players that way and I can tell people what I'm thinking when I make something.

I have a lot of respect for autobiographical work, but at some point, I realized that that's not exactly what I do. For example, *Cibele* is based on an online relationship I really had, but in reality, there were a lot more boring details that I didn't include in the game. I tried to strip away the pointless bits and find the core of the thing. If I were doing autobiographical work, I'd keep those mundane details, but I'm telling human stories, not just my own stories. It's important to me that I'm not just making diary entries. I'm not looking for my own catharsis.

RUBERG :::: Even so, there is still a lot of you in your work. For example, you not only designed _Cibele_, you also starred in the video segments.

FREEMAN :::: The way I put myself into my work is that I ask myself, "What are the moments in my life that I keep coming back to or the stories that I like to tell my friends?" Honestly, my process is really impersonal, even though I make personal stuff. I'm a lot more analytical than people expect. For example, when I was working on _Cibele_, I did a lot of research on myself. I went back and read my old Gchat logs and this private blog I had where I used to vent and I asked myself, "Okay, what was really going on?" I had to give myself critical distance so I could write about that experience honestly. Everyone is flawed; people are complicated. I wanted to show that I wasn't perfect either.

RUBERG :::: You mentioned that you were interested in talking about your games as vignettes. What does that mean for you?

FREEMAN :::: The poets that I was studying in New York, people like Frank O'Hara or Allen Ginsberg, their work is about moments. Take Elizabeth Bishop's poem "In the Waiting Room," for example. It's about her, as a kid, in a doctor's waiting room when she finds an issue of _National Geographic_ with photos of women with big, bare breasts. The whole poem is just about that one moment. That's the kind of thing that inspires me. The idea for _How Do You Do It?_ came from a poem I wrote after college. One stanza from the poem was this vignette about how I remembered playing Barbie dollhouse with my friend and pretending that her Ken doll and my Barbie doll were having sex, but she did it too wildly and ripped the Ken doll's leg off. That one moment is where the whole game came from.

RUBERG :::: What sorts of feedback have you heard from players in response to your games? What elements of your work do players seem to connect with?

FREEMAN :::: Players reach out to me all the time. After _Cibele_ came out, tons of women got in touch to say things like, "I appreciated that the Nina character had low self-esteem. That is something I relate to." I also got lots of emails from people who wanted to share stories about their own online relationships. Sometimes people were going through a lot of drama—like, I got an email from a teenaged girl who had just flown to Europe to meet her online boyfriend. She was like, "He's not as nice as I expected." When men emailed me about _Cibele_, it was mostly comments like, "Wow, your character reminded me of my ex-girlfriend who I dated in *World of Warcraft* and it really helped me understand why she was so pissed at me. I was a total asshole." You'd be surprised how many times I got that exact email. All these dudes play my game and then they want to confess to me that they were really shitty teenagers.

To be honest, it gets a little exhausting, because, at a certain point, I need my personal space and it can be overwhelming to respond to everyone's story. But it's also really encouraging to see that people connect with my work. Besides, after doing all that poetry work for so long, it felt natural to me that people would reach out, because poetry is about very tough, personal stuff. It takes a lot of emotional labor, but making games already takes a ton of emotional labor.

RUBERG :::: Is gender something that you think about as a game designer, either in your work or your own experiences?

FREEMAN :::: Yes, I think about gender a lot these days. When I first started making games, I was naive about gender. I was used to being in the poetry scene, where there are lots of women. I realized pretty quickly though that gender was a big issue in video games and I wanted to do something about it. I was one of the people who helped start the Code Liberation group in New York, which teaches women how to program for games. The problem was that, when I was outspoken about gender issues, I got pigeonholed as "that woman who helps other women get into games," so I've tried to shift out of that role. I want to make the industry better for women, but that's not my only focus as a designer. Almost all of my games are about women, because that's who I am. But that's not the only thing I'm about. The media conversation about women's work unfortunately gets boiled down to, "This person's work is interesting because she's a woman." I'm like, "No, my work stands for itself."

So I've stopped being so visible around issues related to women in gaming and started doing more private mentoring. It's sad that I've had to do that, but it's been a lot better for my work, because now I don't get pigeonholed in the same way. I was thinking about it at the Game Developers Conference this year. When I started making games it felt like it was just me and a bunch of more established women. Now I'm seeing more young women get involved, and that's awesome.

RUBERG :::: Your games have a very femme-y, cute look that's often associated with "girly" things. Are you interesting in reclaiming that aesthetic?

FREEMAN :::: I definitely am. I want everything I make to be super feminine or cutesy. I'm really into magic girl anime, so I draw a lot of inspiration from that. I actually met the artist who worked on *Cibele* at a *Pokémon* zine party. She had a bunch of *Sailor Moon* tattoos and I was like, "Oh my god!" When we were nailing down the look of the game, we watched a lot of Sofia Coppola movies and other things with that feminine, pastel palette.

I really gravitate toward artists who have an aesthetic sensibility like mine—weird, cute, and girly. I played Barbie games a lot growing up. They're a really important part of games history that we don't talk about. Video games shouldn't need to be hyperrealistic or dark to be taken seriously.

RUBERG :::: **What has it been like working on *Tacoma* at Fullbright, given that the game is so different from the work you do independently?**

FREEMAN :::: When I started working at Fullbright, my boss gave me a "reading list" of games to play—things like *BioShock*, *Deus Ex*, and *System Shock*, and *The Last of Us*. I came to Fullbright to be a 3D-level designer, so I spent a while learning from games that are 3D-level-design heavy. I'd never worked on a 3D game before.

I know that all sounds really different from my personal games, but, actually, *Cibele* draws on the same modes of storytelling that you see in those 3D games. Basically, in *Cibele*, you spend most of your time sifting through the contents of a computer and trying to make connections that tell you things about the characters, and that's something immersive sims do as well: they use environment storytelling. That's why the people at Fullbright were interested in my work. With 3D level design, you think about where you're going to place an object and what that means narratively. It's all about telling human stories through the details of the physical space. With *Cibele*, the physical space was the architecture of the desktop: Where are the folders? What's in each one? With *Tacoma*, it's like, "OK, I'm designing someone's bunk. Where do I put this person's personal items? Where do I put the bathroom?" The games are really different, but in both cases, it's about developing characters.

RUBERG :::: **Earlier, you said that you try to shape how people talk about your work. Ideally, what would you like people to say about you?**

FREEMAN :::: I want to be known as a game designer, not as a person who made one specific game. That's what drives me to make so many small, weird things. Ultimately, what would make me happy is if I released a game and somebody played it just because they generally find my work interesting. That's what I want for my career, not to be "the girl who makes sex games" or even "the girl who makes games."

Analog Games: Exploring Queerness through Non-Digital Play

PART VI

Though the majority of game makers featured in this volume make video games, analog games and other non-digital experiences of play are also rich sites for expressing queerness. The contributors in this section take the queer games avant-garde beyond the computer or the television screen. Chapter 16 is "Avery Alder: Queer Storytelling and the Mechanics of Desire." Alder is a tabletop role-playing game designer whose work upends traditional narrative models and embraces the subversive potential of the anticlimax, collective identity (rather than individual characters), and relinquishing sexual agency to the twists and turns of storytelling. In addition, Alder has been influential among queer game makers for her idea of "structural queerness," in which she argues that games can be queer in their systems as well as in their content. The second of the two chapters in this section is "Kat Jones: Bisexuality, Latina Identity, and the Power of Physical Presence." Jones designs analog role-playing games of a different sort than Alder's. Her emphasis is on live-action play, in which players directly embody and act out the roles of characters. Here, Jones discusses her game *Glitter Pits* (2016), which challenges players to identify and subsequently queer dominant beauty norms—or to rip them up and set them on fire. She also speaks about how her interest in foregrounding "queer complexity" through game design emerges from her own experiences of bisexuality and her Latina identity, which have often placed her between shifting cultures. Through their work, these creators demonstrate that games and play in their many forms, whether digital or analog, can create opportunities for resisting heteronormativity and inhabiting other, queerer ways of being in the world.

16 AVERY ALDER

--===---===---===---===---===---===---===---===---==

Queer Storytelling and
the Mechanics of Desire

Avery Alder designs tabletop role-playing games that use alternative storytelling techniques to explore relationships, community, and queer identity. Growing up in a remote town in Sinixt Territory without access to queer community, Alder turned to role-playing games as a tool for understanding herself and the world around her. After years living in a large urban center in unceded Coast Salish territory (colonially "Vancouver"), she has recently returned to the mountains where she grew up, Alder reported in an email from July 2018, roughly one year after this interview took place.

Like many of the game makers interviewed for this project, Alder began creating games of her own at an early age. She describes here how she has always been interested in turning messy interpersonal systems (like her own family) into functional ones. Disappointed by her experiences with existing tabletop role-playing games such as *Dungeons & Dragons*, Alder was originally inspired to make games in order to create richer, more coherent narrative worlds. Her best-known games are *Monsterhearts* (figure 16.1) and *The Quiet Year* (figure 16.2), both of which were initially released in 2012. Her other works include *Perfect* (2006), *Ribbon Drive* (2009), and *Dream Askew* (2013, 2018). Through her designs, Alder challenges traditional structures of storytelling. She develops narrative experiences that value the collective over individual progress and embrace the subversive potential of the anticlimax. Fittingly, Alder is currently training to become a narrative therapist, a field that empowers patients to tell and retell their own stories.

Over the course of her life, games have been entwined with Alder's queer identity. Similar to the connection that Dietrich Squinkifer de-

Fig 16.1 :::: Cover art from Avery Alder's tabletop role-playing game *Monsterhearts* (2012), which uses dice rolls to determine characters' desires

Fig 16.2 :::: *The Quiet Year* (2012), a game that demonstrates how narratives can be "structurally queer"

scribes between their *Dominique Pamplemousse* games and their non-binary and asexual identities, Alder explains how the process of designing *Monsterhearts* paralleled and informed her own process of coming out as a queer trans woman. Stories like Alder's, which point to the intimate yet complex connections between queer games and the lives of their creators, offer valuable alternatives to mainstream narratives about how queer art is supposed to be simply confessional. While Alder's work is inspired by her own experiences, it does not invite straight, cis players to become spectators of her queerness. For Alder, this is one of the most important characteristics of analog game design. When asked why she works in the medium of non-digital games, she describes how tabletop role-playing games invite players to become active participants in storytelling. This, says Alder, makes role-playing uniquely suited for expressing the perspectives of marginalized people because "it allows us to tell stories from the margins that aren't for the benefit of the center. This kind of storytelling can only be created. It can't be consumed."

Within the queer games avant-garde and the academic field of queer games studies, Alder's work has been influential for her groundbreaking claims about what she calls "structural queerness": the idea that game mechanics themselves can be queer. At the 2013 Queerness and Games Conference, Alder co-ran a workshop on queer mechanics with her collaborator Jodi St. Patrick, which has been a source of inspiration for many other indie game makers and scholars who are interested in queerness in games beyond representation.[1] Alder's game *Monsterhearts* exemplifies this idea of structural queerness. As Alder discusses below, a key element of the game is that, rather than allowing players to decide their characters' sexualities, dice rolls determine which characters turn each other on. All game mechanics "create a certain worldview," says Alder. *Monsterhearts* imagines a world in which sexuality is fluid, surprising, uncontrollable, and vibrant. While, among Alder's many games, the role of queerness is most evident in *Monsterhearts*, here she describes how queer thinking has influenced her work more generally. Alder is passionate about subverting dominant narratives and creating platforms for others to do the same. To paraphrase her words from the opening moments of this interview: if you want something to exist in the world, you have to make it.

RUBERG :::: **What draws you to games? How did you get started designing your own games?**

ALDER :::: When I was young, I spent a lot more time making games than playing them. I grew up in a small, isolated, rural logging town without other queer or creative people around me. I felt that something was absent from my life, but I didn't know what. I didn't have a lot of context for figuring out who I was. That strongly informed my sense that if I wanted something to exist, I had to make it.

For a long time, I thought that game design was something I had consciously chosen when I was around eighteen, but looking back, I see that that's not the case. I started inventing games when I was seven. We had family meetings and I was always really excited to invent new systems for distributing chores. I wasn't good at actually doing chores, but I was great at making elaborate board games that would determine who did laundry that week.

My first exposure to role-playing games was at a family reunion when I was eleven. A relative explained to me what *Vampire: The Masquerade* was and I went home and tried to run it for my friends at recess. I had never read the books. I just thought, "That sounds reasonable. I could do that." I really mourn the loss of that childhood arrogance where I just assumed I could make whatever I wanted in an afternoon.

I started playing *Dungeons & Dragons* when I was sixteen, but it was a really underwhelming experience. I'd built up in my head what playing *D&D* would be like. When we sat down to play, it was mostly my friends bickering about their storylines. I felt frustrated that we didn't have a shared vision. My desire to design games really stems from that.

RUBERG :::: **You mentioned that you didn't have a queer community around you when you were young. Was there a point in your life when that changed?**

ALDER :::: I had moved to Vancouver for college. Then, when I was twenty-two, I moved back from Vancouver to a small town. While I was there, I put together a role-playing group. One of the members was a trans woman; she became my first trans woman friend. She was excited about playing characters who brought queer identity issues to the fore and that challenged me to contend with those issues in myself. That was the first time I really engaged with people who I saw my own queer potential reflected in.

RUBERG :::: **What motivates you as a game designer? Where do you turn for inspiration?**

ALDER :::: Frustration motivates me to do interesting work. It gives me something to chew on. When I play something I enjoy, I don't feel an impetus to act. In that sense, the way that I approach game design is similar to how I approach participating in communities. I try to flag recurring problems and highlight tools for overcoming those problems. Approaching a story by asking, "How can I turn this into a game?" is not that different from approaching a dysfunctional community and asking, "How can I turn this into a functional system?"

Another reason why I design games is to create frameworks for understanding issues that I need to learn more about. Games help me make sense of cultural scripts and social expectations, and to work through my own desires. That's not to say that my games are necessarily autobiographical, but I make games that are about topics I'm currently struggling with or celebrating in my own life.

Storytelling is also really important to me. Right now, I'm training towards becoming a narrative therapist. Narrative therapy is based on the idea that we are all multistoried, yet typically we become entrenched in one particular, totalizing story about ourselves. Narrative therapists thicken the plot of those stories. It's a transformative process. There are also politics embedded in the practice of rejecting the belief that problems are things that live inside of us rather than things that relate to the people and power structures around us.

The work I've done designing games really closely parallels the work I'm doing with narrative therapy, especially when it comes to seeking alternate stories that subvert dominant narratives. I'm attracted to stories because I've been attracted to the power that they have to allow us to see ourselves differently. Transformation is a theme that runs through my work.

RUBERG :::: Most contemporary queer indie game makers are creating digital games. Why do you design analog games?

ALDER :::: I have a few answers to that. The first is that we are contending with the ongoing threat of nuclear war. If power networks go down, analog games will still exist. Analog games are things you can play in the woods by candlelight; they are things you can play in a bunker.

Answer number two is that there's something beautiful about tabletop role-playing games where you can play a game once and then you know how to design your own. You engage with the mechanics of the game directly. The same isn't true for digital games. You can't just play video games until you understand the code. Tabletop role-playing games are transparent, replicable, and hackable. You don't need expert knowledge to become a designer in this field.

My third reason for making analog games is that, in tabletop gaming, you—the player—are the one designing the story. You choose the themes; you create the characters. In digital games, you're interacting with stories that someone else has set up. In tabletop games, when you sit down as a player, you're also sitting down as a maker.

Because of that, tabletop games offer opportunities for telling fundamentally different stories—stories about marginalized experiences. You're not creating a narrative that has to cater to a mainstream consumer. You're creating it for each other. There is no external audience. Often, when I explain tabletop role-playing games to people, they ask, "What happens to the story afterwards? Does it get turned into a book? Do you put it up on YouTube?" Sometimes people do watch role-playing games, but mostly the story exists solely in that moment and for that purpose. That's special and profound. It allows us to tell stories from the margins that aren't for the benefit of the center. This kind of storytelling can only be created. It can't be consumed.

RUBERG :::: As a designer, you are well known for your game *Monsterhearts*. Can you describe how the game approaches the mechanics of desire?

ALDER :::: *Monsterhearts* is a game where you play as teenagers who are contending with two kinds of monstrosity. The first is literal monstrosity. Your character is a vampire or a werewolf or a witch or a fairy. The second is metaphorical monstrosity, where you feel shame and alienation. Those feelings might stem from class or race, but the central topic of the game is queerness. Playing the game is about navigating the pressure cooker of high school, with its petty dramas and big feelings.

The main rule that shifts the paranormal romance genre is that you can roll to turn other characters on. When one character turns another on, it doesn't necessarily mean that the two are going to hook up, but the players have to contend with what that desire means for their characters. Players might go into the game with preconceived notions about who their characters are, but the dice roll can challenge that. For example, there might be a character who has always seen himself as straight, but someone in the locker room totally turns him on. What does he do? Maybe he starts cheating on his girlfriend. Maybe he gets defensive and picks a fight. The mechanics of the game don't say what happens next. They just tell you there is something here to contend with.

Game mechanics always imply a certain worldview. How I see the world is that we aren't in control of what we desire or what our bodies want, especially when we're teenagers. What we do get to control is what choices we make in those unexpected circumstances. In *Monsterhearts*, there aren't any explicit motivations built into the game. There is no common enemy to best or predefined plot. What the game cares about is emotions and power and figuring out your sexuality as it changes from moment to moment.

RUBERG :::: You mentioned that transformation is a key theme in your games, and the way that desires can be transformed in *Monsterhearts* highlights that. Do you see your interest in transformation as related to your own experience as a trans person?

ALDER :::: Looking back, it's really telling that all of my games have been about letting go of an understanding of yourself, or about social deviancy, or about navigating turbulent relationships. I've always had a recurring interest in how stories can reconfigure our identities. Being transgender probably has a lot to do with that lifelong preoccupation.

The process of designing *Monsterhearts* was also intimately wrapped up in my own personal coming-out process. I first began conceiving of myself as a queer person when I was seventeen, but I didn't act on that sense of self for a long time. For years I knew that I was probably not straight but I didn't have the self-assurance to step outside what was familiar to me. When I was working on *Monsterhearts* is when I was in the gaming group with my trans woman friend. That relationship did a lot to shape my understanding of myself and my design thinking. It became clear to me that, with *Monsterhearts*, I wanted to make a statement about how attraction and desire work, and I knew I wanted to make those mechanics queer.

All of this was happening at a time when my own queer identity was really uncertain. It felt almost theoretical. It was a time before I'd started having same-sex dates, before I'd realized I was trans. *Monsterhearts* provided an outlet for exploration that let me stay in that theoretical place. Sorting out how I feel about queer relationships and queer communities has been an ongoing process and I imagine it will be for the rest of my life, so it will probably continue to be a central focus of the games that I write.

RUBERG :::: **Is queerness also important to your earlier games, such as** *Perfect*, *Ribbon Drive*, **and** *The Quiet Year*? **If so, what is the place of queerness in those games?**

ALDER :::: Even before I realized I was queer, I was designing with queer themes. *Perfect* was my first major game. I made it in 2006. It's about criminal resistance in a dark Victorian dystopia. My work tends to reject the idea that role-playing games are great because you can do anything in them. In *Perfect*, you commit a specific crime in a specific setting for a specific reason, then we look at the aftermath. The thing about *Perfect* that I'm most proud of is that, every time you tell the story of this crime, you're always successful in committing it. Taking away the focus from success allows players to focus on their vision of the world. It's been more than ten years since I made *Perfect*. I'm proud that I had the insight as a young designer to realize that the question of whether or not you succeed isn't actually very interesting. That certainly doesn't seem un-queer.

The next major game that I designed was *Ribbon Drive*. It's a structureless, free-form game about going on a road trip together and letting go. Each of the characters has two goals that they want to come true in the future. Whether or not you succeed at your goals doesn't actually matter though; that's not the point. As you're playing, you can give up on those futures if they're no longer important for your sense of self. The game ends when someone has crossed out their second future. They've let go of all their expectations for what lies ahead and they're living in the moment. What matters is their identity and their desires. That easily lends itself to queer readings.

The Quiet Year is a cartography-based game where you experience how a community changes. For each week of the year, you draw a card. The game ends when the "Frost Shepherds" arrive. The game doesn't explain who the Frost Shepherds are or what they mean. Once they arrive, that's just the end. I'm interested in anticlimax, in ending on an unresolved, uncertain note. As a culture, we are obsessed with telling a very particular type of story: a story that has a protagonist with clear goals and escalating antagonism, that culminates in a climax and wraps up neatly. Telling only these heavily structured stories is really toxic. It says that the only thing we value about ourselves is winning conflicts.

I see *The Quiet Year* as structurally queer because it rejects the familiar division in storytelling between powerful, freestanding heroes, weak people who need rescuing, and outsider bad guys. That whole framework is based on a very patriarchal vision of power that centers on dominance and individualism. The game troubles that framework by operating outside it. That's a key idea for me: operating outside dominant modes of power and discourse in ways that eat away at the foundation of the dominant. To do that, *The Quiet Year* plays with a fluid relationship to character. Characters are communally owned. The game isn't interested in privileging or even distinguishing individual voices. Challenging the idea that stories have specific characters who stand alone rather than contextualizing those characters within a system of relational forces: that is a way of queering how we tell stories through games.

RUBERG :::: What does it mean to you to "queer" storytelling in games? Does it relate to the talk you gave at the Queerness and Games Conference in 2013 about designing queer game mechanics?

ALDER :::: The significance of the word "queer" has shifted for me over time. These days, to me, queerness means an otherness from dominant narratives and from dominant modes of exchanging power—an otherness that relates to desire, the body, and gender. Queerness is a feeling where you move between anger about and celebration of marginality. Queerness aspires to break down binaries.

When I talk about what it means to make a game queer, my central argument is that games are not made queer because they have queer representation. Games are made queer when they have structural queerness. Structural queerness is fundamentally about challenging the frameworks for how stories get told. It's about subverting systems through queer mechanics and creating new ways of seeing desire.

17 KAT JONES

Bisexuality, Latina Identity, and the Power of Physical Presence

"I've played games that have profoundly affected me because I've played them with my whole, bodily self," says Kat Jones, speaking about the opportunities that analog games give players to explore sexuality, gender, and identity. "For me . . . being able to interact face-to-face is what is most powerful." Jones is an analog game maker who specializes in creating and running live-action role-playing (LARP) games. Currently based in Cincinnati, Jones also travels back and forth from Berlin. When we spoke, she was working remotely on her PhD in sociology from the University of Massachusetts, Amherst; she has since completed her degree. Jones's dissertation examined organizations that promote premarital sexual abstinence. For Jones, game-making is a creative outlet that helps her stay connected to the arts and to her queer and feminist communities while meeting the demands of academia.

As she discusses here, Jones has a complicated relationship with her own identity. This has deeply informed her work as a game maker. She is Latina and bisexual but describes often feeling illegible as both a woman of color and a queer person. She cites queer scholars of color like José Esteban Muñoz, with their commitment to intersectionality and what she calls "queer complexity," as inspirations for her creative practice. "Playing pretend" has been a love of Jones's since she was a child, and she describes her game-making as an attempt to recapture the feeling of uninhibited world-building. Even her most fantastical games tackle real-world issues, however, challenging players to take on roles that disrupt the expectations of their lives outside the game.

Of Jones's many works, the game that engages most directly with queerness is *Glitter Pits* (2016). As Jones describes below, *Glitter Pits* encourages player to confront, destroy, and ultimately queer hegemonic beauty norms (figure 17.1). After identifying what they see as problematic mainstream notions of beauty, players are invited to queer those notions, reinventing beauty itself through a celebration of queer bodies and queer desires (figure 17.2). Beauty norms that players decide cannot be queered are written on cards, ripped apart, and set on fire. Since beauty norms are most insistently imposed on women, a fact that the game itself encourages players to reflect upon, *Glitter Pits* has clear feminist implications. Gender politics also appear as a key theme in other games created by Jones, such as *Glitzy Nails*, a game about the privilege that white women hold over women of color who work in nail salons, which was published in the 2017 "micro-games" anthology *#Feminism*.[1] Another game of Jones's that addresses gender is *All Hail the Pirate Queen!* (2013), a live-action role-playing game about a diverse group of rapscallions on the high seas electing a new pirate queen. In 2018, Jones also helped adapt and organize a U.S. version of the LARP *Just a Little Lovin'* (2011), which she describes as being about "fear of death during the early years of the AIDS crisis."

Like Avery Alder (chapter 16), as an analog rather than a digital game maker, Jones brings an important perspective to the queer games avant-garde. Though the majority of queer indie games being developed today are digital, non-digital games are equally important for exploring the relationship between queerness and play. Many of Jones's games involve acting out particular roles and relationships. As she explains here, these embodied experiences offer unique opportunities for playing with selfhood, culture, and power. Much in the vein of Elizabeth Sampat's *Deadbolt* (chapter 9), Jones's *Glitter Pits* combines live-action and tabletop play, beginning with a traditional game element (cards) and ultimately sending players out into the world to complete the subversive task of setting undesirable social expectations ablaze.

RUBERG :::: **You are Latina but you grew up in a mostly white area in the American Midwest. How would you describe your experience with identity when you were young?**

JONES :::: I am from Muscatine, Iowa, a small city on the Mississippi River. My dad is white; my mother is from Cuba. She was sent to live with a family in Iowa when she was thirteen years old, a few years after Castro took power. I grew up living in two different cultures. Muscatine has a siz-

Fig 17.1 :::: Cards created by players of Kat Jones's *Glitter Pits* (2016), a game about confronting beauty norms

Fig 17.2 :::: Players of a game of *Glitter Pits* sort beauty norms into categories: ones to queer and one to say "fuck it" to

able Mexican American population. I went to a Spanish-language church and a lot of my friends were Mexican American. There was a fair amount of racism and hostility from white people towards immigrants and Mexicans in particular though, so the two cultures I was part of weren't very friendly to each other. Those early experiences really informed how I view the world. They helped me become analytical and critical because I could see different perspectives. They also made me committed to honoring the fact that people have complicated identities.

RUBERG :::: Would you describe your own ethnic identity as "complicated"?

JONES :::: Definitely. I spent a lot of my young adulthood trying to figure out who I was and where I fit and what identities people would allow me to claim. Now I identify as a Latina much more than as a Cuban American. As opposed to someone who grew up in Miami, I don't have the same ties to Cuban American culture. I do feel connected to the Mexican American community though. I care a lot about immigrant rights and the representation of Latinx folks in the media. Those are the stories that I feel most comfortable relating to.

I identify as a person of color but I am also white-passing. I recognize that that means I have a different experience with race than other people of color. I try to be careful of how I take up space in public places because my skin does give me privilege.

I went to college in Iowa, then grad school in Massachusetts, and I've lived in Germany on and off over the last five years. It's interesting to see how people read me in different parts of the world. Because Iowa is so white, I used to get comments about how exotic I was. Because I didn't fit the blond hair, blue-eyed look, people knew I was Latina—but I also got teased by my Mexican American friends for being so fair-skinned. In New England, people saw me as "some sort of ethnic"—like Jewish or Greek—but white. In Europe, people come up to me and speak Spanish. That never happens to me in the U.S.

RUBERG :::: In addition to being Latina, are there other elements of your identity that are particularly important to you?

JONES :::: Because I grew up in a small, conservative city, there was a lot of pressure to conform. If you were different, that wasn't a good thing. I went to Grinnell College, which is also in Iowa, but it was a completely opposite experience. Quirkiness and diversity and progressiveness were all celebrated there. It was this tremendous breath of fresh air. I could finally be myself in a way that I hadn't been able to when I was in high school.

That was when I started exploring my bisexuality, but being bisexual was still a really complicated aspect of my identity. I didn't know many other queer folks of color, and the gay and lesbian scene at Grinnell was hostile toward bisexual people, so it wasn't an identity I felt comfortable claiming publicly. I had some gay friends who told me adamantly that bisexual men were just gay men who hadn't come out yet and bisexual women were really straight and they just wanted to experiment. There was this one moment: I was in the painting studio alone with this lesbian woman I had a crush on. We were looking through this book about Frida Kahlo and there was this picture of Kahlo in an intimate embrace with another woman. The woman was like, "Was Frida Kahlo gay?" and I said, "No, she was bisexual"—like, all excited because I was bisexual, too. The woman I had a crush on just said, "Oh," in this I-found-something-dead-in-the-bottom-of-my-lunch-box tone. I felt so shut down.

As I've gotten older, I've gotten more comfortable with my bisexuality. For most of my early graduate school career, I lived in Northampton, which is this lesbian mecca. It was a space where I could really think about what it meant to be part of a queer community. At this point in my life, it's much more important to me to publicly claim my bisexual and queer identities.

RUBERG :::: Do you identify with both bisexuality and queerness equally, or do they mean different things to you?

JONES :::: On the one hand, I like to use the term "bisexual" because there is so much erasure of bisexual and pansexual folks in queer spaces. On the other hand, for me, "queer" signals a more political identity, so it has a greater specificity. It's about my sexuality but it's also about how I'm living my life and how I'm doing activism through my art.

RUBERG :::: How did you get interested in role-playing games, which are now the focus of your game design practice?

JONES :::: I have always been somebody who loved to play pretend. Growing up, I had a close friend and we were really into playing pretend in her backyard. There came this disappointing moment where we realized, "Now we're teenagers. We're too old to pretend to be pirates." I had a boyfriend at the time who was into *Dungeons & Dragons* so we decided to join his game, thinking it would let us recapture some of that let's-play-pretend spirit. It was horrible. It was like all of the awful *D&D* stories from women about casual misogyny.

My interest in games really solidified when I was in college. At Grinnell, I had a friend who got a bunch of us together to play *Call of Cthulhu*. She was the game master, and she did a really good job of explaining the rules. That was the first time I realized that tabletop role-playing games could be fun. When I studied abroad in London my junior year, I joined the student role-playing group. I was one of the only women, but everyone was really welcoming. That's the point when I started to identify as a gamer.

RUBERG :::: When did you begin designing your own live-action role-playing games? What inspired your shift from player to maker?

JONES :::: When I started graduate school, I looked around for opportunities to do role-playing in the Northampton area. By this amazing coincidence, there was a close-knit group of independent game designers who ran this convention nearby called JiffyCon. It was a magical place for me: there were a bunch of women, a bunch of queer people, and a bunch of people of color. Because so many of them were game designers, it was easy to make that transition from being someone who played games to someone who designed games. Originally, the group was more focused on tabletop role-playing, but eventually a group of us split off and started doing live-action role-playing.

I don't know if I would be a game designer today if I had not been part of that community. I had other women and other POCs and other queer people who were making games as role models. They exposed me to games that were different from the ones I had played before. They were the kinds of games that I wanted to play, but also the kinds of games that I could see myself making.

RUBERG :::: You mentioned how much you loved playing pretend as a kid. Are you trying to recapture that feeling when you design a game?

JONES :::: That has been my constant search, to find games that give me that feeling. That's one of the reasons I went into game design, yes, because I was like, "If I can't find it, I'm going to make it myself." One of the things that was frustrating for me when I first started getting into role-playing games was the unnecessary constraints that were being placed on my imagination. When I was playing pretend, I had this wide-open world that I could explore. Yes, a lot of the games that I create are partially designed to recapture that feeling.

RUBERG :::: In addition to designing games, you're also completing your PhD. Has the creative work of game-making helped you balance the critical work of academia?

JONES :::: I've always been a creative person. As a kid, I did theater; I did speech and debate; I did dance and singing and played musical instruments. When I went to college, I thought I would be an artist or an actor. I ended up as a sociologist, but I didn't want to lose my attachment to creativity. Creating things is something that I need to do. Because I had this supportive community, gaming became an easy outlet for that creative energy. It gave me a way to explore this other part of myself that wasn't being nurtured in my academic life.

RUBERG :::: How would you describe the types of games you design?

JONES :::: I wear a few different design hats. I have some games that are about inhabiting a fantastical space. They tend to be more theatrical. Then I have games that interrogate social systems. I think of those games as more political because they come with a message.

For example, I wrote the game *All Hail the Pirate Queen!* for a LARP convention called InterCon. That year, there were several pirate games that sounded interesting but they filled up. I was really bummed, but then I realized I could just write my own pirate game. If I was going to write a pirate game though, I wanted it to have a lot of women pirates, queer pirates, and pirates who weren't white. I got stuck on this scene from *Pirates of the Caribbean* where they elect the new pirate king. What if it's a pirate queen? The game spun off from there. On the one hand, it's totally this over-the-top game about pirates being awful to each other. The subject matter isn't very political. At the same time, for me, creating a world with all these different types of pirates was a political act.

RUBERG :::: You exhibited your game *Glitter Pits* at the 2017 Queerness and Games Conference. What is that game about?

JONES :::: *Glitter Pits* is different from my other games. It's not really a role-playing game; it's a group ritual. You create cards with beauty norms on them, then you decide which of those norms you want to say "Fuck that" to and which you want to try to queer. If you say "Fuck that" to a beauty norm, it means it's just horrible and it shouldn't exist. You make a pile of those, rip them up, and set them on fire. With the beauty norms that you want to queer, it's this exercise in deciding how to take a norm that makes certain people feel ugly or excluded and open it up to new ideas of beauty.

I wanted the game to be a critical analysis of beauty norms but also to be celebratory. You decorate the cards with stickers and glitter. At the end of the game, you have these fun, funky cards with new beauty norms on them. By the time you're done playing the game, you've not only dissected beauty culture, but you've also created a set of cards you can take with you and use when mainstream beauty norms are getting you down.

RUBERG :::: What are some of the beauty norms that players have decided to queer? How do they queer them?

JONES :::: Because the game is titled *Glitter Pits*, there is a lot of discussion about body hair: leg shaving, armpit hair, eyebrows. For example, with eyebrows, the new queer norm might be, "Shave them off," or it could be sillier, like "Rainbow eyebrows are awesome." In one of the games, someone wrote about how the hourglass shape is over idealized. The group decided to queer that norm with a card that said, "A fruit basket of shapes." They went through and discussed what fruit they each were—like, "I'm a pineapple" or "I'm an avocado."

RUBERG :::: What sort of beauty norms do people say "Fuck it" to? It seems like it would be very cathartic to set those cards on fire.

JONES :::: When people are like, "No, fuck that!," they usually have a personal story about why that norm is so toxic. I was playing with this group where one of the players was a photographer and he had made a card about needing to have flawless skin. The rest of us were like, "Oh, we can queer that," but he said, "No." He told this story about how photographers have to create flawless skin and how models get criticized for any flaws.

One of my students played the game with a group of friends in New York City and they went to a parking lot to set the cards on fire. Apparently, a cop wandered by and they weren't sure if they would get in trouble so they hid behind a dumpster. She said that, on the one hand, it was scary because they didn't want to get arrested, but on the other hand, it really ramped up the sense that they were doing something destructive towards normative society.

RUBERG :::: From what you've observed, do the players of *Glitter Pits* mostly focus on gender norms for women?

JONES :::: It depends on who is playing the game. When cis men play, they often struggle to think of any beauty norms that apply to them, whereas cis women will have whole, long lists. If they take their time though, the cis men will start to realize that there are social expectations placed on them that they find oppressive. The game prompts players to turn that critical gaze on themselves, even if they've never thought about beauty norms before.

RUBERG :::: In addition to appearing as a theme in your work, is queerness important in your approach to making games?

JONES :::: My work really resonates with authors like José Muñoz, queer people of color who talk about holding onto complexity and fluidity and identities. In the games I make, I want to tweak dominant narratives and hold space for new ways of seeing social situations.

For example, instead of just talking about gender in terms of men versus women, we need to understand the ways that women with different levels of privilege oppress each other. My game *Glitzy Nails* comes out of that idea. It's about nails salons—which seem like this fun, innocuous place you go with your girlfriends or whatever—and the power dynamics of immigrant women doing the nails of the women who are either a different race or a different class than them. That's an example of the kind of queer complexity I try to bring to my games.

RUBERG :::: You have also contributed games to the #*Feminism* and *queer gaymes* role-playing anthologies.[2] Have you found feminist and queer communities around role-playing similar to those around indie video games?

JONES :::: #*Feminism* is an anthology of free-form games that was originally made for a convention in Denmark that has a reputation for being an all-boys club. The editors reached out to their networks and got a group of game designers, most of them women, to write games on feminist topics. As they were putting it together, the anthology evolved into this beautiful, glossy magazine full of feminist games. The games in it have been played all over the world now. #*Feminism* did a really great job of not just creating an anthology but also creating this sense of community of feminist game designers. The *queer gaymes* collection is also an anthology but it's not as extensive. As queer role-playing game designers, we haven't done much community-building yet.

RUBERG :::: Why make live-action role-playing games? What draws you to the medium?

JONES :::: There's no one-size-fits-all method to game design. There are some experiences that fit well in the digital format and other experiences that gain a lot of power from taking place in the physical world. I've played games that have profoundly affected me because I've played them with my whole, bodily self. With gender and sexuality, which are so connected to the physicality of the body, interactions between people in the same physical space can tap into different emotional experiences than digital games can.

I'm organizing a live-action experience this summer called *Just a Little Lovin'*. It's about a community dealing with the AIDS crisis. So much of the game is about sharing physical space with other people—being able to hug them, touch them. I gave a presentation about *Just a Little Lovin'* at the Queerness and Games Conference and somebody came up to me afterwards and said, "I don't understand why you didn't just make a digital game." That didn't make sense to me. From their point of view, that would be great, because then anybody could play it. For me, embodying characters and being able to interact face-to-face is what is most powerful.

Making Queer Games, Queer Change, and Queer Community

PART VII

This final section of the book looks at the "how" of the queer games avant-garde: the nuts and bolts that underlie the structure of queer games as they exist today and as they might exist in the future. *How* are queer indie games made and what obstacles do aspiring queer game makers face? *How* are queer games bringing change to the mainstream video game industry, and, conversely, *how* does the mainstream game industry regard queer games? *How* has the work of community organizers fostered and shaped contemporary queer indie game-making? These questions are driven by a spirit that is hopeful but also pragmatic. In chapter 18, "Mo Cohen: On Self-Care, Funding, and Other Advice for Aspiring Queer Indie Game Makers," Cohen discusses the development of *Queer Quest* (expected 2020), a point-and-click adventure game about how queer communities process loss. Here, Cohen offers advice for those hoping to make their own indie video games. She speaks to the financial and emotional challenges of the work, as well as the importance of remaining connected to LGBTQ communities. Chapter 19, "Jerome Hagan: Are Queer Games Bringing 'Diversity' to the Mainstream Industry?" considers the perspective from the world of AAA game development. Hagen, who works as a user researcher for Microsoft's Xbox division, leads the company's LGBTQ inclusivity program; he is also a player of queer games and a participant in queer game spaces, which offers him insight into the interplay between the traditional commercial industry and the queer games avant-garde. What emerges from Hagan's interview is a mixed picture in which queer game makers are influencing the mainstream, but not necessarily to the benefit of those who are marginalized. Finally, chapter 20, "Sarah

Schoemann: The Power of Community Organizing," features the founder and leader of the Different Games conference, an event that has been instrumental in bringing together and supporting contributors to the queer games avant-garde.

18 MO COHEN

--===---===---===---===---===---===---===---==

On Self-Care, Funding, and Other Advice for Aspiring Queer Indie Game Makers

Developing indie video games as a queer person comes with unique challenges. As more artists enter the queer games avant-garde, many are finding that making video games that engage with non-heteronormative experiences is both highly rewarding and surprisingly taxing. The mainstream narrative that surrounds the contemporary rise of "diversity" in video games often neglects to mention that making indie games requires considerable financial, educational, and emotional resources. Even as we celebrate the increasing democratization of video game development, it is crucial to recognize that the "accessibility" of game-making still only means accessible for some. For queer people and other marginalized folks, the cost of developing games can be particularly high.

Here, Mo Cohen shares candid advice about the material realities of developing queer indie games. Cohen is currently working on their game *Queer Quest* (expected 2020), a point-and-click adventure (figure 18.1). *Queer Quest* features the story of two queer women of color, Lupe and Alexis, and what it means for their queer community when Alexis mysteriously goes missing. In promotional materials, Cohen describes the game as a "point-and-*clit* adventure game."[1] Much like Dietrich Squinkifer (chapter 1), Cohen finds inspiration in the classic point-and-click games from the 1990s. "Think [of *Queer Quest* as] a gay *Monkey Island* meets feminist *Leisure Suit Larry*," Cohen writes. Cohen also points to the 2016 Pulse shootings in Orlando as a major influence for *Queer Quest*. Though the game has an upbeat tone and a colorful look, Cohen identifies grief and loss as some of its key themes. Cohen even has plans to make grief an "object" in the game—reimagining the notion of the collectible object, standard in the point-and-click genre, as a metaphor for the feelings that a person carries with them. In addition to their work on *Queer Quest*, Cohen is the developer of *Queertastrophe* (2013), set in a queer dance party, and the recently released first chapter of their newest project, *Bottoms Up: A Historic Gay Bar Tycoon* (2018) (figure 18.2). Cohen discusses *Bottoms Up* at the end of this interview, which was conducted when the development of the game was still in its earliest stages.

Cohen lives in Portland, Oregon. Originally from New Jersey, they spent parts of their life in California and New York City before settling in the Pacific Northwest. Rather than the artistic network of the queer games avant-garde, Cohen's main creative community is the local Portland Indie Games Squad (PIGSquad). In 2016, Cohen ran a Kickstarter for *Queer Quest* to support themself during the development process and compensate their collaborators. Despite Cohen's considerable efforts, the Kickstarter did not reach its goal, and Cohen received none of the pledged funding. This proved to be a crucial moment in Cohen's path as an indie game maker, because it forced them to confront their own frustrations with the challenges of funding queer games. It has also inspired them to share their story in order to help others.

This interview is particularly valuable for those who are interested in developing their own socially conscious indie video games. *Queer Quest* is still a work in progress. Therefore, this discussion focuses less on *Queer Quest* itself and more on what other indie game designers can learn from Cohen's experiences. Here, Cohen speaks frankly about the important yet often overlooked logistics that make the day-to-day work of a queer indie game maker possible: how to run a crowdfunding campaign, how to make the development process sustainable through self-care, when to reach out for assistance in conscientiously representing a range of queer voices, and how to respond constructively if your game gets called out for problematic content.

Also among the valuable perspectives that Cohen brings to queer indie game-making is their position in the tech industry as a programmer. Cohen's background is in nonfiction writing. They explain that, while they never expected to become a coder, they learned to program in order to create queer video games. In a contemporary moment when many well-intentioned educational initiatives insist on the empowering potential of teaching women to code, Cohen tells a more pragmatic and less idealized story. Their knowledge of programming has allowed them to build what they call their "dream game," but they also find coding itself tedious, and they encounter sexism in their workplaces. In this way, Cohen's experi-

Fig 18.1 :::: Mo Cohen's game *Queer Quest* (expected 2020), featuring queer women of color

Fig 18.2 :::: *Bottoms Up: A Historic Gay Bar Tycoon* (2018), one of Cohen's recent projects

ence with programming offers an important counterpoint to the often-repeated misconception that queer indie games are being built by artists without technical skills. Most queer game makers do indeed have—and often need—computational expertise. For Cohen, the "steep emotional learning curve" of programming is just one of the prices they have paid for getting to make their passion project, which they describe exuberantly as "this really fucking gay game."

RUBERG :::: You use the word "queer" in the title of your game, *Queer Quest*, and the name of your company, QueerMo Games. Do you identify as queer? What does queerness mean to you?

COHEN :::: I definitely identify as queer. Other words I identify with are Jewish, dyke, nonbinary, and boi. Pick an identity and, at some point, it has probably resonated with me. That's why I like the word "queer." It's a good catchall.

Queerness for me is like family. If I'm in a new city by myself, I will look for queer bars so that I don't feel alone. I remember one night, I had to travel to Texas for work. A friend of mine had just passed away and I couldn't be there for their funeral. So I went to a queer bar and befriended some drag queens. It helped. There's just this comfort in queerness.

RUBERG :::: *Queer Quest* is your first longer-term game design project. How did you get involved in making queer indie video games?

COHEN :::: Before I knew I wanted to make video games, I was really into nonfiction writing. My family is all writers. I was an English major in college and I went to New York for my MFA in creative writing, but I dropped out almost right away. I was in a writing workshop and this woman turned in an awful story. I thought, "She got into the same program as me. Screw it, I'm going to drop out." The story had to do with the song "Don't Stop Believing." Whenever I hear that song now, I know I'm on the right path.

After I dropped out of grad school, I was living in New York working as a barista. I didn't know what I was going to do with my life. I had a Tumblr where I posted video game latte art I made. One day, I thought, "Why am I making video game latte art when I could be making video games?" I read Anna Anthropy's book about video games as zines and that was a huge influence. I knew I wanted to start with a point-and-click adventure game because that was what shaped me the most as a kid. I grew up playing games like *Leisure Suit Larry* and *Monkey Island* with my sister.

The first little game I made was called *Queertastrophe*. You're at a dance party, trying to avoid your exes while bringing drinks to cuties. Now I'm working on *Queer Quest*. I basically learned programming for the sake of making the game. I'm about a third of the way through now. My plan is to release it in 2020. For a long time, I was really worried that someone would make *Queer Quest* before me. Other queer point-and-click adventure games have come out, like *Read Only Memories*, but none of them are like *Queer Quest*.

RUBERG :::: In addition to making queer indie games, you also work full-time in the tech industry. Do you find that work fulfilling?

COHEN :::: I have a day job as a programmer at a tech company. It's one of those places where they ask questions like, "What is your experience as a woman in tech?" For all the feminism in the tech industry these days, there's a lot of red tape when it comes to talking about gender. At my previous job, I surveyed women about their experiences in tech, and I got in trouble with HR. It's frustrating, but it's nice to work at a place that has benefits so I can make my dream game on the side. Working on *Queer Quest* balances me out.

RUBERG :::: So many initiatives these days encourage women to learn to code because it is supposedly empowering. Has that been your experience?

COHEN :::: I like programming as a tool to solve problems but it's not actually that interesting. Sometimes I do feel like it gives me power—like when I'm at a male-centric game conference and all the men say, "What are you, an artist?" and I'm like, "No, I'm a programmer."

There's a really steep emotional learning curve to programming though because it makes you feel like you know nothing. My friend just started a coding bootcamp. She's maybe four weeks in and she's having panic attacks. I get that. I never thought I would be a programmer. I'm not disappointed about it, but I'm also not excited. I'm just happy that I get to make this really fucking gay game.

RUBERG :::: You're involved with the Portland Indie Games Squad (PIG-Squad). Would you say that you're also part of a broader queer games community?

COHEN :::: PIGSquad has had a huge impact on me. When I was first learning how to make games, I was living in New York. I tried to get involved with [the art games organization] Babycastles but it was really intimidating. I volunteered but I never felt like I was a part of the community. When I moved back to Portland, I found PIGSquad. I was so scared the first time I went to one of their meetings that I took my girlfriend with me. Afterward, she was like, "I can't believe you were so nervous to meet all those nerds." I was so impressed though, because they were doing exactly what I wanted to do.

PIGSquad is still mostly white men. That's why going to the Queerness and Games Conference [QGCon] for the first time this year was amazing. I got to meet all these other queer developers. Before QGCon, I'd had very little interaction with other people who make queer games. I still do feel like I'm part of a queer games movement, though.

RUBERG :::: How did you decide to make *Queer Quest* as your first game? Where did the idea for Lupe and Alexis's story come from?

COHEN :::: A few years ago, there was a homophobic hate crime in Portland. The queer community's response was to hold hands across a bridge. I didn't go. I was so cynical; I thought it was pointless. I had some idea about the right way to respond to grief, but the truth is that there isn't a right way to respond. Now, years later, I've been to many hand-holding events and I see why they are powerful. As a result of that, a lot of *Queer Quest* is about how community responds to tragedy.

One of my biggest influences in making *Queer Quest* has been the Pulse shooting. The night that it happened, my friends and I went to a big queer party. It was a bizarre way to mourn, but we needed to be in a physical queer space together. There was this heaviness that I felt the need to dive into with the lens of a game developer. Maybe that's my coping mechanism.

RUBERG :::: It's surprising to hear that tragedy was an inspiration for *Queer Quest*, since the game's tone is so lighthearted and funny.

COHEN :::: Point-and-click adventures are known for their campiness. I use humor to tackle serious issues. I don't think I could get through real life without humor.

RUBERG :::: Has your interest in exploring grief shaped the design of the game?

COHEN :::: Definitely. Lupe has moments of very intense feeling. At one point, you can lie on the ground and just stare at the sky. It doesn't help you progress; you just need to process. Some people have said that *Queer Quest* seems like a twist on a typical damsel-in-distress game, but you never see Mario cry for Peach.

Grief also appears as this object that breaks the standards of the point-and-click genre. Point-and-click adventure games are very inventory-based. Normally, you have items that help you solve problems. At the moment Alexis get kidnapped, an item appears in Lupe's inventory that is "grief." It doesn't help you in any traditional way. If you use it, it triggers statements like, "I wish I could have done something differently" or "I'm so angry!" or "Why couldn't it be me instead?"

RUBERG :::: **What responses have you gotten to *Queer Quest* when you've showed the demo at game events?**

COHEN :::: Sometimes little kids play it. The youngest to beat it so far was an eight-year-old. I always get nervous when parents are like, "Oh, can my kid play your game?" I'm thinking, "Probably, but it has the word 'pussy' in it." I was ten when I was playing *Leisure Suit Larry* though. Why shouldn't an eight-year-old play a queer, sex-positive game?

Sometimes, when I show the game, people see the title and make this squinty, judgy face. They're trying to tell whether the game is going to be offensive—like, "Is this going to make fun of queer people or support queer people?"

RUBERG :::: **On your blog, you've written about interviewing a wide range of queer people so that you can bring a diversity of voices to *Queer Quest*.[2] Why has that been important to you?**

COHEN :::: I want *Queer Quest* to represent the full texture of queer people's experiences in the real world. For example, I have trans characters in the game, so I interviewed trans femmes about representation. That's how I learned about the Topside Test. It's like the Bechdel Test, but it's with trans characters. When two trans character are talking but they aren't talking about being trans, then they pass the Topside Test. Next up on my list is to talk to folks who identify as bisexual, because they're queer but often they're invisible in queer communities.

There are a lot of people of color in the game, too. Alexis and Lupe are Latina and Latinx. I knew I couldn't make a video game with white people as the main characters. We have plenty of that already. I've also been interviewing people about race, but that has been a slower process, unfortunately, because Portland is such a white city.

A lot of what I'm learning are things I know from my background in writing. I was talking to a friend of mine about physical disabilities. He asked me, "When did this character end up in a wheelchair? How did that happen?" With characters of color, I need to ask myself questions like, "What is this character's cultural identity? What is their family heritage?" Those are things that a lot of game makers never think about. Their characters aren't influenced by the past. They're only influenced by what the player does. They use white-dude characters like blank slates, because they have the privilege of not needing any background. To me, that is a real failing of character development. The details are vitals.

RUBERG :::: It sounds you've tried to be very conscientious about how you represent marginalized folks in your games. Have there been times when you've found that challenging?

COHEN :::: I'll tell you about a time when I fucked up. When I was promoting the Kickstarter for *Queer Quest*, the *Huffington Post* wrote an article about the game. In the article, I describe a puzzle where Lupe is at a bar and there's a drag show, but there are too many straight people in the bar and you need to get them to leave to make room for the queer people. In the quote, I describe the straight people as "breeders." When I used that word, I didn't realize that I was hurting bi, trans, and pansexual folks. A lot of people left comments telling me the word was offensive. It was a funny experience of getting called out by the people I wanted to support. I'm glad I've been in enough intersectional and feminist spaces that I know to use it as a chance for self-reflection. I talked to a lot of friends who said, "Oh, you can't make everyone happy." But I was like, "This is a game about queer community. If it's going to make anyone happy, it should be queer people."

RUBERG :::: You gave a talk at the Queerness and Games Conference this year about the importance of self-care for queer indie game makers. What are some of your own self-care practices?

COHEN :::: Indie game makers usually have to do everything themselves, so it's easy to burn out. It's important to take care of yourself. For me, friendship has really helped—and so have cat GIFs. While I was working on my Kickstarter campaign, I had a little altar with some candles where I could set my intention for the day. Another thing that worked well for me was making fun of internet trolls. Someone online left a comment about the game that said, "I bet a white straight guy did the kidnapping, right?"

I had the honor of replying, "I'm sorry, there's no one in this game that fits that description."

Other things didn't work as well for me. I was bad at delegating. Also, I tried taking Ritalin and writing three blog posts in one night. I showed them to my friend the next morning and she was like, "Wow, these make it sound like you're on drugs." Not good.

RUBERG :::: Are there lessons that you learned from your Kickstarter campaign that would be helpful for other indie game makers who are figuring out how to fund their work?

COHEN :::: It takes so much to run a successful Kickstarter campaign. You need to build up a reputation. You also need friends who have money, which I didn't have. I wasn't going to be like, "Hey, broke-ass queer community, help me fund this game." I tried appealing to tech people, but it was also weird to be like, "Hey rich, straight people, pay for me to make this game that isn't about or for you."

In retrospect, I wish I'd picked Indiegogo instead of Kickstarter, since Indiegogo lets you keep the money, even if the campaign doesn't reach its goal. Since then, I've moved to Patreon, which is much better. It's more creator-oriented and interactive.

I also struggled with people's perceptions of how much money it should take to make a video game. The goal for the *Queer Quest* Kickstarter was around $40,000. People would always say, "Oh gosh, you're asking for so much money." Some trolls would even be like, "You're a greedy Jew." Who are these people? The way I see trolls, it's like if you went to a supermarket and you picked up a can of beans and you were like, "I hate you, beans!" Why are you telling me that? Who asked you? I don't like you either, so we're even.

RUBERG :::: Over the last few years, there has been a lot of talk about how anyone can make an indie video game these days, even without expertise or money. Given how much effort you've put into learning to code and raising funds, it sounds like you would disagree.

COHEN :::: To anyone who thinks that, I would say, "That's ridiculous." It's true that a lot of development tools are free these days, but no one has all the skills to make a game. Let's say I want to hire an artist or a musician. I have to pay them. Their time is worth money.

Also, a big part of the cost of making an indie video game is emotional. If you are making queer games, then you're putting yourself out there on the internet, and the internet can be really harsh. Sometimes it's vital to just walk away—to be like, "Okay, I'm pouring my heart into this thing in my computer, but also, if I close my eyes and breathe, there is my heart. It's right there in my chest." When I knew my Kickstarter was going to fail, I went to a hippie retreat in the woods for a few days with no internet or cell reception. I really needed it.

RUBERG :::: **Are there self-care techniques that you recommend specifically for queer people?**

COHEN :::: Consume a lot of queer art. For me, things like *Steven Universe* and *Sense8* are really helpful reminders of why I'm making this game. Also, spend time with other queer people. I was doing some work with a friend and they were like, "Let's take a break." Five minutes later, I was ready to work some more. My friend said, "Are you kidding me? That was not a break." We went out to a queer party. It was great because I got to interact with the community I'm making the game for.

RUBERG :::: **Once you're finished with** *Queer Quest***, are there other queer games you'd like to make?**

COHEN :::: After *Queer Quest*, I want to make a historic gay bar tycoon game inspired by the ONE Archives collection [at the University of Southern California]. They have all these magazines about queer bar culture. You would start the game in a gay bar in the 1920s. How do you get people there if you can't be openly gay? How do you keep the cops away? Bars are such an important part of queer history, but all the lesbian bars are closing, and a lot of gay bars, too. The queer community has a generational issue. I really want to help keep the stories from older queer people alive.

19 JEROME HAGEN

--===---===---===---===---===---===---===---===---==

Are Queer Games Bringing "Diversity" to the Mainstream Industry?

Are queer indie video games inspiring change in the mainstream video game industry? Are developers who work inside large companies influenced by the games emerging from the queer games avant-garde? The games industry is increasingly pushing to strengthen its engagement with "diversity," yet this word leaves many queer creators understandably wary. Corporate, profit-based agendas rarely align with the politics of radical art. At the same time, there are many queer makers and players who believe in the importance of bringing positive change to video games on a broad scale. As some queer game makers interviewed here point out, such as Aevee Bee (chapter 3), the vectors of influence between the queer games avant-garde and the mainstream games industry are not always direct. It is also important to remember that, even when we talk about large-scale game development companies, those companies are made up of individuals with their own experiences, beliefs, goals, and identities. As Kara Stone (chapter 10) notes in her interview, change does not happen all at once. Progress does not necessarily follow a straight line.

Jerome Hagen is uniquely situated to speak about queer games and LGBTQ inclusivity from the perspective of the AAA games industry. He is a user researcher in the Xbox division of Microsoft. Originally from eastern Washington State, Hagen has lived in Seattle for the past two decades. In college he began working at Microsoft, where he has been employed ever since. Unlike most of the interviewees in this book, Hagen is not a designer or an artist. His role is to look at how players interact with games—to study what they do, what they like, and how these insights can help developers build more compelling games. As Hagen himself points out, hundreds if not thousands of people contribute to the development of each Xbox game title. His is just one of the numerous capacities in which games industry professionals help shape the finished product. For Hagen, conducting user research represents an important opportunity to bring diverse perspectives to the development process. His job, says Hagen, is to make sure that a game's designers are taking into account feedback from voices that would not otherwise be heard.

In addition to his role as a user researcher, Hagen is an active contributor to Microsoft's corporate inclusion efforts, specifically Xbox's "Gaming for Everyone" program. In 2015, he founded Xbox's LGBTQ task force. Through this group, Hagen headed the organizational team for the first annual "LGBTQ in Gaming" event (figure 19.1) at the 2017 Game Developers Conference: a large social gathering for queer games professionals that hosted more than two hundred attendees in its inaugural year. As a gay man working in the games industry, Hagen says that he himself is drawn to independent and experimental video games. This allows him to speak to the interplays between queer indie games and the big corporations that continue to set the cultural tone of mainstream gaming.

The picture of the interplay between queer indie games and the games industry that emerges from Hagen's interview is ambivalent. Hagen's discussion of the "LGBTQ in Gaming" event epitomizes this. While the event did offer queer game professionals an opportunity to build community, it also served as free marketing research for Xbox executives. As Llaura McGee (chapter 4) warns in her interview, even when queer game makers influence mainstream developers, the question remains: Who benefits from that influence? Hagan also describes running a game club for his fellow user researchers at Microsoft in which they play and discuss experimental games. Yet, Hagen admits, the group has never played a queer game because doing so, he says, is logistically more complicated than playing a game available for a home console. This may appear to be a small point, but in fact it speaks volumes about the ways that game publishing affects the reach of queer indie games. Because queer games are rarely published on consoles, people who make and consume console games are less likely to play them.

RUBERG :::: **How did you get your start in AAA video games? What has your path through the industry been like so far?**

HAGEN :::: I largely got into the games industry by accident. At the time, when I was going to college in the late 1990s, there weren't many programs

People who are LGBTQ are already underrepresented in gaming, and so I think it's really important to have these kinds of events

Fig 19.1 :::: Still from a promotional video about Xbox's "LGBTQ in Gaming" event at the 2017 Game Developers Conference

for studying game development, so I studied psychology, which was a good fit for me, because it combined the scientific stuff I was good at with my interest in people. I was working in a research lab and I heard from one of the grad students that somebody at Microsoft was starting up a video games research program. I began at Microsoft as a part-time research assistant. There wasn't an established group focusing on understanding player experience yet. This was 1998.

I've been at Microsoft ever since, which is highly unusual in the games industry. Throughout my whole career, I've been with what is now called the Xbox research group. It used to be called "games user testing," since, when I started, Xbox didn't exist yet.

RUBERG :::: **How would you describe your work as a games user researcher? Do issues of diversity and inclusion come up in your research?**

HAGEN :::: I work with development teams to get feedback from players during the process of developing a game. Understanding player experiences helps make games better. We collect data in all sorts of ways: observations, interviews, surveys, direct recordings of player behavior, etc.

Right now, I conduct research specifically for the *Minecraft* franchise. Before *Minecraft*, I worked on the *Halo* franchise, and a number of other franchises before that.

My work as a researcher is definitely related to diversity. It's core to my job, because what I do is bring different voices into game development. We always say to developers, "You are not your player. Not everyone who plays this game will have the same background as you." User research really pushes you to think about which voices aren't being heard. Diversity is also a part of the way we conduct research itself. It's important for us to make sure that the participants in our studies reflect a wide array of perspectives. There are some games where that is more important than others, like games that have romance in them. Also, when you think about gender expression, any game where you have a choice about your characters, it matters more to have more types of people represented in the research.

RUBERG :::: **What has your experience been like as a gay man working in the mainstream games industry, which is often considered unwelcoming to queer folks?**

HAGEN :::: In the overall, it's been a really good experience. I've always been out. I've never felt the need to hide. At the same time though, in the tech industry and the gaming industry as a whole, there isn't a ton of diversity. I've never been on a team where it was the default for me to think, "Oh, yeah, people here are probably queer." It hasn't led to a lot of issues. It's just about how many people you do or don't see around you who you can identify with.

RUBERG :::: **Over the last two decades that you've worked at Microsoft, have you seen changes in how the company handles issues of sexuality, gender, and inclusivity?**

HAGEN :::: When I first started working in the tech industry, Microsoft was a very stereotypically masculine environment. Considering people's differences was not really at the center of things. Microsoft as a company has always had inclusion as a core value, but the tech industry was built by twenty-something men who started these companies, so . . . as Microsoft has grown and evolved, the culture evolved around it. Today, you see people in positions of power in the company who really demonstrate Microsoft's thoughtfulness toward inclusion.

RUBERG :::: Do you think that your position as a queer person working inside the AAA industry gives you a unique perspective?

HAGEN :::: Absolutely. I've always been somebody who feels a little like an outsider in whatever space I'm in. At some point when I was growing up, I started to realize that that had to do with being queer.

For me, being a researcher is a perfect role because having an outside perspective is helpful. My work is all about understanding how other people see things. A lot of what I do is communicate to designers, "This is the experience your players are having." When I do that, I draw from my experience of feeling like an outsider and ask myself, How do I connect people who are different? Maybe that's why my research group has so many queer people in it, because we share that outsider perspective.

One of the things that people don't realize about AAA is that games get made by huge teams of people who all have different perspectives. There's this auteur theory in games. People assume that there is one vision-holder whose mind is represented on the screen, but actually there are so many people contributing in different ways. Take user research. People don't know that it can be really exciting to help make a game better by getting more voices included. There's a lot more to making AAA inclusive than coming up with the ideas for games.

RUBERG :::: You're currently the head of Xbox's LGBTQ group. What is your history with activism and how did you get involved with the diversity initiatives at Microsoft?

HAGEN :::: It's something that has been important to me for a long time. I came out when I was sixteen, when I was still living in Spokane. There was a city-sponsored queer youth group that I got involved in as a teenager, where we did things like visit kids in juvenile detention centers to answer questions about what it was like to be queer. Over the years since then, I've volunteered with lots of different groups.

My involvement with diversity initiatives in Microsoft started relatively recently, within the last few years. Microsoft has an employee group called GLEAM [Gay and Lesbian Employees at Microsoft], which has been around for a very long time. GLEAM has been behind Microsoft's push for things like partner rights and trans health care. Last year, here in Washington, there was an attempt to get an antitrans bathroom bill on the ballot and Microsoft was one of the major sponsors of the group trying to keep it off the ballot.

Even though I've been at Microsoft a long time, I hadn't gotten involved with GLEAM because, I guess, I had a hang-up where I thought, "Oh, I'm over in Xbox so I don't really know how the rest of Microsoft works." A couple years ago though, Xbox started this new initiative called "Gaming for Everyone" that was about things like gender, race, ethnicity, disability, and sexual orientation. As part of the initiative, they were looking to start more groups within Xbox focused on specific communities. I went to one of the early meetings and I asked, "Who is helping out with the LGBTQ side of things?" They said, "Nobody! Would you like to help?"

RUBERG :::: **What made you say yes? That was 2015, shortly after the rise of #GamerGate. Did that make you more eager to support an LGBTQ initiative?**

HAGEN :::: Well, in general, LGBTQ issues in video games are really important to me. Queer employees within a company should be able to connect with other queer folks. I think the reason I hesitated at first in terms of volunteering is that, in queer spaces, people who share my identities are already the most heavily represented. White, cis men tend to dominate those spaces and that was something I definitely did not want to do. I was happy to help out, but I wanted to be very aware of being inclusive of everybody.

At the time, there were five queer people even just in my research group, so that was a great place to start listening to other voices and getting feedback, for example from some of my bi and pansexual coworkers, who have had bad experiences in the past in spaces that were supposedly queer-inclusive but where they felt unwelcome. They encouraged me to use the "Q" in LGBTQ, since they said that was a clue to them of who was or wasn't more inclusive of queer identities.

It's definitely true that #GamerGate was a big thing at the time. It was very frustrating to just see people who claimed they represented video games promote the message that certain voices aren't allowed in gaming. These gamers who are angry about people who aren't like them being able to play games—those aren't the players we want to cater to, as an industry. That's a philosophical perspective, but also companies have to think financially. Making games that as many people as possible can enjoy is part of that.

RUBERG :::: **What sort of work have you done as the leader of Xbox's LGBTQ group?**

HAGEN :::: This year, we ran our first "LGBTQ in Gaming" event at the Game Developers Conference. Last year, we did a very small, private roundtable event of LGBTQ people within the game industry. Xbox executives came so they could get a better understanding of what it's like for LGBTQ people. It was a listening session where the execs could sit down and observe instead of standing up and representing Microsoft. It was really enlightening for people within Xbox and that's partly why we did a larger event this year. This year's event was more about serving the community, but there were several Microsoft execs there. They weren't at the center of things; they were just hanging out and hearing from the community. The event was a great success. Our tickets sold out really quickly. There is a Gay Gaming Professional party that has been going on at the Game Developers Conference for eleven years, but we wanted to provide an event that wasn't a party space, one that is inclusive of people who aren't cis, gay men.

That's something that I really loved at the Queerness and Games Conference. I went to the conference for the first time this year and it was really exciting to me as someone trying to set up queer spaces for the Xbox LGBTQ group. What was wonderful was the feeling that there was no default, that there were lots of people and lots of identities and you couldn't assume that someone had a certain perspective, which led to wonderful conversations. I'm someone who has always felt most comfortable in mixed queer spaces. It's funny because people often assume that a cis, white, gay man will feel at home with other cis, white, gay men. That's never how it's felt to me. The more homogenous a space that I'm in, the more assumptions people make about me that aren't true—assumptions about who I am, what my interests are, and how I am as a gay person. People get concerned that, in diverse spaces, they won't be able to be themselves, but to me it feels like those mixed spaces are where I can just *be*.

RUBERG :::: From your perspective inside the AAA industry, do you think that queer indie games influence mainstream video games?

HAGEN :::: Personally, I don't think of AAA games and indie games as being all that separate. At Microsoft, we have the IDeAte Xbox program, which is indie developers publishing on Xbox and Windows. In terms of queer games, *Fragments of Him* was released last year through IDeAte and *Read Only Memories* will be out soon. There is also *Kitty Powers' Matchmaker*. I think Microsoft sees it as critical to help indie folks be successful.

RUBERG :::: **The queer games you mention are largely by and about gay, cisgender men, though. Are there other games that are "too queer" for Microsoft?**

HAGEN :::: It's less about what's "too queer" and more about what a gaming audience on a console platform is or isn't going to understand or connect with. The gaming industry is designed around making money. Personally though, I'm really interested in experimental games—especially interactive fiction. At the Queerness and Games Conference, I played a game called *Downtown Browns*. Some people would say, "That's not a game," but that doesn't matter to me. My husband really likes point-and-click adventures and walking simulators, so within my own household, there's a pretty broad definition of a game. It's not all things that are guaranteed to sell five million copies.

RUBERG :::: **Have the experimental and queer games you play personally come up in your conversations with coworkers at Xbox?**

HAGEN :::: People definitely talk a lot about different games they play. Within our research group, I run a games club where we play a different game every month and discuss it. A ton of those have been indie games. I don't think the group has ever played a queer game, though. We decide by a voting system, and we've definitely had queer games in the pool, but they've never been chosen. People like to choose games they can play on consoles, and there aren't a huge number of queer games that have shown up on consoles yet. It's just a logistical thing.

20 SARAH SCHOEMANN

--=≡≡---≡≡≡---≡≡≡--≡≡≡---≡≡≡---≡≡≡--≡≡≡--≡≡≡---≡≡

The Power of Community Organizing

Sarah Schoemann is the cofounder and lead organizer of the Different Games conference, an annual event (and now an ongoing collective) started in 2013 (figure 20.1) that has been instrumental in fostering the queer games avant-garde and other areas of "diverse" indie game-making. Like the Queerness and Games Conference, Different Games brings together game makers and academics to share their work and open conversations around video games, artistic expression, and social justice (figure 20.2). Originally based in New York City, the Different Games Collective has also hosted related events in San Francisco and Toronto, and the 2018 conference will take place in Worcester, Massachusetts. As Schoemann discusses here, the conference grew out of—but also in resistance to—the indie games scene in New York. Schoemann, frustrated by the male-dominated New York games culture she found at the time, first envisioned Different Games as a feminist event. However, the conference has become a space for many types of creators, thinkers, and players who are "different," including a notable number of queer game makers. Though Schoemann herself does not develop queer games, her community organizing efforts and those of her collaborators represent invaluable if at times overlooked contributions to the current network of queer indie game-making.

Schoemann plays many roles. She is an organizer, an academic, and an artist. Like Kara Stone (chapter 10), her background is in "weird" video art and experimental performance. Originally from New York City, Schoemann moved to Boston for college and received her undergraduate degree from the School of the Museum of Fine Arts at Tufts University. She later returned to New York City, where she worked in video- and games-based education before taking part in the Integrated Digital Media master's

Fig 20.1 :::: Attendees playing a game in the 2016 Different Games Conference arcade

Fig 20.2 :::: Participants share during a workshop about marginalization in the games industry at the first annual Different Games Conference in 2013

program at NYU's Tandon School of Engineering: the same program attended by others who have worked within and alongside the queer games avant-garde, including Mattie Brice (chapter 11), Nina Freeman (chapter 15), and Catt Small, co-organizer of Game Devs of Color Expo. While completing her master's degree, Schoemann studied with game designers and researchers like Kaho Abe and Katherine Isbister. Schoemann currently lives in Atlanta, where she is working toward her PhD at Georgia Tech.

Community organizing is a thread that can be traced across Schoemann's history. Her organizing work began during her time in Boston, where she collaborated with other artists on events related to music and comics. Today, a major focus of Schoemann's dissertation centers around organizing community events and shows at Charis, the longest-running feminist bookstore in America, which is located in Atlanta. Indeed, many of her efforts have been driven by the desire to create feminist spaces for games or to bring games into feminist spaces. Schoemann speaks here about what models like Charis can teach those who make and study games about creating intergenerational spaces that support feminist, queer, and transgender community members.

Of the many interviews in this volume, this discussion with Schoemann hits the closest to home for me as an interviewer. Schoemann and I inhabit very similar positions: we have both dedicated ourselves to organizing grassroots events focused on diversity and inclusion in games, we are both career academics studying games who are trying (and not always succeeding) to maintain our own creative practices, and we both find ourselves navigating the rich yet fraught territory between academia and game-making performed by marginalized artists. On both a professional and a personal level, I value Schoemann's reminder, expressed below, that the logistical and affective work that supports the queer games avant-garde is crucial in its own right, and that this labor, though it takes place in conjunction with academic institutions, is itself deeply precarious. Building community is important—for queer games and for queer people. Organizers like Schoemann are managing the day-to-day realities of creating space for difference and building structures that sustain the radical work of making "different" games.

RUBERG :::: Can you describe your background? You currently work in academia, but you have your own creative practice as well, right?

SCHOEMANN :::: Yes, I have a fine art background. I went to undergrad at the School of the Museum of Fine Arts in Boston where I did performance art. I chose that school because they didn't have a foundation year and I was like, "I know that I want to make art that's not necessarily about making objects. I'm not interested in fine tuning my drawing skills. I want to go somewhere where they're already ready for me to get weird."

At the time, I was really interested in the question of documentation versus liveness, and when documentation is a barrier to the enjoyment of work. My senior year project was a performance where I was surrounded by an apparatus of video cameras and lighting equipment that was so densely packed that people had to watch through and around it. What it captured was this really controlled, beautiful video of me doing absurd stuff like popping balloons full of whipped cream with my feet while I was wearing a bikini. The idea was that the ability to observe was being obscured by all this cinematic apparatus.

RUBERG :::: What did you do after you finished your undergrad degree? How did you transition to games?

SCHOEMANN :::: I worked in public schools doing media arts residencies there. We led video editing and filmmaking projects with low-income youth of color. That's where I became aware of video games being used in education. Then I did work with Quest to Learn, which is the charter school that Katie Salen started. They had a summer program where we were making QR-code, location-based games with smartphones . . . After that I did my master's degree at NYU.

RUBERG :::: What is the game scene like in New York?

SCHOEMANN :::: In general, the New York game scenes is unique because there isn't a games industry there in the way there is in other places. No AAA studio has been able to survive the cost of rent in New York. You end up having these smaller, weirder studios and independent developers, or people who are connected to academia as a stabilizing source of income. That's just who can make it in New York. It's a different creative landscape.

RUBERG :::: What was the experience like for you personally in the New York?

SCHOEMANN :::: I get the sense that things have really changed in New York over the years, but back then, from like 2009 to 2012, I would go to game events and be the only woman there. That was the way things were. I felt really alienated and isolated.

Even [the game art gallery] Babycastles, when it first started, was a space that felt extremely gendered. It was so much a vestige of the New York independent music scene, and it brought with it the baggage of that scene, the way that punk scenes in general tend to be white and tend to be male. Add to that the internalized sexism of games and computer culture. The worst parts of nerd culture were being imported into the worst parts of the DIY scene. It created, on the one hand, this really revolutionary thing: this idea of games as a form of independent culture. On the other hand, it felt really marginalizing that there were no games by women being displayed. Seriously, for the whole first year, Babycastles showed zero games made by women and had zero events that were curated by women. They had to have a "come to Jesus" moment where it was like, "OK, yes, this space was started by two brown guys, and that's super important, but that's also not an excuse for being sexist."

I've always liked being part of a scene. The game scene really appealed to me but also there were things about the community that were loathsome. I started putting together meetup groups for women so we could talk about our experiences. One of our first events was a panel where we sat on the cabaret stage of a bar and discussed what it was like to be a woman in the games scene in New York.

RUBERG :::: **Is that how Different Games got started, as an effort to build a community for women in the New York games scene?**

SCHOEMANN :::: Starting Different Games was about getting together people who wanted to organize around inclusion. Also, we wanted to create a space where academics and game designers could be in conversation. There are a lot of spaces that exist for that now. The Queerness and Games Conference, GaymerX, and IndieCade are some of them. Back then, though, you didn't see the same critical discussions at game events that were happening in academic spaces. Now we have lots of conversations where we talk about representation and procedurality, but at the time those conversations were very separate. Different Games was an attempt to get game developers in the same room with scholars, and to get designers to think through how representation functions in their work.

I wasn't deep enough down a game studies hole yet to understand the narratology versus ludology debate, but I did understand that there was this hostility toward critically engaging with games using media studies. I knew that hostility was coming out of places like NYU Game Center and the Practice conference, which is an event that is supposed to be a pure exploration of game design—as if design were completely divorced from cultural meaning-making. That event was a big inspiration for Different Games in terms of wanting to be the antithesis of something.

RUBERG :::: How would you describe the value of an event like Different Games? What opportunities does it bring to the people who share their work there?

SCHOEMANN :::: I think what's been valuable for people who participate in the event and want to get into indie games is that it's an early career experience with a low barrier to entry. We want work that's not polished and finished. Over the years, we've had people who were part of the conference go on to do amazing work. It's exciting that Different Games is the place where they met people they later collaborated with or who clued them in to other opportunities. Recently, Different Games has been shifting, both in terms of how the event works and how many people we reach. That's OK though. There are more diversity events out there and more resources now. When Different Games was getting started, people were just meeting each other.

Different Games has never blown up. On the one hand, I'm like, "Why haven't we started getting a billion submissions?" Then again, it makes perfect sense. When your event is systemically organized so that you privilege the voices of marginalized people, you don't really run the risk of getting thousands of entries. Video games still have a diversity problem. Different Games is a place where people who are underrepresented can rise to visibility.

RUBERG :::: The term "different" is quite broad. What topics or identities does that encompass for you? For example, queerness isn't the focus of Different Games, but it seems to be an important presence.

SCHOEMANN :::: Initially, Different Games could easily have been a feminist conference. That could have been our focus: feminist games. We decided not to go that route since there are a lot of people who don't identify with feminism as a movement because of its history of being exclusionary, either toward queer people or people of color. The decision to make the conference a space that was more committed to "diversity and inclusion" was an attempt to make sure that we were placing ourselves in an intersectional context. We wanted it to be clear that it was a space for people who were marginalized along lots of different axes of privilege and oppression.

RUBERG :::: Events like Different Games run largely on volunteer labor. Do you ever wrestle with the fact that this conference, which is designed to support marginalized communities, is built on the labor of marginalized people? As the organizer of an event that operates similarly, I think about that a lot.

SCHOEMANN :::: In terms of the people who help organize the conference, it's all based on what they have to give. The labor has to be worth it. I think about it in a very straightforward way: Is this serving your career? Is it connecting you with people? Is it sustaining you, even though it's not sustaining you with money? Some people will do it for a couple years and then realize they have to concentrate on their jobs or finish school. There are ebbs and flows, and you have to deal with the ways that institutional knowledge gets transferred and gets lost. It can be difficult, but part of doing this work responsibly is encouraging people to make the choice that's right for them.

RUBERG :::: There's also the question of compensating speakers, which community events like Different Games or the Queerness and Games Conference unfortunately rarely have the budget to do. That's been a source of some friction, since participants from different backgrounds have different expectations.

SCHOEMANN :::: The issue of money and funding is one that has been really hard for me to wrap my head around. We're one of the few conferences that puts resources toward helping speakers get to the event. Travel sponsorship is not normally part of speaking at a conference. Explaining that to people is really tough. There was this vitriol directed at IndieCade a few years back when people were like, "How come the speakers aren't being paid?!" We have to think about what we're here to do, and who this space is for. Academics think of conferences as opportunities to aspire to. That's really different than talking at a big, corporate event. That's hard to explain to someone with real resource constraints though. I'm sure it sounds ludicrous that someone would agree to speak at an event for free and pay their own way to get there.

I also feel incredibly self-conscious as a white woman who presents as cis being the leader of a diversity conference. It has not gotten past me that that's problematic. I think about that a lot: whether it makes sense for me to occupy this position. On the other hand, doing the labor of organizing the conference is something I can contribute. At the end of the day, in a position like mine, you end up doing a lot of the labor that other people don't want to do. It's not all fanfare. It's a lot of boring, hard work and spreadsheets.

RUBERG :::: **In addition to co-organizing Different Games, you have been collaborating with the feminist bookstore Charis in Atlanta as part of your dissertation. How would you describe Charis and the work you're doing there?**

SCHOEMANN :::: Charis is the oldest feminist bookstore in the country. It's almost forty-three years old. Only about ten feminist bookstores still exist in the United States. Charis has always been a feminist bookstore, not a women's bookstore, though. That's an important distinction. In the 1970s and '80s, Charis became a center for queer and specifically lesbian subculture in Atlanta, so historically it's had this role as a community anchor for queer folks as well as feminists. There are lots of different kinds of events that happen at Charis, from author readings, to support groups for queer and trans youth, to antiracist parenting groups. Charis is really remarkable as a space. I've learned a ton from being exposed to the way they do organizing.

These days, in the games worlds, we have projects like Dames Making Games that are explicitly feminist DIY spaces for making media. They're referencing all the infrastructures created by places like Charis. Some of those places still exist. I wanted to know what we could learn from them. My proposition to Charis was, "What if we were to bring an arcade cabinet in here? What if we were to do talks by people like Adrienne Shaw?" It's been a codesigned project with people from the Charis community who have helped us figure out what sorts of events will appeal to this audience while also bringing games and technology to the fore.

RUBERG :::: **Would you say you've been successful in bringing games and folks who work on games into this queer, feminist space?**

SCHOEMANN :::: Our work with Charis has definitely drawn people to the bookstore who have never been there before, and it's also brought women from the Charis community into discussions about technology. When #GamerGate was going on, Charis's nonprofit director was like, "Can you do an event that just explains what #GamerGate is?" We did a panel with a media studies student and a game developer who answered questions about what was going on. Apparently, older women had been calling the bookstore being like, "Have you heard about this #GamerGate?

This sounds horrible." The same thing happened with *Pokémon Go*. We did a *Pokémon Go* discussion group because there were all these people being like, "What is this thing? Is there a PokéStop here?" We had a discussion about the political ramifications of the game. Also, younger people who may not have been to the bookstore before took out their phones and showed older people the game.

Charis has been able to stick around even though feminist bookstores are a dying breed because they have this very open process of inviting people of any age and experience level to be part of their board. So they have this mixed intergenerational group of leaders. Because of that, they've maintained a connection to newer generations of feminists, which has kept Charis a vibrant and relevant space in a way that similar spaces haven't been able to do. For example, trans inclusion, which unfortunately can be an intergenerational source of conflict for feminists, is not an issue for Charis. Charis is incredibly trans inclusive. They're very committed to the multiplicity of feminisms and particularly ones that we might associate with contemporary, younger feminists.

RUBERG :::: **Do you think about the intergenerational element of your own community organizing? Even if we're not talking about literal generations, is longevity and maybe eventually passing Different Games on to new leaders something on your mind?**

SCHOEMANN :::: Definitely. One of the reasons why I'm excited that Different Games is working with Worchester Polytechnic Institute this year is that there are undergraduates there who run a diversity in games club, and they're helping with the logistics of organizing the conference. I was anxious, because every time you move an event to a new institution, you have to learn all of these logistics that seem small from the outside but they're really important. Like, who is the person you ask about accessing the freight elevator for getting the food up to the space? Things like that: that knowledge is gold. That's the stuff the students are coordinating. Even if it's not the most exciting work, it's gotten them involved. Now they're helping make the curatorial decisions about which speakers and games will be at the conference. It's great to have a younger generation of people working with us.

AFTERWORD   The Future of the Queer Games Avant-Garde

What does the future look like for the queer games avant-garde? For that matter, what does the future of video games look like with the queer games avant-garde as its vanguard? More than a year after these interviews were conducted, as I write this afterword, the work of the queer games avant-garde continues to grow and change. As it does, it pushes the medium of video games in new directions that are exciting, strange, challenging, and above all playful in their resistance to the status quo of both games and society more broadly. As Naomi Clark states in the epigraph to the introduction of this book, "If you're really interested in queering games, you can never rest."

It has been one of the goals of this book to demonstrate how the constellation of artists that make up the queer games avant-garde is leading a larger shift toward inclusion and experimentation in video games—a shift that undermines and reimagines expectations about what games should look like and whose stories games can tell. In this way, the queer games avant-garde brings to fruition what Alexander Galloway, referenced in the introduction, imagines as an "independent gaming movement" that "redefine[s] play itself and thereby [realizes] its true potential as a political and cultural avant-garde." Yet queer indie game-making is not just any avant-garde. These works and their creators are redefining play through *queerness*. Its politics are queer politics. Its culture is queer culture. This is an avant-garde *of* queer people, *about* queer people, and (more often than not) *for* queer people. Given video games' long-standing history of exclusion and discrimination, as well as the ongoing marginalization of queer people in the world at large, that makes the queer games avant-garde far more revolutionary than Galloway could have imagined.

At the same time, the voices of queer game makers that have been included in this volume productively complicate the vision of the queer games avant-garde as a unified force pushing video games forward. Taken as a whole, these interviews highlight the connections but also the points of disagreement and tension between contributors to the queer games avant-garde. Many of the questions raised through the juxtaposition of these conversations remain unresolved. Should queer creators make games that transform straight players into allies or should they refuse to cater to heteronormative culture? Should they represent or resist representing queer identities? If we take one thing from these interviews, it is that there are no clear, tidy answers and no obvious singular path to follow. To move straight ahead into the future of games would, after all, be counter to the spirit of queerness.

In a sense, these interviews speak to a specific moment in time: a tipping point at which the queer games avant-garde was spreading, picking up speed, and breaking free from the cultural narratives that described queer indie game-making as "niche." To the contrary, queer indie games were becoming an undeniable force in broader conversations about video games as art and as culture. Today, admittedly, much is the same. Game makers, players, and commentators who are seen as "different" continue to face harassment from reactionary gamers. Queer indie game-making continues to constitute precarious labor. However, there is also much that is different. Since these interviews were conducted, many compelling new queer games and queer game makers have made their appearances. Some have gained levels of visibility that would have been hard to imagine only a few years ago. Among these games are interactive visual novels like Brianna Lei's *Butterfly Soup* (2017) (figure A.1), Aevee Bee and Mia Schwartz's *Heaven Will Be Mine* (2018), and Christine Love's *Get in the Car, Loser!* (2018). *Tacoma*, the 2017 game from Fullbright, includes LGBTQ characters, though its queer content is admittedly less prominent than in the studio's previous game, *Gone Home* (2013). Beyond North America, the German "playful media" festival A MAZE. has presented the work of a number of queer and trans game makers, including British artist Natalie Clayton, South African artist Bahiyya Khan, Polish artist Zuzanna Buchowska, and Finnish artist Elie Abraham.

In addition, a number of topics have gained prominence in the work of the queer games avant-garde in the last year. Among these topics are indigeneity, afrofuturism, astrology, radical softness, the queerness of interface, queer temporality, parallels between games and immersive theater,

Fig A.1 :::: *Butterfly Soup* (2017) by Brianna Lei, a visual novel about a group of queer Asian girls

the politics of cuteness, and a reclamation of femme aesthetics. Intersectional concerns are generally becoming more central. Those who make and support queer games are expressing their commitment to addressing interlocking causes of social injustice.

In keeping with the methods of this book, I close here with brief profiles of four emerging game makers: new voices who are up-and-coming in the queer games avant-garde. The information in these profiles was drawn from short interviews with the artists, conducted over email in the summer of 2018. These profiles offer a taste of the ongoing work of queer indie game-making and the issues that are rising to the surface as a new wave of game makers enters the queer games avant-garde.

RYAN ROSE ACEAE AND HEATHER FLOWERS: QUEER MONSTERS

In 2018, Ryan Rose Aceae and Heather Flowers released GENDERWRECKED: *Post-Apocalyptic Genderpunk* (figure A.2). GENDERWRECKED, as Flowers describes it, is "a visual novel about talking, fighting, and making out with monsters thousands of years after an event that shredded the world." Flowers and Aceae are both graduates of the University of Southern California, where Aceae founded and ran the Transgender Advocacy Group and Flowers was part of the Interactive Media + Games Division. Flowers describes herself as privileged in her development as an artist, even in try-

Fanny
Would you still like to kiss me, jenna?

Fig A.2 :::: *GENDERWRECKED: Post-Apocalyptic Genderpunk* (2018) by Ryan Rose Aceae and Heather Flowers, a game about talking, fighting, and making out with monsters

ing moments. During her time at the University of Southern California, she says, "I found a loving queer community, came out as transgender, and experienced the trauma of watching our nation descending ever-further into fascism: all events that have shaped my artistic process drastically." Mental health has also played a significant role in both Aceae's and Flowers's game-making. Aceae, who has bipolar disorder, describes how their experiences with psychosis have come to define their art. Says Flowers, in a related vein, "I want to make art that expresses how it feels to be trans, queer, and mentally ill, to feel like something at your very core is broken because you're assembled from scars and broken glass and pieces of trash, so that others who feel the same way can take away the lesson that they are not alone in this world."

Asked to describe her games, Flowers responds, "I make games for people who feel like they've been crushed by systems beyond their control, people who find themselves at odds with their own bodies, people who are filled to the brim with trauma." She continues, "Much of my work is about chasing those moments of love and hope in a world that often seems to lack both: love letters inside a brutalist hellscape, moments of relief and confidence in a society built on shame, music after the end of the world. That juxtaposition is what drives most of my work." Says Flowers, on the subject of her artistic inspirations, "I do my best work when I take inspiration from as many sources as possible." Among the things that are currently inspiring Flowers, she lists music by the Mountain Goats, poetry by 1990s trans zine cocreator Xanthra Phillips MacKay, and, in appropriately poetic gesture, "this one sign in my hometown that's been broken for over a year, just flashing different colors and the words 'A/V NO SIGNAL.'" Aceae describes their own work in a collage of imagery and ideas: "Gender and magic, queerness and monsters, building a community that finally makes you feel seen. Brains breaking and being pieced back together again. How easy it is to fall in love and how complicated it is to stay in it. Fully automated luxury gay space communism."

Both artists report that they now consider themselves to be "separate creators" and do not plan to collaborate again in the future. "Heather and I made GENDERWRECKED together because we wanted to create something that we loved as much as we loved each other," says Aceae. "It was a manifestation of the relationship we were in at the time." Though they are no longer collaborators, Flowers says that working with Aceae greatly improved her skill as an artist. Aceae and Flowers's experience as cocreators speaks to the emotional as well as the creative complexities of artistic collaboration. It also serves as a reminder that queer interpersonal relations are often inextricable from queer games.

Aceae is now working on a solo project: a dating sim called *Gay Monster Kiss Club*, which is about "a dragon that's super rude and like ten times the size of any of the love interests." *Gay Monster Kiss Club* explores themes like the "intersection between queerness and monstrosity, . . . building a community, and figuring out tough shit like mental illness and gender." Following GENDERWRECKED, Flowers's current project is EXTREME MEAT-PUNKS FOREVER: *Powered by Blood*. Flowers describes the game as "a serial visual novel/mech brawler about gay disasters beating up neonazis in giant robots made of meat." The game, says Flowers, "expresses a lot of things I've been thinking about, from leftist politics to being at odds with your own body to the existential horror of growing up queer in the void between the South and the Midwest."

Fig A.3 :::: Art from
Santo Aveiro's
current project,
*DON'T WAKE THE
NIGHT*, developed
through her indie
game studio
Brujería @ Werk

SANTO AVEIRO: COMMUNITY EDUCATION
AND FINDING "PEOPLE LIKE ME"

Santo Aveiro is a queer game maker of color and a community organizer
and educator. Their current work in progress is *DON'T WAKE THE NIGHT*
(figure A.3). The game is scheduled for release in 2019 from Aveiro's indie
studio Brujería @ Werk, whose name references Latin American traditions
of witchcraft. Fittingly, *DON'T WAKE THE NIGHT* is about witches and community conflict resolution. Aveiro reports that they are also working on
a "secret side project" about cyberpunk themes and indigeneity. "I love to
make games that are nonlinear and don't have a conclusive ending," says
Aveiro. "That is what makes games so powerful, that they can go in any
direction. Usually my games also contain a lot of unanswered questions.
In life, we generally don't have the answer to everything. We might never
have the answer. That's okay."

Like Flowers, Aveiro's biggest inspirations are not games. In particular, Aveiro is drawn to post-apocalyptic and cyberpunk work, like the
film *Akira*. "However," says Aveiro, "I do find that post-apocalyptic and

cyberpunk narratives often ignore issues of colonialism and capitalism, so when I come across a story that genuinely tries to address these issues, it sticks with me forever." As an example of art that succeeds in this area, they point to Janelle Monáe: "Her work is incredibly powerful and challenges our expectations around sci-fi conventions."

In addition to making games, Aveiro is currently the codirector of Dames Making Games, a Toronto-based nonprofit organization that runs workshops and other events that focus on teaching marginalized creators to develop games. Aveiro's own background is in animation. As an undergraduate, they took part in a game development program, but they were disappointed by its lack of diversity. In response, they sought out local communities where, they say, "I could meet people like me." This brought them to Dames Making Games.

Aveiro recalls how their early experiences with the organization gave them newfound confidence to speak at game events. When Dames Making Games approached them to join their board in 2016, they accepted with excitement. At the same time, Aveiro is frank about the challenges of community organizing. "I care a lot about our community members, which can cause stress at times because I always want to make sure they're safe and looked after," they say. For Aveiro, the challenge is worth it, though. "Knowing the members of my community are safe and have access to the same resources I did when I was starting out is a huge reward."

JESS MARCOTTE: PHYSICAL-DIGITAL HYBRIDS

Soft interfaces, intimate controllers, queer embodied experiences: these are some of the themes that cross Jess Marcotte's work. Marcotte calls their pieces "human-assisted physical-digital hybrid games," which "basically means games that use alternative and unusual interfaces with digital programs and a human moderator or facilitator." Along with Dietrich Squinkifer (chapter 1), they are the cocreator of *Rustle Your Leaves to Me Softly* (2017) (figure A.4), "an ASMR plant dating sim" in which players stroke the leaves of houseplants to generate a sensual soundscape, and *The Truly Terrific Traveling Troubleshooter* (2017), a role-playing game about emotional labor contained with a suitcase. At the moment, Marcotte is working on a new game called *Flip the Script*, which, says Marcotte, uses puppets to prompt players "to talk about personal experiences that reflect larger systems of privilege and oppression." Among their inspirations, Marcotte lists game designer and teacher Pippin Barr, whose instruction

Fig A.4 :::: Jess Marcotte demonstrates their game *Rustle Your Leaves to Me Softly* (2017), a dating simulator in which players stroke the leaves of houseplants

to make games that "tease rather than please" has stuck with Marcotte since taking Barr's class, Curious Games Studio. Marcotte also points to the work of Christine Love, Ida Toft, and Kara Stone (chapter 10).

Their goal with these physical-digital hybrid games, as Marcotte describes it, is to "commiserate." Asked what they hope to communicate with their work, Marcotte responds, "I want to communicate about alienation and our subjective experiences in the world." For Marcotte, sharing these games with players itself generates intimacy: "Because of the nature of my work, with interfaces that need someone to care for them and games that need facilitation, I get to experience these moments with players quite closely." Marcotte has also made what they refer to as "purely digital" games. By contrast, with these games, Marcotte says, "I'm trying to reach through the screen to make a rueful joke or offer a mug of something warm and soothing. My digital games tend to be about a line between sincerity and cynicism, whereas my hybrid games create possibility spaces where players can reflect on ways of thinking about the world." Whether it is analog or digital, Marcotte sees their work engaging with intersectional feminist discussions around topics like stereotypes about women and negotiating consent. They approach game-making through the "Reflective

Game Design" framework, which they explain privileges "questions over answers," allowing them to create games that "aim to open discussion."

Marcotte currently lives in Montréal, where they are pursuing their doctoral degree at Concordia University in conjunction with the Technoculture, Art and Games (TAG) lab. Both their undergraduate and master's degrees are in English and creative writing—which, says Marcotte, provided them with the training in reading media objects as texts that lets them approach their own work through "critical thinking, textual analysis, and making." They began making games in 2013. As Marcotte explains, "While writing an article about the Global Game Jam in Montréal, I wound up joining a team and making a game. From there, I never stopped." Marcotte describes the game-making scene in Montréal, and especially organizations like Pixelles and Critical Hit, as a valuable source of education and support. The Queerness and Games Conference, of which Marcotte is now the lead organizer (as of 2019), was hosted in Montréal in 2018 and is returning to the city in 2020. "It's a credit to the [local] community that . . . there were always people to encourage me to make my weird little games . . . I was privileged to be in Montréal."

LIVING IN THE FUTURE

These profiles, though short, give us a glimpse at the work that is emerging from the queer games avant-garde today. They also hint toward where queer indie game-making might go in the future. Some of the experiences that Flowers, Aceae, Aveiro, and Marcotte describe resonate with comments made by game makers at various points in this book. The call from Aveiro and Flowers to look for inspiration in areas of art and culture beyond games is echoed, in one form or another, in each of the interviews in this volume. Flowers's haunting comment about the "existential horror of growing up queer in the void between the South and the Midwest" recalls the childhood stories of Avery Alder (chapter 16), Llaura McGee (chapter 4), Liz Ryerson (chapter 6), and all those contributors to the queer game avant-garde for whom queer game-making has been a way to confront or move beyond a personal history characterized by isolation. Simultaneously, there are elements of these profiles that bring new issues and insights to the fore. Marcotte and Aveiro both stress the importance of local game-making communities in encouraging them to develop their own games, for example. This suggests that the labor of community organizers like Sarah Schoemann (chapter 20) is beginning to bear fruit, bringing forth a new generation of queer game makers, queer games thinkers, and queer games activists.

If this rhetoric of "next generations" and "bearing fruit" seems to fall back on heteronormative metaphors of reproductive futurity, this is, strangely enough, on purpose. Of course, we must remain wary of teleological narratives about progress toward a "better" future—for queer folks and all those who are marginalized and oppressed. Yet, I would argue, there is indeed a sort of reproductive futurity to the queer games avant-garde, though one that is far from heteronormative. Contributors to this movement create art that sparks new art. They push boundaries in ways that encourage others to push boundaries further. This mode of reproduction is fundamentally queer. It follows a genealogy that is not straight or clear but twisting and diffuse, born of moments of hope and togetherness but also of moments, as Flowers points out, of pain and trauma. These experiences can be productive, but what they will produce is a radical unknown.

If the queer games avant-garde is the future of video games, and if that avant-garde is thriving all around us (it is), it is tempting to say that we are already living in that future. To make that claim sounds celebratory, even idealistic, and to an extent it is. Yet it is worth remembering that the futurity that these queer games themselves present is a deeply ambivalent one. Their visions of futurity are ones that both long for and fear the future. It is no coincidence that three of the artists profiled in this afterword make work about queerness after the apocalypse. Through the lens of games, the queer games avant-garde moves beyond the world of today and gives players the chance to play in and play with the world of to. It uses games to confront what comes *after*. As queer people in Ameri are now living in the future that we feared: one where our elected officia. lend their vocal support to white supremacists, where immigrants seeking aid are forcibly separated from their loved ones, where the threat of bigotry being written into law looms over us in new ways each day. Now more than ever, we need the queer games avant-garde and the alternative visions of the future that it allows us to explore through play.

Perhaps, rather than saying that we are living in the future, it would be more accurate to say that we are getting closer to that queer future on the horizon—which we may never reach but which the queer games avant-garde pushes us ever closer toward. The future is always a work in progress. At the same time, queer games, along with those who make, support, study, and play them, must remain rooted in the present. These games and their creation represent the work of the body, of touch, of intimacy, of feeling, of political resistance that manifests as self-care, of queer identity and queer desire as a source of power. Queer games put the medium of video games to new purpose. Through these games, we, as queer players and queer people, are invited to reimagine our pasts and our futures, but also, and perhaps most importantly, the realities of our present.

APPENDIX   Queer Indie Games to Play at Home
                               or in the Classroom

Games are an interactive medium. No understanding of the queer games avant-garde would be complete without playing queer games. The following is a list of queer indie games, both digital and analog, that are currently available to play, download, or otherwise purchase as of October 2018. Compared to mainstream AAA video games, many of these games are short and inexpensive (although it is crucial to fairly compensate marginalized artists for their work whenever possible). Games sold through Steam usually cost between $10 and $20. Games sold through itch.io often allow customers to name their own price.

Most the games listed here have been developed by the game makers interviewed in this book, though other interesting and important titles have also been included. A number of additional queer games have been left off this list—such as playable art installations and games that use one-of-a-kind alternative interfaces—not because they are not important but because they are not widely accessible. In other cases, queer game makers themselves have decided to remove their own works, including popular games like Anna Anthropy's *Dys4ia* and merritt k's *Lim*, from the internet.

This list of queer indie games is a helpful resource for scholars, students, and educators. The brief descriptions below provide a quick snapshot of each game.

» *Analogue: A Hate Story (2012)*, **Christine Love**

A visual novel that Love describes as "a mystery featuring transhuman-ism, traditional marriage, loneliness, and cosplay." *Analogue: A Hate Story* is the sequel to Love's earlier game *Digital: A Love Story* (2010). The game can be purchased and downloaded from Steam.

» *Be Witching (2015)*, **Anna Anthropy**

An analog game about fashion balls for witches involving drawing and group choices. The printable game elements can be purchased and down-loaded from itch.io.

» *Become a Great Artist in Just 10 Seconds (2013)*,
  Michael Brough + Andi McClure

A playful art-making program that produces glitchy, chaotic visual works. The game can be downloaded for free from McClure's website at https://msm.runhello.com/p/987.

» *Bottoms Up: A Historic Gay Bar Tycoon (2018)*, **Mo Cohen**

A point-and-click adventure about the challenges of operating a queer speakeasy in the 1920s. The first chapter of the game can be downloaded for free from itch.io.

» *Butterfly Soup (2017)*, **Brianna Lei**

Lei describes the game as "a visual novel about gay Asian girls playing baseball and falling in love." The game can be downloaded for free from itch.io.

» *Cibele (2015)*, **Nina Freeman**

A semiautobiographical game about a sexual relationship between a young woman and a young man who play video games together online. The game can be purchased and downloaded from Steam.

» *Cobra Club (2015),* **Robert Yang**

One of Yang's "gay sex games," *Cobra Club* is a game about "dick pics" in which players take and share naked photos of their characters' genitals in an imaginary, Grindr-esque mobile app. The game can be purchased and downloaded from itch.io.

» *Coming Out Simulator (2014),* **Nicky Case**

A game about how, when, and whether to come out as queer to one's family. The game can be played for free using a web browser at https://ncase.me /cos.

» *Coming Out on Top (2014),* **Obscurasoft**

A gay dating sim featuring romance and sex between normatively attractive cisgender male characters. The game can be purchased and downloaded from Steam.

» *Conversations We Have in My Head (2015),* **Dietrich Squinkifer**

A game about what it might be like to talk to friends from one's past about current issues of gender, romantic orientation, and mental health. The game can be downloaded for free from Squinkifer's website: https:// squinky.me/2015/07/23/conversations-we-have-in-my-head.

» *Curtain (2014),* **Llaura McGee** (DREAMFEEL)

A highly stylized game with surrealist elements in which players walk through the apartment of two women in an emotionally abusive relationship. The game can be purchased and downloaded from itch.io.

» *Cyber Sext Adventure (2015),* **Kara Stone**

A gamelike experience in which players interact with an erotic bot via text message. The game can be purchased and downloaded from itch.io.

» *Dominique Pamplemousse and Dominique Pamplemousse in "Combinatorial Explosion!" (2017)*, Dietrich Squinkifer

The sequel to *Dominique Pamplemousse in "It's All Over When the Fat Lady Sings!"* (2013), the game is also a musical that follows a genderqueer detective. The game can be purchased and downloaded from itch.io: https://squinky.itch.io/dompam2.

» *Dominique Pamplemousse in "It's All Over When the Fat Lady Sings!" (2013)*, Dietrich Squinkifer

A point-and-click musical adventure game with a noir aesthetic and handcrafted visual elements that features a nonbinary protagonist. The game can be purchased and downloaded from itch.io: https://squinky.itch.io/pamplemousse.

» *Downtown Browns (2016)*, Lishan AZ, Tonia B******, Luciana Chamorro, Allison Comrie, Jazmin Garcia, Emilia Yang

A series of interactive web videos that uses gamelike elements to prompt players to consider the perspectives of three women of color living in Los Angeles. The videos can be accessed for free at http://downtownbrowns.weebly.com.

» *Dream Daddy: A Dad Dating Simulator (2017)*, Game Grumps

A dating simulator in which players, in the role of the father of a teenage daughter, choose which other dads in a new town to romance. The game can be purchased and downloaded from Steam.

» *The Earth Is a Better Person than Me (2018)*, Kara Stone

A visual novel in which the protagonist, a young woman who has run away into the forest, forms romantic and sexual connections with different elements of nature. The game can be purchased and downloaded from itch.io.

» *Escape from Pleasure Planet (2016),* **Luke Miller**

A sequel to *My Ex-Boyfriend the Space Tyrant, Escape from Pleasure Planet* is described by its creators as a "gay-themed," science-fiction adventure game. The game can be purchased and downloaded from Steam.

» *EXTREME MEATPUNKS FOREVER: Powered by Blood (2018),*
   Heather Flowers

A visual novel with fighting elements about "four gay disasters beating up neonazis in giant robots made of meat." The game can be purchased and downloaded from itch.io.

» *Fragments of Him (2016),* **Sassybot**

A narrative game about the death of a bisexual man and how those close to him reflect on his life and their loss. The game can be purchased and downloaded from Steam.

» *GENDERWRECKED: Post-Apocalyptic Genderpunk (2018),* **Ryan Rose**
   Aceae + Heather Flowers

A visual novel that uses body horror and humor to address gender and dysphoria. The game can be purchased and downloaded from itch.io.

» *Genital Jousting (2016),* **Free Lives**

A colorful, humorous multiplayer game in which players, each represented by a moving penis, attempt to penetrate one another. The game can be purchased and downloaded from Steam.

» *Glitter Pits (2017),* **Kat Jones**

An analog game in which players write down, discuss, and then queer or destroy beauty norms. Instructions for the game are available as part of *queer gaymes: a collection of games by queer people about queer experiences,* which can be purchased through Amazon.

» *Glitzy Nails* (2016), **Kat Jones**

An analog game about the privilege that white women hold over women of color who work in nail salons. Instructions for the game are available as part of the *#Feminism* micro-games anthology, which can be purchased online through Pelgrane Press.

» *Gone Home* (2013), **Fullbright**

A first-person, narrative game. Players explore a family home to uncover a love story between two young women. The game can be purchased and downloaded from Steam.

» *Heaven Will Be Mine* (2018), **Aevee Bee + Mia Schwartz**

A visual novel about giant fighting robots and queer women pilots. The game can be purchased and downloaded from Steam.

» *How Do You Do It?* (2014), **Nina Freeman**

A browser-based game in which a young girl moves two naked dolls together in humorous combinations in an attempt to figure out sex. The game can be played on Freeman's website: http://ninasays.so/howdoyoudoit.

» *Hurt Me Plenty* (2014), **Robert Yang**

A game about spanking that emphasizes communication and consent. The game can be purchased and downloaded from itch.io: https://radiatoryang.itch.io/hurt-me-plenty.

» *The Isle Is Full of Noises* (2016), **Llaura McGee** (DREAMFEEL)

A highly stylized "flat game" about sailing a boat through a storm inspired by McGee's return from Scotland to Ireland. The game can be purchased and downloaded from itch.io.

» *Kitty Powers' Matchmaker* (2014), **Magic Notion**

A humorous dating simulator hosted by drag queen Kitty Powers. The game can be purchased and downloaded from Steam.

» *Ladykiller in a Bind* (2016), **Christine Love**

An erotic visual novel about "girls tying each other up." The game can be purchased and downloaded from Steam.

» *Lesbian Spider-Queens of Mars* (2011), **Anna Anthropy**

A game about a spider dominatrix collecting her slaves in a series of mazelike levels. The game can be purchased and downloaded from itch.io: https://w.itch.io/lesbian-spider-queens-of-mars.

» *The Longest Couch* (2016), **Sean Wejebe**

A game for two players about boys awkwardly shuffling toward one another on a sofa as they attempt to kiss. The game can be purchased and downloaded from itch.io.

» *Mainichi* (2012), **Mattie Brice**

A short, RPG-style game about navigating daily life as a black trans woman. The game can be downloaded from Brice's website: http://www.mattie brice.com/mainichi.

» *Mighty Jill Off* (2008), **Anna Anthropy**

A game about a submissive with a boot fetish who must climb a tower to reach her queen. The game can be downloaded from http://mightyjilloff .dessgeega.com.

» *Monsterhearts 2* (2016), **Avery Alder**

The second edition of Alder's game *Monsterhearts*, a tabletop role-playing game about teenagers, monsters, and the mechanics of desire. The game can be purchased on Gumroad.com.

» *My Ex-Boyfriend the Space Tyrant (2014)*, **Luke Miller**

A point-and-click adventure game featuring white, cisgender gay male characters. The game can be purchased and downloaded from Steam.

» *Queers in Love at the End of the World (2013)*, **Anna Anthropy**

A Twine game in which the player has ten seconds to interact intimately with their partner before the world ends. The game can be played for free using a browser at https://w.itch.io/end-of-the-world.

» *Queertastrophe (2013)*, **Mo Cohen**

A browser-based game about dancing at a party, trying to avoid your exes, and bringing drinks to cuties. The game can be played using a web browser at https://gamejolt.com/games/queertastrophe/14195.

» *The Quiet Year (2009)*, **Avery Alder**

A tabletop role-playing game about cartography and post-apocalyptic community that challenges normative narrative structures. The game can be purchased on Gumroad.com.

» *Quing's Quest VII: The Death of Videogames! (2014)*, **Dietrich Squinkifer**

A text-based game with sparkling, musical elements about a monarch traveling through space who must decide whether to destroy the planet Videogames. The game can be played on Squinkifer's website: https://games .squinky.me/quing.

» *Problem Attic (2013)*, **Liz Ryerson**

An intentionally garbled, glitchy, nonlinear platformer with a message about navigating the upsetting inner workings of one's own mind. The game can be played using a browser at itch.io: https://lizryerson.itch.io/ problem-attic.

» *Realistic Kissing Simulator (2014)*, **Jimmy Andrews + Loren Schmidt**

A colorful, absurdist browser-based game in which two players lick one another with long, floppy tongues. Features consent mechanics. The game can be played on Schmidt's website: http://jimmylands.com/experiments /kissing.

» *Rinse and Repeat (2015)*, **Robert Yang**

In this game, the player-character washes another man in a group shower at the gym. The game can be purchased and downloaded from itch.io: https://radiatoryang.itch.io/rinseandrepeat.

SABBAT (2013), **Eva Problems**

A Twine game about satanic rituals and shifting monstrous bodies. A release of the game can be purchased and downloaded from itch.io: https:// ohnoproblems.itch.io/sabbat-directors-kvt.

» *Starcatchers (2017)*, **Sean Wejebe**

A game about boyfriends on a date looking at the stars and gazing into each other's eyes. The game can be purchased and downloaded from itch.io: https://wedgiebee.itch.io/starcatchers.

» *Stick Shift (2015)*, **Robert Yang**

The player changes gears to pleasure a car in a metaphor for masturbation. The game can be purchased and downloaded from itch.io: https://radiato ryang.itch.io/stick-shift.

» *Succulent (2015)*, **Robert Yang**

A game in which the player moves a melting Popsicle sensually in and out of a man's mouth. The game can be purchased and downloaded from itch.io: https://radiatoryang.itch.io/succulent.

» *Tacoma (2017)*, **Fullbright**

A first-person, science-fiction narrative game including some LGBTQ characters, from the studio that developed *Gone Home*. The game can be purchased and downloaded from Steam.

» *The Tearoom (2017)*, **Robert Yang**

A game about cruising in public restrooms. The game can be purchased and downloaded from itch.io: https://radiatoryang.itch.io/the-tearoom.

» *Transgalactica: A Tune Your Own Adventure (2018)*, **Jess Marcotte + Dietrich Squinkifer**

A transgender person travels through space while listening to a radio. Gameplay takes place through the mechanic of tuning to different channels. The game can be played online using a web browser at https://games .squinky.me/transgalactica.

» *Triad (2013)*, **Anna Anthropy + Leon Arnott**

A puzzle game about trying to fit three lovers together in one bed. The game can be downloaded from itch.io: https://w.itch.io/triad.

» *2064: Read Only Memories (2015)*, **MidBoss**

A cyberpunk adventure game with a cast of LGBTQ characters. The game can be purchased and downloaded from Steam.

» *Undertale (2015)*, **Toby Fox**

A role-playing game with additional fighting elements and a variety of queer characters. A child of unspecified gender falls into a world of monsters and must find their way back to the earth's surface. The game can be purchased and downloaded from Steam.

» *We Know the Devil (2015),* **Aevee Bee + Mia Schwartz**

Part visual novel, part horror game. The game features three queer protagonists who spend a week at a religious sleepaway camp in the woods. The game can be purchased and downloaded from Steam.

» *With Those We Love Alive (2014),* **Porpentine**

A text-based game that instructs players to draw symbols on their arms. The game can be played on Porpentine's website: http://slimedaughter .com/games/twine/wtwla.

NOTES

INTRODUCTION

1   Katherine Isbister, *How Games Move Us: Emotion by Design* (Cambridge, MA: MIT Press, 2016), xvii.

2   Anna Anthropy, *Rise of the Videogame Zinesters: How Freaks, Normals, Amateurs, Artists, Dreamers, Drop-outs, Queers, Housewives, and People Like You Are Taking Back an Art Form* (New York: Seven Stories, 2012).

3   Eric Zimmerman, "Manifesto: The 21st Century Will Be Defined by Games," *Kotaku*, September 9, 2013, https://kotaku.com/manifesto-the-21st-century -will-be-defined-by-games-1275355204; Kirk Skaugen, "The Game Changer," *Technology@Intel* (blog), August 18, 2015, https://blogs.intel.com /technology/2015/08/the-game-changer.

4   T. L. Taylor, *Play between Worlds: Exploring Online Game Culture* (Cambridge, MA: MIT Press, 2009), 113.

5   Katherine Cross, "Press F to Revolt: On the Gamification of Online Activism," in *Diversifying Barbie & Mortal Kombat: Intersectional Perspectives and Inclusive Designs in Gaming*, ed. Yasmin B. Kafai, Gabriela T. Richard, and Brendesha M. Tynes (Pittsburgh: ETC Press, 2016), 23–34.

6   Allegra Frank, "Overwatch's New Comic Confirms Game's First Queer Character," *Polygon*, December 24, 2016, https://www.polygon.com/2016 /12/20/14028604/overwatch-gay-tracer; Brian Crecente, "Varus: The Remaking of a 'League of Legends' Hero," *Rolling Stone*, November 30, 2017, https://www.rollingstone.com/glixel/features/varus-league-of-legends-hero -remade-with-gay-storyline-w512929.

7   Megan Condis, *Gaming Masculinity: Trolls, Fake Geeks and the Gendered Battle for Online Culture* (Iowa City: University of Iowa Press, 2018).

8   Chelsea Stark, "Atari's LGBTQ-Friendly Mobile Game Misses What Pride Is Actually About," *Mashable*, January 28, 2016, http://mashable.com/2016 /01/28/pridefest-atari.

9   Adrienne Shaw and Bonnie Ruberg, "Imagining Queer Game Studies," in
    Queer Game Studies, ed. Bonnie Ruberg and Adrienne Shaw (Minneapolis:
    University of Minnesota Press, 2017), x.

10 Carly A. Kocurek, *Coin-Operated Americans: Rebooting Boyhood at the Video
    Game Arcade* (Minneapolis: University of Minnesota Press, 2015), xiv.

11 Bonnie Ruberg, "Creating an Archive of LGBTQ Video Game Content: An In-
    terview with Adrienne Shaw," *Camera Obscura* 32, no. 2 (2017): 165–173.

12 Eddie Makuch, "'It Can't Be All White Males,' EA Exec Says about Diversity
    in Gaming: Electronic Arts Is Actively Looking to Increase Its Diversity,"
    Gamespot, September 5, 2015, http://www.gamespot.com/articles/it-cant
    -be-all-white-males-ea-exec-says-about-dive/1100–6430348.

13 Alison Harvey and Stephanie Fisher, "Everyone Can Make Games! The Post-
    Feminist Context of Women in Digital Game Production," *Feminist Media
    Studies* 15, no. 4 (2015): 576–592.

14 Philip Jones, dir., *Gaming in Color* (MidBoss, 2015).

15 Kishonna L. Gray, "Gaming Out Online: Black Lesbian Identity Development
    and Community Building in Xbox," *Journal of Lesbian Studies* 22, no. 3 (2017):
    282–296; Soraya Murray, *On Video Games: The Visual Politics of Race, Gender
    and Space* (New York: I. B. Tauris, 2018); Lisa Nakamura, "Queer Female of
    Color: The Highest Difficulty Setting There Is? Gaming Rhetoric as Gender
    Capital," *Ada* 1 (2012), https://adanewmedia.org/2012/11/issue1-nakamura/;
    David J. Leonard, "Not a Hater, Just Keepin' It Real: The Importance of Race-
    and Gender-Based Game Studies," *Games and Culture* 1, no. 1 (2006): 83–88.

16 Janine Fron, Tracy Fullerton, Jacquelyn Ford Morie, and Celia Pearce, "The
    Hegemony of Play," in *Situated Play: Proceedings of the 2007 Digital Games Re-
    search Association Conference*, edited by Baba Akira (Tokyo: University of To-
    kyo, 2007).

17 Mary Flanagan and Helen Nissenbaum, *Values at Play in Digital Games* (Cam-
    bridge, MA: MIT Press, 2014), 3.

18 Shaw and Ruberg, "Imagining Queer Game Studies."

19. Diana [Teddy] Pozo, Bonnie Ruberg, and Chris Goetz, "In Practice: Queerness
    and Games," *Camera Obscura* 32, no. 2 (2017): 153–163.

20 Adam Koebel (@skinnyghost), "Can we please have more queer games that
    aren't visual novels?," Twitter, July 26, 2018, 5:59 p.m., https://twitter.com
    /skinnyghost/status/1022602263489961984?lang=en.

21 Nadia Nova (@littanana), "With steam straight up deleting our lgbt tag,
    this is a great reminder to put your past and future games on itch instead if
    you already haven't," Twitter, June 9, 2018, 6:02 a.m., https://twitter.com
    /littanana/status/1005389623093284864; Flames within Black Feathers,
    "'LGBT' tag was purged," Steam, June 9, 2018, 4:44 p.m., https://steam
    community.com/discussions/forum/0/1697175413681679054.

22 Judith [Jack] Halberstam, *The Queer Art of Failure* (Durham, NC: Duke Uni-
    versity Press, 2011), 2.

23 Mary Flanagan, *Critical Play: Radical Game Design* (Cambridge, MA: MIT
    Press, 2009), 243.

24 Cara Ellison, "Anna Anthropy and the Twine Revolution," *The Guardian*, April 10, 2013, https://www.theguardian.com/technology/gamesblog/2013/apr/10 /anna-anthropy-twine-revolution.

25 Aaron Trammell and Emma Leigh Waldron, "Playing for Intimacy: Love, Lust, and Desire in Pursuit of Embodied Design," in *Rated M for Mature: Sex and Sexuality in Video Games*, ed. Matthew Wysocki and Evan W. Lauteria (New York: Bloomsbury Academic, 2015), 177–192.

26 Graeme Kirkpatrick, "Early Games Production, Game Subjectivation and the Containment of the Ludic Imagination," in *Fans and Videogames: Histories, Fandom, Archives*, ed. Melanie Swalwell, Helen Stuckey, and Angela Ndalianis (New York: Routledge, 2017), 19–36.

27 Melanie Swalwell, "1980s Home Coding: The Art of Amateur Programming," in *The Aotearoa Digital Arts Reader*, ed. Stella Brennan and Su Ballard (Auckland, NZ: Aotearoa Digital Arts and Clouds, 2008), 192–201.

28 Jaroslav Švelch, "Keeping the Spectrum Alive: Platform Fandom in a Time of Transition," in Swalwell et al., *Fans and Videogames*, 57–73.

29 Anne-Marie Schleiner, *The Player's Power to Change the Game: Ludic Mutation* (Amsterdam: Amsterdam University Press, 2017), 19.

30 Brendan Keogh, "Just Making Things and Being Alive about It: The Queer Games Scene," *Polygon*, May 24, 2013, https://www.polygon.com/features /2013/5/24/4341042/the-queer-games-scene.

31 Stephanie Boluk and Patrick LeMieux, *Metagaming: Playing, Competing, Spectating, Cheating, Trading, Making, and Breaking Videogames* (Minneapolis: University of Minnesota Press, 2017), 33.

32 Felan Parker, Jennifer R. Whitson, and Bart Simon, "Megabooth: The Cultural Intermediation of Indie Games," *New Media & Society* 20, no. 5 (2018): 1953–1972.

33 Lisa Nakamura, "The Unwanted Labour of Social Media: Women of Colour Call Out Culture as Venture Community Management," *New Formations* 86 (2015): 106–112.

34 Peter Bürger, *Theory of the Avant-Garde* (Minneapolis: University of Minnesota Press, 1984); Hal Foster, *The Return of the Real* (Cambridge, MA: MIT Press, 1996).

35 Miguel Sicart, *Play Matters* (Cambridge, MA: MIT Press, 2014), 61.

36 Schleiner, *Player's Power*, 7.

37 Flanagan, *Critical Play*, 96, 183, 87.

38 Keith Stuart, "Roger Ebert Re-Enters the 'Games as Art' Debate," *The Guardian*, April 20, 2010, https://www.theguardian.com/technology/gamesblog /2010/apr/20/roger-ebert-games-as-art.

39 Eddo Stern, "20 Years of Game Art: Reflections, Transformations, and New Directions," paper presented at Digital Games Research Association Conference, Turin, Italy, July 2018.

40 Alexander Galloway, *Gaming: Essays on Algorithmic Culture* (Minneapolis: University of Minnesota Press, 2006), 126.

41 Flanagan, *Critical Play*, 1–2, 6.

42 Brian Schrank, *Avant-Garde Videogames: Playing with Technoculture* (Cambridge, MA: MIT Press, 2014), 1, 3.

43 John Sharp, *Works of Game: On the Aesthetics of Games and Art* (Cambridge, MA: MIT Press, 2015), 12.

44 Simon Parkin, "Zoe Quinn's Depression Quest," *The New Yorker*, September 9, 2014, https://www.newyorker.com/tech/elements/zoe-quinns-depression -quest.

45 Colleen Macklin and John Sharp, *Games, Design and Play: A Detailed Approach to Iterative Game Design* (London: Pearson Education, 2016), 25–26.

46 Luke Karmali, "Why We Need More Gay Characters in Video Games," *IGN*, March 14, 2013, http://www.ign.com/articles/2014/03/14/why-we-need-more -gay-characters-in-video-games; Joe Parlock, "Why Gaming's Gay Male Representation Needs to Change," *The Telegraph*, February 24, 2016, http:// www.telegraph.co.uk/gaming/what-to-play/why-gamings-gay-male -representation-needs-to-change.

47 Jennifer Malkowski and TreaAndrea Russworm, eds., *Gaming Representation: Race, Gender, and Sexuality in Video Games* (Indianapolis: University of Indiana Press, 2017), 2.

48 Patrick Gann, "Playing at Empathy: Anna Anthropy's *Dys4ia*," *Gamechurch*, January 2, 2013, http://gamechurch.com/playing-at-empathy-anna -anthropys-dys4ia; Dan Solberg, "The Problem with Empathy Games," *Kill Screen*, January 19, 2016, https://killscreen.com/articles/the-problem -with-empathy-games.

49 Shira Chess, *Ready Player Two: Women Gamers and Designed Identity* (Minneapolis: University of Minnesota Press, 2017), 16.

50 Claudia Lo, "Everything Is Wiped Away: Queer Temporality in *Queers in Love at the End of the World*," *Camera Obscura* 32, no. 2 (2017): 185–192; Whitney Pow, "Reaching Toward Home: Software Interface as Queer Orientation in the Video Game *Curtain*," *Velvet Light Trap* 81 (2018): 43–56; Diana Mari [Teddy] Pozo, "Queer Games After Empathy: Feminism and Haptic Game Design Aesthetics from Consent to Cuteness to the Radically Soft," *Game Studies* 18, no. 3 (2018), http://gamestudies.org/1803/articles/pozo.

51 Cara Ellison, *Embed with Games: A Year on the Couch with Game Developers* (Edinburgh: Birlinn, 2016); merritt kopas, ed., *Videogames for Humans: Twine Authors in Conversation* (New York: Instar, 2015).

52 Jacqueline Bryk and K. N. Granger, eds., *queer gaymes: a collection of games by queer people about queer experiences* (self-published, 2016); Misha Bushyager, Lizzie Stark, and Anna Westerling, eds., *#Feminism: A Nano-Game Anthology* (London: Pelgrane Press, 2017).

53 Elizabeth Freeman, *Time Binds: Queer Temporalities, Queer Histories* (Durham, NC: Duke University Press, 2010), 22.

54 Macklin and Sharp, *Games, Design and Play*, 117–130.

55 Švelch, "Keeping the Spectrum Alive," 57.

56 Paolo Ruffino, *Future Gaming: Creative Interventions in Video Game Culture* (Cambridge, MA: MIT Press, 2018), 4.

57 Ruffino, *Future Gaming*, 7, 8.

58 Lee Edelman, *No Future: Queer Theory and the Death Drive* (Durham, NC: Duke University Press, 2004); José Esteban Muñoz, *Cruising Utopia: The Then and There of Queer Futurity* (New York: New York University Press, 2009); Kathryn Bond Stockton, *The Queer Child, or Growing Sideways in the Twentieth Century* (Durham, NC: Duke University Press, 2009); Halberstam, *Queer Art of Failure*; Freeman, *Time Binds*.

CHAPTER ONE. DIETRICH SQUINKIFER

1 Dietrich Squinkifer, "Conference, Conventions, Conversations, and *Coffee*," *Camera Obscura* 32, no. 2 (2017): 175–183.

CHAPTER TWO. ROBERT YANG

1 Robert Yang, "If You Walk in Someone Else's Shoes, Then You've Taken Their Shoes: Empathy Machines as Appropriation Machines," *Radiator Blog*, April 5, 2017, http://www.blog.radiator.debacle.us/2017/04/if-you-walk-in-someone -elses-shoes-then.html; Robert Yang, "For Better or for Worse," *Radiator Blog*, November 7, 2016, http://www.blog.radiator.debacle.us/2016/11/for-better -or-worse.html.

CHAPTER THREE. AEVEE BEE

1 *We Know the Devil*, Steam store page, http://store.steampowered.com/app /435300/We_Know_the_Devil, accessed September 30, 2019.

2 Aevee Bee, "Against Representation," *Medium*, April 13, 2016, https://medium .com/mammon-machine-zeal/against-representation-97bc44b4d609.

CHAPTER FOUR. LLAURA MCGEE

1 Llaura McGee, personal website, http://dreamfeel.org/curtain.

2 In a follow-up communication from July 2018, McGee clarified that, in the year between when this interview was conducted and the present, she felt the indie games scene in Ireland had become significantly more diverse.

CHAPTER FIVE. ANDI MCCLURE

1 Andi McClure, *Run Hello* (blog), https://msm.runhello.com.

2 Andi McClure, "'Games?,'" *Run Hello* (blog), https://msm.runhello.com/anti -games, accessed September 30, 2019.

CHAPTER SIX. LIZ RYERSON

1 Brendan Keogh, "Just Making Things and Being Alive about It: The Queer Games Scene," *Polygon*, May 24, 2013, https://www.polygon.com/features /2013/5/24/4341042/the-queer-games-scene.

2 Liz Ryerson, "Healing from Past Wounds," *Ellaguro* (blog), December 8, 2015, http://ellaguro.blogspot.com/2015/12/healing-from-past-wounds.html.

CHAPTER SEVEN. JIMMY ANDREWS + LOREN SCHMIDT

1 "About Realistic Kissing Simulator," Indiecade.com, http://www.igf.com /realistic-kissing-simulator, accessed September 30, 2019.

CHAPTER EIGHT. NAOMI CLARK

1 Naomi Clark, "What *Is* Queerness in Games, Anyway?," in *Queer Game Studies*, ed. Bonnie Ruberg and Adrienne Shaw (Minneapolis: University of Minnesota Press, 2017), 3–14.

CHAPTER NINE. ELIZABETH SAMPAT

1 Elizabeth Sampat, *Empathy Engines: Design Games That Are Personal, Political, and Profound* (self-published, 2016), https://www.amazon.com/Empathy -Engines-Personal-Political-Profound/dp/1548761516.

CHAPTER TEN. KARA STONE

1 Kara Stone, "The Mystical Digital @ Babycastles," May 2016, https:// karastonesite.com/the-mystical-digital-babycastles.

CHAPTER ELEVEN. MATTIE BRICE

1. Mattie Brice, "Play and Be Real about It: What Games Could Learn from Kink," in *Queer Game Studies*, ed. Bonnie Ruberg and Adrienne Shaw (Minneapolis: University of Minnesota Press, 2017), 77–82.

CHAPTER TWELVE. SEANNA MUSGRAVE

1 Robert Yang, "'Take Ecstasy with Me': A Manifesto for Gay VR," *Radiator Blog*, March 21, 2017, http://www.blog.radiator.debacle.us/2017/03/take-ecstasy -with-me-manifesto-for-gay.html.

CHAPTER THIRTEEN. TONIA B****** + EMILIA YANG

1 Emilia Yang, "Downtown Browns: Interactive Web Series, Intersectionality and Intimacy," *Confessions of an Aca-Fan* (blog), April 13, 2017, http://henryjenkins.org/blog/2017/04/downtown-browns-interactive-web-series-intersectionality-and-intimacy.html.
2 "Team," Downtown Browns, http://downtownbrowns.weebly.com/team.html, accessed September 30, 2019.

CHAPTER SIXTEEN. AVERY ALDER

1 Naomi Clark, "What *Is* Queerness in Games, Anyway?," in *Queer Game Studies*, ed. Bonnie Ruberg and Adrienne Shaw (Minneapolis: University of Minnesota Press, 2017), 4.

CHAPTER SEVENTEEN. KAT JONES

1 Misha Bushyager, Lizzie Stark, and Anna Westerling, eds., *#Feminism: A Nano-Game Anthology* (London: Pelgrane, 2017).
2 Jacqueline Bryk and K. N. Granger, eds., *queer gaymes: a collection of games by queer people about queer experiences* (self-published, 2016).

BIBLIOGRAPHY

Anthropy, Anna. *Rise of the Videogame Zinesters: How Freaks, Normals, Amateurs, Artists, Dreamers, Drop-outs, Queers, Housewives, and People Like You Are Taking Back an Art Form.* New York: Seven Stories Press, 2012.

Bee, Aevee. "Against Representation." *Medium*, April 13, 2016. https://medium.com/mammon-machine-zeal/against-representation-97bc44b4d609.

Brice, Mattie. "Play and Be Real about It: What Games Could Learn from Kink." In *Queer Game Studies*, edited by Bonnie Ruberg and Adrienne Shaw, 77–82. Minneapolis: University of Minnesota Press, 2017.

Bryk, Jacqueline, and K. N. Granger, eds. *queer gaymes: a collection of games by queer people about queer experiences.* Self-published, 2016.

Bürger, Peter. *Theory of the Avant-Garde.* Minneapolis: University of Minnesota Press, 1984.

Bushyager, Misha, Lizzie Stark, and Anna Westerling, eds. *#Feminism: A Nano-Game Anthology.* London: Pelgrane Press, 2017.

Chess, Shira. *Ready Player Two: Women Gamers and Designed Identity.* Minneapolis: University of Minnesota Press, 2017.

Clark, Naomi. "What *Is* Queerness in Games, Anyway?" In *Queer Game Studies*, edited by Bonnie Ruberg and Adrienne Shaw, 3–14. Minneapolis: University of Minnesota Press, 2017.

Cohen, Mo. "Having Trans Women+Femme Characters in a Game (When You Aren't One)." *Queermo Games Dev Blog*, December 19, 2016. https://queermogames.tumblr.com/post/154693704345/having-trans-women-femme-characters-in-a-game.

Condis, Megan. *Gaming Masculinity: Trolls, Fake Geeks and the Gendered Battle for Online Culture.* Iowa City: University of Iowa Press, 2018.

Crecente, Brian. "Varus: The Remaking of a 'League of Legends' Hero." *Rolling Stone*, November 30, 2017. https://www.rollingstone.com/glixel/features/varus-league-of-legends-hero-remade-with-gay-storyline-w512929.

Cross, Katherine. "Press F to Revolt: On the Gamification of Online Activism." In *Diversifying Barbie & Mortal Kombat: Intersectional Perspectives and Inclusive De-*

signs in Gaming, edited by Yasmin B. Kafai, Gabriela T. Richard, and Brendesha M. Tynes, 23–34. Pittsburgh: ETC Press, 2016.

Edelman, Lee. No Future: Queer Theory and the Death Drive. Durham, NC: Duke University Press, 2004.

Ellison, Cara. "Anna Anthropy and the Twine Revolution." The Guardian, April 10, 2013. https://www.theguardian.com/technology/gamesblog/2013/apr/10/anna-anthropy-twine-revolution.

Ellison, Cara. Embed with Games: A Year on the Couch with Game Developers. Edinburgh: Birlinn, 2016.

Foster, Hal. The Return of the Real. Cambridge, MA: MIT Press, 1996.

Flanagan, Mary. Critical Play: Radical Game Design. Cambridge, MA: MIT Press, 2009.

Flanagan, Mary, and Helen Nissenbaum. Values at Play in Digital Games. Cambridge, MA: MIT Press, 2014.

Frank, Allegra. "Overwatch's New Comic Confirms Game's First Queer Character." Polygon, December 24, 2016. https://www.polygon.com/2016/12/20/14028604/overwatch-gay-tracer.

Freeman, Elizabeth. Time Binds: Queer Temporalities, Queer Histories. Durham, NC: Duke University Press, 2010.

Fron, Janine, Tracy Fullerton, Jacquelyn Ford Morie, and Celia Pearce. "The Hegemony of Play." In Proceedings of the 2007 Digital Games Research Association Conference, ed. Baba Akira. Tokyo: University of Tokyo, 2007.

Galloway, Alexander. Gaming: Essays on Algorithmic Culture. Minneapolis: University of Minnesota Press, 2006.

Gann, Patrick. "Playing at Empathy: Anna Anthropy's Dys4ia." Gamechurch, January 2, 2013. http://gamechurch.com/playing-at-empathy-anna-anthropys-dys4ia/. Accessed August 1, 2008.

Gray, Kishonna L. "Gaming Out Online: Black Lesbian Identity Development and Community Building in Xbox." Journal of Lesbian Studies 22, no. 3 (2017): 282–296.

Halberstam, Judith [Jack]. The Queer Art of Failure. Durham, NC: Duke University Press, 2011.

Harvey, Alison, and Stephanie Fisher. "Everyone Can Make Games! The Post-Feminist Context of Women in Digital Game Production." Feminist Media Studies 15, no. 4 (2015): 576–592.

Isbister, Katherine. How Games Move Us: Emotion by Design. Cambridge, MA: MIT Press, 2016.

Jones, Philip, director. Gaming in Color. MidBoss, 2015.

Karmali, Luke. "Why We Need More Gay Characters in Video Games." IGN, March 14, 2013. http://www.ign.com/articles/2014/03/14/why-we-need-more-gay-characters-in-video-games.

Keogh, Brendan. "Just Making Things and Being Alive about It: The Queer Games Scene." Polygon, May 24, 2013. https://www.polygon.com/features/2013/5/24/4341042/the-queer-games-scene.

Kirkpatrick, Graeme. "Early Games Production, Game Subjectivation and the Containment of the Ludic Imagination." In *Fans and Videogames: Histories, Fandom, Archives*, edited by Melanie Swalwell, Helen Stuckey, and Angela Ndalianis, 19–36. New York: Routledge, 2017.

Kocurek, Carly A. *Coin-Operated Americans: Rebooting Boyhood at the Video Game Arcade*. Minneapolis: University of Minnesota Press, 2015.

kopas, merritt, ed. *Videogames for Humans: Twine Authors in Conversation*. New York: Instar, 2015.

Leonard, David J. "Not a Hater, Just Keepin' It Real: The Importance of Race- and Gender-Based Game Studies." *Games and Culture* 1, no. 1 (2006): 83–88.

Lo, Claudia. "Everything Is Wiped Away: Queer Temporality in *Queers in Love at the End of the World*." *Camera Obscura* 32, no. 2 (2017): 185–192.

Macklin, Colleen, and John Sharp. *Games, Design and Play: A Detailed Approach to Iterative Game Design*. London: Pearson Education, 2016.

Makuch, Eddie. "'It Can't Be All White Males,' EA Exec Says about Diversity in Gaming: Electronic Arts Is Actively Looking to Increase Its Diversity." *Gamespot*, September 5, 2015. http://www.gamespot.com/articles/it-cant-be -all-white-males-ea-exec-says-about-dive/1100-6430348.

Malkowski, Jennifer, and TreaAndrea Russworm, eds. *Gaming Representation: Race, Gender, and Sexuality in Video Games*. Indianapolis: University of Indiana Press, 2017.

Muñoz, José Esteban. *Cruising Utopia: The Then and There of Queer Futurity*. New York: New York University Press, 2009.

Murray, Soraya. *On Video Games: The Visual Politics of Race, Gender and Space*. New York: I. B. Tauris, 2018.

Nakamura, Lisa. "Queer Female of Color: The Highest Difficulty Setting There Is? Gaming Rhetoric as Gender Capital." *Ada* 1 (2012), https://adanewmedia.org /2012/11/issue1-nakamura/.

Nakamura, Lisa. "The Unwanted Labour of Social Media: Women of Colour Call Out Culture as Venture Community Management." *New Formations* 86 (2015): 106–112.

Parker, Felan, Jennifer R. Whitson, and Bart Simon. "Megabooth: The Cultural Intermediation of Indie Games." *New Media & Society* 20, no. 5 (2018): 1953–1972.

Parkin, Simon. "Zoe Quinn's Depression Quest." *The New Yorker*, September 9, 2014. https://www.newyorker.com/tech/elements/zoe-quinns-depression -quest.

Parlock, Joe. "Why Gaming's Gay Male Representation Needs to Change." *The Telegraph*, February 24, 2016. http://www.telegraph.co.uk/gaming/what-to -play/why-gamings-gay-male-representation-needs-to-change.

Pow, Whitney. "Reaching Toward Home: Software Interface as Queer Orientation in the Video Game *Curtain*." *Velvet Light Trap* 81 (2018): 43–56.

Pozo, Diana Mari [Teddy]. "Queer Games After Empathy: Feminism and Haptic Game Design Aesthetics from Consent to Cuteness to the Radically Soft." *Game Studies* 18, no. 3 (2018).

Pozo, Diana, Bonnie Ruberg, and Chris Goetz. "In Practice: Queerness and Games." *Camera Obscura* 32, no. 2 (2017): 153–163.

Ruberg, Bonnie. "Creating an Archive of LGBTQ Video Game Content: An Interview with Adrienne Shaw." *Camera Obscura* 32, no. 2 (2017): 165–173.

Ruffino, Paolo. *Future Gaming: Creative Interventions in Video Game Culture*. Cambridge, MA: MIT Press, 2018.

Ryerson, Liz. "Healing from Past Wounds." *Ellaguro* (blog), December 8, 2015. http://ellaguro.blogspot.com/2015/12/healing-from-past-wounds.html.

Sampat, Elizabeth. *Empathy Engines: Design Games That Are Personal, Political, and Profound*. Self-published, 2016, https://www.amazon.com/Empathy-Engines-Personal-Political-Profound/dp/1548761516.

Schleiner, Anne-Marie. *The Player's Power to Change the Game: Ludic Mutation*. Amsterdam: Amsterdam University Press, 2017.

Schrank, Brian. *Avant-Garde Videogames: Playing with Technoculture*. Cambridge, MA: MIT Press, 2014.

Shaw, Adrienne, and Bonnie Ruberg. "Imagining Queer Game Studies." In *Queer Game Studies*, edited by Bonnie Ruberg and Adrienne Shaw, ix–xxxiii. Minneapolis: University of Minnesota Press, 2017.

Sharp, John. *Works of Game: On the Aesthetics of Games and Art*. Cambridge, MA: MIT Press, 2015.

Sicart, Miguel. *Play Matters*. Cambridge, MA: MIT Press, 2014.

Skaugen, Kirk. "The Game Changer." *Technology@Intel* (blog), August 18, 2015. https://blogs.intel.com/technology/2015/08/the-game-changer.

Solberg, Dan. "The Problem with Empathy Games." *Kill Screen*, January 13, 2016. https://killscreen.com/articles/the-problem-with-empathy-games.

Squinkifer, Dietrich. "Conference, Conventions, Conversations, and *Coffee*." *Camera Obscura* 32, no. 2 (2017): 175–183.

Stark, Chelsea. "Atari's LGBTQ-Friendly Mobile Game Misses What Pride Is Actually About." *Mashable*, January 28, 2016. http://mashable.com/2016/01/28/pridefest-atari.

Stern, Eddo. "20 Years of Game Art: Reflections, Transformations, and New Directions." Paper presented at Digital Games Research Association Conference, Turin, Italy, July 2018.

Stockton, Kathryn Bond. *The Queer Child, or Growing Sideways in the Twentieth Century*. Durham, NC: Duke University Press, 2009.

Stuart, Keith. "Roger Ebert Re-Enters the 'Games as Art' Debate." *The Guardian*, April 20, 2010. https://www.theguardian.com/technology/gamesblog/2010/apr/20/roger-ebert-games-as-art.

Švelch, Jaroslav. "Keeping the Spectrum Alive: Platform Fandom in a Time of Transition." In *Fans and Videogames: Histories, Fandom, Archives*, edited by Melanie Swalwell, Helen Stuckey, and Angela Ndalianis, 57–73. New York: Routledge, 2017.

Swalwell, Melanie. "1980s Home Coding: The Art of Amateur Programming. In

The Aotearoa Digital Arts Reader, edited by Stella Brennan and Su Ballard, 192–201. Auckland, NZ: Aotearoa Digital Arts and Clouds, 2008.

Taylor, T. L. *Play Between Worlds: Exploring Online Game Culture*. Cambridge, MA: MIT Press, 2009.

Trammell, Aaron, and Emma Leigh Waldron. "Playing for Intimacy: Love, Lust, and Desire in Pursuit of Embodied Design." In *Rated M for Mature: Sex and Sexuality in Video Games*, edited by Matthew Wysocki and Evan W. Lauteria, 177–192. New York: Bloomsbury Academic, 2015.

Yang, Emilia. "Downtown Browns: Interactive Web Series, Intersectionality and Intimacy." *Confessions of an Aca-Fan* (blog), April 13, 2017. http://henryjenkins .org/blog/2017/04/downtown-browns-interactive-web-series-intersectionality -and-intimacy.html.

Yang, Robert. "For Better or for Worse." *Radiator Blog*, November 7, 2016. http:// www.blog.radiator.debacle.us/2016/11/for-better-or-worse.html.

Yang, Robert. "If You Walk in Someone Else's Shoes, Then You've Taken Their Shoes: Empathy Machines as Appropriation Machines." *Radiator Blog*, April 5, 2017. http://www.blog.radiator.debacle.us/2017/04/if-you-walk-in-someone -elses-shoes-then.html.

Yang, Robert. "'Take Ecstasy with Me': A Manifesto for Gay VR." *Radiator Blog*, March 21, 2017. http://www.blog.radiator.debacle.us/2017/03/take-ecstasy -with-me-manifesto-for-gay.html.

Zimmerman, Eric. "Manifesto: The 21st Century Will Be Defined by Games." *Kotaku*, September 9, 2013. https://kotaku.com/manifesto-the-21st-century -will-be-defined-by-games-1275355204.

INDEX

Bold page numbers refer to figures